This book ~~~~~~~~~~~~~~~~~~~~~~~ branch of the
Lancashire County Library ~~~~~~ ~~e the date

Praise for *Another Little Piece of My Heart*

'Extraordinary' Darren Reidy, *Rolling Stone*

'Vivid and eccentric ★★★★' *Billboard Magazine*

'The history of a seismic era … *Another Little Piece of My Heart* is a genuinely essential addition to the bibliography of the revolutionary sixties' Barney Hoskyns, *Guardian*

'Tinged with an autumnal sense of loss and the self-examination of a 70-year-old man looking back on his life … As well as being very funny, *Another Little Piece of My Heart* is an affecting meditation on the author's "budding queerness" and acceptance, finally, that he was gay' Ian Thomson, *Independent*

'A pithy memoir of the sixties counterculture by a rock critic who saw beyond the hype … A fond eulogy to misplaced idealism and expectations … Goldstein writes with pithy insight into the counterculture's foibles and failings ★★★★' Mick Brown, *Daily Telegraph*

'*Another Little Piece of My Heart* provides unique views of some of the time's most colourful figures, including Janis Joplin, Jim Morrison, Susan Sontag and Andy Warhol. But most of all, it shows us how one electric consciousness – Goldstein's own – emerged and evolved as America itself became new' Ann Powers, author of *Weird Like Us: My Bohemian America*

LANCASHIRE COUNTY LIBRARY

3011813323798 6

'Goldstein gives a deeply felt and largely compelling portrait of an age that indelibly marked everyone who took part in it. Indispensable for understanding the culture of the sixties and the music that was at its heart' *Kirkus*

'His advantage as fan, street freak, political rad and literate academic distinguished him from trade and teen rag rats. Given this singularity, he invented his gig – and his description of the process is fascinating' Michael Simmons, *Mojo*

'His memoir (a curate's egg) is pithy and touching on the foibles of sixties idealism and counterculture ★★★★' Mick Brown, *Sunday Telegraph*

'Goldstein manages to condense his formative writing years – and one of the most tumultuous decades in rock 'n' roll history – into relatable, poignant prose … He's self-aware, unabashedly enthusiastic (at times even nerdy), sparing no shame in admitting to his own awkwardness while encountering the artists he admired … Establishing an emotional connection to the reader' *Village Voice*

'Equal parts confessional, acerbic, honest, lyrical and intimate, *Another Little Piece of My Heart* is a memoir that upends the idea that if you remember the 1960s, then you weren't there. Goldstein was there, all right – in the vibrant, vivid and dissenting thick of it' Tony Clayton-Lea, *Irish Times*

'Goldstein recalls a tumultuous culture with humility and a healthy perspective' *Publishers Weekly*

'Very well written ★★★★★' *Western Mail*

A NOTE ON THE AUTHOR

RICHARD GOLDSTEIN is one of the founders of rock criticism, beginning with his Pop Eye column in the *Village Voice* in 1966 when he was just twenty-two. His reporting led to a long career as a commentator on culture, politics and sexuality. His work has appeared in many newspapers and magazines, including the *New York Times*, *New York*, *Harper's*, *Artforum*, the *Guardian*, and the *Nation*, and he served as arts editor and then executive editor of the *Village Voice*. His gay activism earned him a GLAAD award as columnist of the year. His books include the bestselling *The Poetry of Rock*, *Reporting the Counterculture*, and *Homocons: The Rise of the Gay Right*. He is currently an adjunct professor at Hunter College of the City University of New York where he teaches, among other classes, a course on the sixties.

richard goldstein

another little piece of my heart

my life of rock and revolution in the '60s

B L O O M S B U R Y

LONDON · OXFORD · NEW YORK · NEW DELHI · SYDNEY

Bloomsbury Paperbacks
An imprint of Bloomsbury Publishing Plc

50 Bedford Square	1385 Broadway
London	New York
WC1B 3DP	NY 10018
UK	USA

www.bloomsbury.com

BLOOMSBURY and the Diana logo are trademarks of Bloomsbury Publishing Plc

First published in Great Britain in 2015
This paperback edition first published in 2016

© Richard Goldstein, 2015

Richard Goldstein has asserted his right under the Copyright, Designs and Patents Act, 1988, to be identified as Author of this work.

This book is a work of non-fiction based on the life, experiences and recollections of the author. In some limited cases names of people, places, dates, sequences or the detail of events have been changed solely to protect the privacy of others. The author has stated to the publishers that, except in such minor respects not affecting the substantial accuracy of the work, the contents of the book are true

All rights reserved. No part of this publication may be reproduced or transmitted in any form or by any means, electronic or mechanical, including photocopying, recording, or any information storage or retrieval system, without prior permission in writing from the publishers.

No responsibility for loss caused to any individual or organization acting on or refraining from action as a result of the material in this publication can be accepted by Bloomsbury or the author.

British Library Cataloguing-in-Publication Data
A catalogue record for this book is available from the British Library.

ISBN:	HB:	978-1-4088-5811-0
	TPB:	978-1-4088-5812-7
	PB:	978-1-4088-5810-3
	ePub:	978-1-4088-5809-7

LANCASHIRE COUNTY LIBRARY	
3011813323798 6	
Askews & Holts	16-Feb-2016
780.422 GOL	£9.99
SOR	

Printed and bound in Great Britain by CPI Group (UK) Ltd, Croydon CR0 4YY

To find out more about our authors and books visit www.bloomsbury.com.
Here you will find extracts, author interviews, details of forthcoming

In memory of my parents, Mollye and Jack,
known by their friends as Malke and Yankel

Contents

Wretched Refuse

It's 1962. I'm eighteen, terrified and turned on by everything. School is the only place where I feel safe. I'm about to enter college, the first member of my family to learn the difference between Hegel and a bagel. I read the way other kids in the neighborhood fuck—constantly (according to them).

I live in a housing project in the Bronx. My parents think of it as a big step up from the tenements of Manhattan where they were raised, but I have a different trajectory in mind. For me, Manhattan is the locus of a better life, the life of guys in corduroy who play the banjo like they come from Kentucky and girls whose breath doesn't smell like cigarettes; of poets with beards like the one I can't grow yet, but want to; of "angel-headed hipsters" like the madmen in "Howl," which I've read and recited to myself dozens of times. Every weekend I set out for the streets where such poems are lived, sorting through the clothing I need for the journey, counting my spending money and deciding whether to wear my beret. (Of course I will.) I slip into the grungy sweater I've worn every day for a year. My jeans have sweat holes in the crotch—I sweat a lot, and I rarely bathe. I envy the sleek kids, the boys with tail-fin hair who can unhook a bra on a girl as easily as they tie their shoes. I envy them but I don't want to be them. I'm from the Bronx but not *of* it. I'm bound for Greenwich Village.

Every week I cross the Bronx, by several buses, in order to reach the only newsstand in the borough that carries the *Village Voice*. I keep a bottle of Dubonnet in the fridge so I don't have to drink soda with the boiled chicken and canned fruit we gulp while talking loudly over the TV. Late at night, while my family is asleep, I curl up in the bathtub with my transistor radio tuned to WBAI, a small FM station that features radicals, artists, holy men from the Himalayas, and folksingers. To me these are typical inhabitants of the city whose towers are visible from my window as tiny spires in the distance. I can reach its magic streets for fifteen cents—the subway fare in 1962.

I know every curve and swerve the El makes as it courses through the Bronx, skirting the edges of buildings where people at their windows can almost touch the train, and then plunging into the tunnel to Manhattan. As soon as it goes underground I lose the knot in the belly that is my constant companion in the neighborhood. I've managed to pass the test I must take every time I leave the project for the zone of possibility. It's a danger unimagined by my parents, harsh as their life in the slums was. Thanks to the New York City Housing Authority, I've been spared their ordeal of heatless winters, toilets in the hall, dead siblings, and gangsters rubbed out on the stoop. But I have to deal with something nearly as fearsome. I need to get out of the Bronx with my sandals.

Nobody wears sandals in the project. If I dare, the guys who guard the gates of masculinity will see them as a crossing over into faggot territory and stomp on my feet. So when I leave the house my feet are in camouflage—Keds. I keep the sandals in a paper bag, but when I get to the Village I put them on. I don't care that my toes are freezing or that the straps chafe. One doesn't wear socks in the Village, or so it seems to me. I'm obsessed with dressing right, since I don't feel like I belong here. But I do, at least on the three-block strip that runs south from Washington Square. Hundreds of kids like me are clogging the pavement. I'm safe among my peers, seeing and being seen on MacDougal Street.

Generations of bohemians hover over this scene. My heroes, the Beats, look down from placards outside the bars where free jazz once mixed with free verse. Folk music fills these clubs now, and the real Beats have departed for less illustrious digs, leaving MacDougal Street to the wretched refuse of the outer boroughs—us. We don't know from the ways of Zen or the world of art in Greenwich Village. Our culture is hanging out. For hours we brood, sipping espresso in the recesses of the Fat Black Pussycat, or we wander over to the Square, where a year ago we rioted and won the right to sing. In this swarm of guitars I will find the first incarnation of what is not just a new life for me but a new era for my generation—a time of sex and drugs, of revolution for the hell of it, and, most important, music. Music will be for us what it always is for youth: a way to know you're not alone.

I was a fat boy, helpless before my weight. I was so hungry—for food, for sex, for attention—that I could never fill the maw inside me. I would wake up in the middle of the night with the feeling that invisible hands were choking me. My survival, my very breath, depended on the small group of misfits that I called my friends.

They were rich, or so I thought. They didn't live in the project but in small brick houses with yards the size of beach blankets. Some of them lived in a cluster of apartments that had been built by the Communist Party for its members. The Party called these buildings cooperatives, but we knew them as the Coops, and in 1962 they were a very cooped-up place. The residents led apprehensive lives, never sure that Joe McCarthy was really dead. My best friends were the children of these pariahs.

They were the first people I met who didn't have the TV on perpetually. Their homes were fascinating to me, with real paintings on the walls and Danish Modern furniture, not Louis-the-Something fakes covered in plastic, my mother's idea of elegance. There were records by performers I'd never heard of, Paul Robeson and Odetta, and no one minded if we sat on the floor singing loyalist songs from the Spanish Civil War. My mother liked the idea that I was hanging out with radicals. She associated Communism with upward mobility—as a girl she'd made it a point to dance with Reds because she was sure those boys would become doctors. "My little Communist," she liked to call me with a grin.

The myth that all Jews have intact families didn't apply to my parents. As a child, my father sometimes lived in foster institutions or on the street. My mother grew up in a "broken home," and her own mother, who couldn't read and barely spoke English, struggled to support the brood. I heard endlessly about how this blessed *bubbie* put out the stove when her kids left for school and sewed all day in the cold flat. There's an old ghetto yarn about maternal sacrifice, which I often endured. A son cuts out his mother's heart in order to sell it. On the way to see the buyer, he trips and drops it, and the heart says, "Did you hurt yourself, dear?" I don't think my mother regarded this tale as even a little over the top, but I saw it as a feeble attempt to induce guilt in me. Now I realize that she was actually lecturing herself. She strained against a maternal role that thwarted her worldly ambitions. Motherhood was so central to her self-image that she never dealt with her rage at its constrictions, and so she directed a burning ball of drive toward her eldest son. It's an old story. My father was a frustrated man, and he sometimes took it out on me. In my family, the belt was what the time-out is today. But he also nurtured my creativity. I owe my lust for fame to my mother, and my artistic urges to him. Both traits propelled me toward the role I would play in the sixties.

For much of my childhood I thought of myself as a TV network broadcasting my experiences. Nothing seemed as real to me as entertainment, and my father fed this fantasy by taking me to all sorts of exotic spectacles, from foreign movies with glimpses of tit to Yiddish melodramas that turned on the conflict between love and God's law. We would leave the Bronx in the morning, when ticket prices were reduced, and catch the stage show at a giant midtown theater. I have a vivid memory of the wild-man drummer Gene Krupa—a jazz precursor of the Who's Keith Moon—rising out of the orchestra pit, his kit sparkling in the spotlight. I wanted to be a singer until my voice changed. (Fortunately, writing doesn't require vocal cords.)

My father was a postal worker, and all sorts of high-tone publications passed through his hands en route to their subscribers. He would tear off the address labels so that the magazines ended up in the dead-letter office, and then he would bring them home to me. As a result I read art and theater journals unheard of in the Bronx. Once a month we'd travel to a discount bookstore in Times Square and I'd come home with a pile of classics. He pumped me full of culture, though it was alien to him, just as my mother drilled me in the social skills that meant success, though she hardly knew what they were. The result was a conflict between respect for his modest achievements and loyalty to her dreams. I tried to resolve this dilemma by becoming a beatnik (hence the beret). It was upwardly mobile, but definitely not anyone's idea of making it.

I can only guess at the scenario that my friends grew up with, but I don't think it was much different from mine. Mixed messages from our parents were what we had in common—and not just us. In 1962, a huge cohort of kids, whose families barely qualified as middle-class, was about to enter a rapidly expanding economy. As beneficiaries of the postwar education boom, we felt entitled to be creative, but we were trained to move up, and these clashing desires produced the youth culture that descended on MacDougal Street, among other places in other cities. Folk music was the perfect outlet for our split sensibility. It was proletarian in its sympathies, yet distinct from the taste of the masses. The other kids in my project didn't know from this music, and they would have found it utterly without the rhythmic energy that signified life. But I found a future in it.

On my jaunts to the Village I frequented the folk clubs, huffing my kazoo (an instrument I chose because it didn't demand any musical skill) at open-mike events called hootenannies, or I heard the pros play for very little money. In one of those small rooms—Gerde's Folk City or possibly the Cafe Wha?—I saw Bob Dylan perform. He was well-known to my friends, had been since his first concert at Carnegie Hall in 1961, which we all attended (I still have the program), so I was aware of his legend long before he became legendary. My father called him "the hog caller" and pleaded for relief from his raspy voice on the record player. Dylan would soon be the emblem of my evolution from a folkie to a rocker, as he was for many people my age. But there was a specter haunting me when I left the Bronx for the peaceful village where the lion sleeps tonight. It was the specter of girl groups.

Black girls, white girls, didn't matter. I was tuned to their voices, especially those sirens of stairwell sex, the Ronettes. Also the Marvelettes, the Crystals, and the Shirelles. Their music snapped like chewing gum. It was everything that tempted me in the project—big hair, fierce moves— and it drove me to fantasies that literature didn't provide. My favorite jerk-off dream involved Dion, the Bronx-bred singer in the Belmonts (as in Belmont Avenue), fucking *all* the Shirelles. I was the only kid at the hootenanny who knew the words to "Baby, It's You."

In high school, doo-wop meant as much as sex to me. It was my link to the gods of the project, the Italian boys. Jews weren't allowed into the gang system ("It would be like fighting girls," my friend Dominick explained), but these barriers didn't apply when we sang together, howling in curlicue scales, as if we were actually momentarily black. Our definition of doo-wop was flexible enough to include nearly any hit song with elaborate vocal parts. As we launched into a number, the tough kids softened and I was welcomed in. This was the only time when I felt truly competent as a male. It distracted me from my anguish in a way that folk songs never could. Certain pop melodies would enter my body and make my mind go blank. I identified with performers as intensely as I did with authors. The gyre that was Elvis, the leaps of Jerry Lee Lewis, the shrieks of Little Richard—to me it was clear: they were as hungry as me.

Folksingers didn't have fierce moves. Try to imagine Joan Baez doing hand jive or Pete Seeger leaping out of a coffin. Robust and even gritty were fine, randy was not. When I think of this scene, the image that comes to mind is a girl cradling an autoharp and radiating purity, not the stuff of my wet dreams. Folk music had a righteous, optimistic attitude that seemed very middle-class, and I went for it with the enthusiasm of a wannabe. But the gutter remained, hot and tarry, within me. I kept it under tight control, just as I struggled to tame my budding queerness. I was sure that if I gave myself over to the rock 'n' roll side of me, I would never rise. My new life depended on mastering the codes of the only society that would have me, the boho left. But in 1962, I lucked out, because those codes were about to change. To the shrieks of girls reaching for their first orgasm, the Beatles would soon arrive.

It wasn't just their capacity to wring the juices out of female fans that made them fascinating. Elvis had done that too, with his body and his seductive voice. But with the Beatles it was a more elaborate package. Their Liverpool accents sounded sophisticated but were really working-class. They had neat suits and androgynous hair, yet behind the cherubic look you could tell that they were horny devils. Their songs, which seemed conventional on first hearing, were laced with unexpected harmonies, octave leaps, and such. Ringo's blunt drumming and Paul's loping bass tied the band to rock 'n' roll, but everything else seemed subject to outside influences. From the start there was something about this band that spoke of potential—theirs and mine. They, too, were streetwise guys, very ambitious and interested in making art, or at least being arty. I was perfectly positioned to take advantage of everything they represented.

I realized soon enough that I should write about them, so I did, constructing an audacious thesis about Beatlemania signaling a cultural shift that went far beyond pop. I called my essay "The Second Jazz Age," and it would eventually run in the college paper, my first piece on the music soon to be called rock. Propelled by enthusiasm, I had stumbled onto something that would turn out to be a career—and, even more unexpectedly, an identity. Within a few years, at the unready age of twenty-two, I would become the first widely read rock critic and a media sensation, a designated arbiter of hip. I had no idea what hip meant—no one did. But for a time, I pretended that I knew, and as a result I moved easily among rock stars, artists, intellectuals, and celebrities in the mash-up that was culture in the sixties. If they wanted publicity, I was on their radar.

In 1962, all of this was unimaginable to me. I was Richie from the projects, wide open and shut down, heedless and needy, full of myself and ready to be filled. And I was hungry.

Nearly Naked Through the Not Exactly Negro Streets at Dawn

Her real name was Roberta, but if you saw her flaming red hair falling in turbulent curls around her eyes, her teeth jutting into her grin, her conversation constant (the product of a manic personality on speed), you'd know right away that she had to be called Tom. She was a misfit among misfits, an oddity even among my friends. But she was the only one of them who grasped my feelings for the Beatles and my ideas about them. "No one's writing stuff like this," she said. I knew right away that she was as unrooted in the world of normal expectations, as riven with ambition and anxiety, as me.

Tom had been raised in Queens, but the subway system meant that any city college was within easy reach, and Tom ended up at the Bronx branch of Hunter (now it's called Lehman). That was where we met, in one of the faux-Gothic buildings, or maybe on the sloping lawns where students strummed guitars and necked. There were no dorms; you either resided at home or convinced your parents to get you an apartment near the campus. That was what Tom had done. In 1962, the derelict caves around the Grand Concourse could be had for scratch. She lived in one of them, with God knows how many of her friends, who occupied sheet-less mattresses in rooms bare of everything except books and instruments.

I was eager to visit, convinced I'd find a bordello with folk music, and I wasn't entirely wrong. It was easier to get laid there than to find something to eat in the rancid fridge. Naturally I came back often, and on one of those visits Tom introduced me to her latest roommate. His name was . . . well, it didn't matter. The look in his eyes was welcoming, his lips curling into a slight smile, over which lurked a downy excuse for a mustache, his black hair falling in clumps around his neck, his bony shoulders and arms tethered to a sunken chest. But there was something about this guy that seemed to float above his physique. I guess that aura was his calling card, because he lived in Tom's place rent-free. All he had to do for his board was fuck.

Which he did, basically servicing all the women who wandered through the place. Tom kept a supply of raw eggs to feed him, because she thought the protein would increase his potency. But as far as I could tell he didn't need nutritional supplements. He walked around with a ready bulge in his jeans. I studiously looked away, but he noticed my interest and sent me a signal that said, "Let's be friends. I *need* a friend in this place."

He treated me to my first joint, smoked on his lumpy mattress. I felt dizzy, also horny, and I was relieved when he picked up his guitar and began to play. He hit the strings badly but beautifully, fragments of melody spilling from his fingers. There were no lyrics, just humming in a voice that broke into a sinus-driven thrum. I listened, transfixed, until he shot me a smile and said, "Think I'm gonna crash." I retreated to the living room, where a pile of people were going at it. I insinuated myself into the grunting heave, touching and licking, and I left feeling very impressed with myself. But what stuck with me about that day was the guy with the guitar.

"He's amazing," I said to Tom.

"Yeah," she replied. "He can fuck you and make it feel like a feather."

"Wow."

"That's why we keep him."

Tom was a writer, naturally. There were manuscripts all over her room, carpeting the paisley bedspread. She was avidly drawn to journalism, and in her mind that meant reporting your inner news. Tom didn't believe in punctuation, except for the occasional !!!!!!!!! But she had found a home for her musings, a publication that circulated among people who didn't mind text creeping up the sides of pages. There were all sorts of similar rags floating around lower Manhattan in those days. Cheap printing technologies had given every faction of style and radical politics a voice. By the end of the decade a network of underground newspapers would spring from this matrix, but back then there were only splotchy things stapled together. They were the zines of their day.

Tom was my guide to this hidden milieu. Thanks to her, I got to be the mascot of a black writers' collective that published an influential journal called *Umbra*. (I didn't know about its rep, but I liked the vibe, and I had the feeling that Tom was working her way through the masthead.) I also discovered *Fuck You: A Magazine of the Arts*, whose main appeal to me was that each copy had a drop of the publisher's sperm on the cover. Stoking my meager courage, I wandered into the magazine's headquarters on East 10th Street, a storefront called the Peace Eye Bookstore. There I met the copious publisher himself. Ed Sanders was a tall man with ruddy cheeks, curly blond hair, and a prairie accent, all of which reminded me of Mark Twain. Years later, he would wrap his arms around my head to protect me from police charging at a demo. But back before we heard the crack of billy clubs, and a decade before punk inherited the earth, when it was still possible to be sincere on the Lower East Side, Sanders sang in one of the most unlikely rock groups of the sixties, the Fugs. I don't think he imagined, when I met him in 1962, that beatniks in a band could possibly have a fan base, but he certainly seemed like a star to me. He represented everything hardcore and handmade about the scene I'd begun to explore.

Sometime that spring, under Tom's prodding, I ventured far east of MacDougal Street to Tompkins Square, a large patch of mottled green surrounded by avenues named for letters of the alphabet—*A, B, C,* and *D*. They were pretty mean streets. The park had a decrepit air, incredibly attractive to me. There were hippies hanging out before there were hippies, and they mingled with old Ukrainians willing to sit near anyone who wasn't a junkie. The area was full of European restaurants that specialized in borscht and butter-slathered challah. They were filled with young people who wanted off the doctor-lawyer track, kids like me. We would fortify ourselves with soup and wander through the park, just sort of soaking up the wreckage—children playing in a dogshit-infested sandbox, street people noodling on badly strung guitars, wanderers who had arrived from every Omaha in America, and the occasional bullet flying. Yes, it could be perilous. But that was where Tom felt most at home.

On one of our trips from the Bronx, she led me into a tenement, up three flights of chipped stone stairs, and down a barely lit corridor slicked with cooking grease. I heard the familiar sound of guitars coming from an open door. Inside, on a wall you wouldn't lean against unless you wanted cement dust on your jacket, was a giant drawing of the Buddha with a machine gun strapped to his belly. This is my most vivid memory of the publication that ran Tom's musings. I've forgotten its name, and so, with apologies to an underground paper that was actually called *The Rat*, I'll call this rag *The Rodent*.

The articles snaked around tiny ads from homemade jewelry shops and notices of political meetings with an obscure Trotskyite pedigree. The house style was a variant of what the Beats called "automatic writing." The lead might refer to an arcane work of Eastern devotion, leading to a description of police brutality and ending with some quote from Kierkegaard. I'm kidding, though not by much. Deciphering the prose felt like walking through a maze, but it was lively and engaged. And the most interesting thing about *The Rodent* was that anyone could write for it, provided they were willing to work for free.

The editor was the oldest person in the place, and he had the jaded look of someone who had been through many careers. I didn't ask about his relationship to Tom, but it was clear that, at the least, she amused him. He greeted her as "Brenda Starr, reporter." She flung a few pages into his hand, and he read them, nodding in agreement every now and then, whipping out a pencil and circling a word or two. "Tell you what," he said. "If you let me add a few periods I'll print it."

"Fuck you," Tom negotiated. But I knew she would agree, because, under all that flaming hair and speed-driven chaos, she was as ambitious as me, and any chance to appear in print pushed her buttons, even if it meant using punctuation.

"Hey," she grunted to the editor. "Meet my friend Richie."

He checked me out warily. "Okay, write something."

"What should I write?" I stammered.

He shrugged. It was all the input I got from him.

But that night, in the tiny room I shared with my younger brother—when the bed was open there was no space to walk—I lay awake trying to think of a subject. I could hear my father snoring through the wall. I could hear the laugh tracks from TV shows audible through the ceiling. To live in the project was to join a community of coughers, moaners, and TV-rerun insomniacs. The building seemed to breathe as one, especially when a baseball game was on. And when something important happened, like the Yanks winning the Series, the cheers reverberated from every window. It was all raw material to me.

I never told my friends about the role writing played in my life. It put me in a timeless daze, a comfort zone where nothing could hurt me. Creating a story with a beginning, middle, and end was a way to give the jumble of my feelings a shape—it was a model for making sense of painful chaos. And I was enchanted by words, especially rhymes, had been ever since the age of four, when my parents enrolled me in a poetry class at the Henry Street Settlement. As soon as I could write my name I scrawled it on the blank pages of every book in our house, convinced that I was the author. I wrote poems as a kid, and as a teenager I branched out into short stories. My subject was the life I didn't feel part of, the worker's world of roles assigned, accepted, and eroticized. Lustiness radiated from my neighbors' bodies, thick and pocked or gnarled and muscled. (Some of the men still wore sailor hats from their navy days.) I wanted to smell every cranny of their flesh, women and men, girls and boys alike. Instead I began to keep detailed notes on them, the music they liked, the way they danced, the precise sounds of their speech. I didn't have a plot or a plan, but I wrote every day, filling pad after pad until my hand ached.

During the summer that I turned eighteen, I went on a serious diet. Eventually I would shed about eighty pounds, and, probably as a result, I had several sexual encounters. Not that I was new to the nasty. When I was maybe nine, I grabbed the luscious breasts of my best friend's mother. I had no idea why I'd done that, but she slapped me. I ran home only to hear a knock on the door, and I shrank into my bed as my parents let her in. To my immense relief I heard her apologize for the slap. They never mentioned the incident to me, and so my career as a fiend proceeded undisturbed. And there were many opportunities in the project, even for a fat kid. I was initiated into fucking by a girl I didn't even like—I think I was fourteen, and it confused the hell out of me. But in high school, I had a different kind of experience, with a boy, sprawled across the front seat of his Pontiac. (I still remember the Madonna on the dashboard.) After that, I felt like a radio dial that couldn't settle on a station. The sense of being suddenly exposed to my desires in all their ambiguity was terrifying.

Looking back, I think I was heading for schizophrenia—it ran in my father's family. I was saved by many things, including the love of my friends, but nothing was as powerful as the impact of a certain book. Lying on the chicken-bone-strewn sands of the local beach, I pored through James Joyce's *Ulysses*. No novel had ever held me so tightly in the sinews of its prose and its landscape of the interior. It was one of those times when incipient mental illness meets the palpability of literature. I didn't get the modernist references or the allusions to *The Odyssey*, just the breathtaking flow and the intense feeling of empathy it called up in me. That summer I decided to be the James Joyce of the Bronx. I might as well have imagined blonde maidens with parasols strolling on the Grand Concourse.

Journalism was a much easier reach, but making the move from a college paper to *The Rodent* seemed very scary. Despite its tiny circulation, it signified Downtown and its contempt for uncool kids like me. I was afraid to go to Tom's house because I knew she would noodge me about my piece, but I couldn't stay away for long. Fortunately, she was out when I arrived. In a corner of the kitchen I saw the stud with the magic guitar. Actually, I saw his ass bobbing up and down. I stood there, queasy. After it was over, he grinned at me dreamily. "Wanna jam?" he asked.

At first I thought he meant sex, but then I realized that he wanted to play for me. Relieved, and a bit regretful, I followed him into his room. He picked up his guitar.

"I can't think of what to write," I whined.

"Well," he said. "What do you like? Write about that."

"I like . . . you," I blurted (probably blushing).

His smile said, *Of course you do, but besides that . . .*

"Well . . . I like poetry—the Beats. And folk music. I play."

"Guitar or banjo?"

"Kazoo."

I could tell that he didn't regard that as a real instrument.

"What else do you like?" he asked.

"I don't know. I guess rock 'n' roll."

He looked baffled. "Frankie Avalon?"

"No, no. That's crap. I like doo-wop."

"But what about new stuff? Like, the Beatles."

"Sure. Absolutely. They're amazing."

"Okay!" he said. "Write about them."

Well, I'd already done that, and there was nothing to stop me from recycling the Beatles piece that I intended to publish in my college paper. So, with Tom along for support, I brought it down to *The Rodent*. But

I made the mistake of telling the editor where it had previously run, and he wasn't up for sloppy seconds. Only when Tom insisted did he look at my manuscript. "Just stop wearing that dumb beret," he groused as he read the lead.

Then he delivered his verdict: "It's not for us."

I wasn't just wounded; I was baffled. I couldn't understand why my piece wasn't right for a paper willing to publish anything. Now I realize that it had to do with its readership, which didn't include rock 'n' roll fans. *The Rodent* may have been an open book, but its editor had an unerring sense of what would offend its readers. Prose poems about sacrilege and oral sex were welcome, as was coverage of the Women's Strike for Peace, but not an article about pop music. Pop was too vulgar for this crowd. It was part of the same tide that had brought the black-list, the hula hoop, and the TV dinner to the center of American life. Like the Cold War, it had to be resisted.

I learned a lesson that would stay with me for the rest of my career. Writers and publishers are fire and ice. We're in it for the words and the attention; they're out to make a buck. I know there are exceptions, but nonprofit partisans are no more likely than media barons to embrace what threatens their values, and in 1962 their values were the only options. The blogosphere has made everyone a writer, but back then, there was no alternative to the limitations of print. Publications had stables of writers, and for a wild-eyed kid like me it was very hard to break in. The most adventurous journals, such as *Evergreen Review*, limited themselves to work by credentialed radical intellectuals. I was invisible to a magazine that published Albert Camus. Music mags were only interested in jazz or folk, and in fan books, writing was beside the point. As for the fledgling underground press, it, too, was a business—so I concluded. If I wanted to join the word trade, I'd have to accept that. Or not.

Sometime in the next few years (I'm not sure when), Tom died. She over-dosed—on heroin, I presume, but it could have been amphetamines, or both. These were the so-called hard drugs that only the most reckless of us went near. In the course of the sixties, that changed. I would know many junkies, friends who stank of sedatives, speed freaks whose teeth chattered as they spoke. Most of these people were dear to me, especially the women. It may be that I'm drawn to women who radiate a sense of doom as they blaze with energy. Something always stopped me from hitting on them; I think I feared that they would suck me into their addictions. But that didn't stop me from wanting to protect them, or from feeling, when it proved impossible, that I'd failed at a sacred duty. Thinking back on it, I realize that Tom was a model for my attachment to Janis Joplin.

I didn't go to Tom's funeral because I didn't want to see her in the grasp of her family. I was sure that they were every bit as bourgie (a word I'd just learned) as she was not. But a week later I stopped by her place. The apartment was empty. All her roommates, including the guy with the guitar, were gone. I felt bereft of a community I never thought I'd find. From now on I would have to face the fact that hanging out in the Village was not the same as living there. I was from the Bronx, and that was a place where creativity meant leading a solitary life.

But just a year later, when I was verging on nineteen, I felt a shock of recognition that would change my sense of possibility. The radio was tuned to a Top 40 station. Suddenly, I heard a song I knew from the folk clubs, Bob Dylan's civil rights anthem "Blowin' in the Wind." It didn't belong on the charts, but there it was, in a rather anodyne version by the folk trio Peter, Paul and Mary. The beat was about as driving as a tuna melt, and the lyrics were far from the simple (though often poetic) patter that hit songs required—but still, I was stunned. It meant that something I'd regarded as the sole passion of my coterie was popular. Even in a place like Santa Barbara, where I pictured teenagers whose brains ebbed and flowed with the ocean tide, kids would soon be singing songs like this on the beach. Rock 'n' roll was about to make a fateful leap, though it wasn't evident yet. Surf music dared not tread where Dylan did, and not even the Beatles ventured into his literary terrain—not yet. But I was sure that this unlikely hit was a sign of more than musical change. I sensed that something was stirring, shuddering on its foundation. The present was beginning to feel different from the past. Nothing was stable, and that thrilled me.

It crossed my mind to try writing about Dylan's role in this transition, but I was far too busy to think about journalism in the summer of 1963. I joined the civil rights movement, along with all my college friends. There was no need to find our identity in a song. *We* were the answer blowing in the wind.

White Like Me

Race was at the core of nearly everything in the sixties. Even more than sitars and exotic beats, it shaped the structure of rock. Even more than the war in Vietnam, it dominated politics. Even more than LSD, it defined the consciousness of my generation. Look at any aging boomer and you'll see someone who was formed in the crucible of civil rights. The man I am emerged when I joined a campaign against job discrimination at the age of nineteen. I came to see my neighborhood—and my father—in a new way, and I broke with them, decisively. In other words, I became me.

I was itching for something to believe in as passionately as I didn't believe in myself. And there were all sorts of causes to choose from in 1963: nuclear disarmament, environmental destruction, the Cold War and its absurdities. (Having failed to topple Fidel Castro, the CIA was trying to kill him with exploding cigars.) But I was riveted by images of black students in the South braving fire hoses and police dogs. There was something personal about fighting racism; it had a payback that working for peace did not. Yes, I believed in social justice, but it was also about identity. Marching for civil rights meant connecting with a tradition that went much deeper than my roots in America. It was a way to be come what my grandparents were not and what my parents wanted to be—a Yankee.

There were other reasons why I was drawn to the civil rights movement. It had something to do with my sense of oppression as a fat kid, and quite possibly with my incipient queerness. But I also had a deep aversion to racism. It was absurd—rock 'n' roll had taught me that—and repugnant. This feeling was instilled in me, as it was for many people my age, when I saw pictures in the paper of a black teenager named Emmett Till. He'd been lynched in the South for whistling at a white girl. His body was swollen grotesquely, but his mother had insisted on an open coffin at the funeral. This was 1955; I was eleven. His mutilated face was the most horrible thing I'd ever seen.

If it had ended there, I might have lulled myself into believing that racism was a southern sin. After all, we had black next-door neighbors, and my brother and I had a few black friends. No one cared who came and went in the Bronx. But it was different in Manhattan. There were parts of that borough where black kids weren't supposed to be.

As a teenager, I often went downtown with friends to see movies or rock 'n' roll shows, and this time my companion was a black kid I liked a lot (perhaps because he never taunted me for being fat). We were on our way to Times Square when a cop stopped us and ordered us to get off the street. That had never happened to me, and I knew right away why it was happening now, as did my friend. The look on his face, frozen with fear, caused a reaction that I still have when someone makes a racist remark. I was nauseated. The power of that cop, the utter certainty with which he reduced us to helplessness, made me feel like vomiting. I think it was the first moment in my life when I wanted to strike out against authority, a reflex that had so much to do with the way I acted in the sixties. And I was hardly alone—many young people who ran wild in the streets during those years were reacting to a string of events like the one I've described. So it wasn't just a projection of my insecurities that led me to join the movement. It was the memory of standing passively by while the police menaced my friend and glared at me. By the time I turned nineteen, I was old enough to know that I wanted to do something about it.

A number of my college friends were Freedom Riders. I was tempted to join them, but my cowardice overcame my ideals, so I decided to stay close to home, and I set out to integrate my parents' "beach club." It was basically a strip of concrete and lawn on the Bronx side of the Long Island Sound. A large swimming pool was the only luxury, but for working-class Jews this was the closest thing to a golf course, and they wanted the perks that came with such a retreat, including racial segregation.

That summer everyone there was reading *Exodus* and sighing over the plight of Jewish refugees trying to make their way to Palestine. I wanted to teach them a lesson in hypocrisy by bringing a black friend to the club as my guest. We figured that she'd be turned away, and our plan was to document it with the tape recorder in her bag; then we'd take the evidence to the city's Human Rights Commission and, voilà, a blow for justice. But she made such a fuss that the attendant at the front gate let her in. We had the whole pool to ourselves, since everyone else got out of the water when we jumped in. I knew they weren't actually horrified; they were imitating those who would have done the same thing to them. It was still common in the fancy suburbs—where we would drive just to ogle the elegant homes—to bar Jews from country clubs, and deeds had clauses that forbade selling property to Jews. But here in the Bronx, we were kings.

Word quickly spread around the club, and my parents were mortified when I came by to introduce my black friend to them. My father sat silently on his beach chair, hands gripping the sides, but my mother's reaction surprised me. She scolded, half in jest. "Richard," she said, referring to a pair of pet rodents I'd once sneaked into the house, "this is worse than the hamsters."

Though I didn't realize it at the time, the civil rights movement signaled my arrival at the point where my mother wanted me to be. I had entered a world of noble ideals and, not incidentally, upward mobility. That was why she hadn't really objected to my stunt. After all, the black friend I'd brought with me was middle-class, as were all the people I met in the struggle, blacks as well as whites. And I have to say, because it was obvious, that the whites weren't exactly white—they were Jews.

My mother instructed me to call colored people Negroes, adding, "Remember, they're human too." This wasn't exactly the Gettysburg Address, but it was a departure from the spirit of the project, where certain firecrackers were called "nigger chasers" and we chose up sides in ball games with a chant that went, "catch a nigger by the toe." (I never realized, until I became an adult, that this had anything to do with race.) My mother bragged that she allowed my brother's black friend to eat off our plates, but she also complained that we were too poor to afford a *schvartzer*, the Yiddish word for maid and also for black people. This contradiction wasn't lost on me, and it became the seed of a conflict that would threaten my solidarity with the family, especially my father. He didn't hate Negroes, only the idea that they could advance beyond him at the post office. "They got the world by the balls and they're squeezing," he would snarl. It was easier to explain their success as racial favoritism than to admit that they'd done better than he on civil-service exams. This is a typical story of the white working class— can you say Reagan Democrats?—but back then I had no perspective on his feelings, and even less sympathy. At nineteen, you don't cut your father slack.

That summer I became a member of the Congress of Racial Equality (CORE), which ran picket lines and sit-ins at places that discriminated by race, including lunch counters that wouldn't serve blacks. Some of them were located in midtown Manhattan, not far from where that cop had accosted my friend. But I volunteered for a campaign in the Bronx. I wanted everyone in the neighborhood to see what I was up to.

Our target was the White Castle chain, which at the time wouldn't hire blacks to work at the counter. I loved their burgers—grease and onions with a square puck of meat—and I could scarf eight at a sitting, which I often did at the stand about ten blocks from the project. There were several White Castles in the Bronx, and we picketed all of them. I'd been trained by CORE in the techniques of nonviolent protest. I learned to fall, covering my head if someone took a swing at me; how to dress in layers so that scalding coffee wouldn't burn if it got thrown; how to handle taunts with a hymn. Anyone who resorted to violence, no matter how justified, would be thrown off the line. These preparations were hardly a drill, since all of the above would happen during the campaign. The risks were real, and so was the bonding on the picket line. It was a major inducement to interracial friendship, also dating, and I was a wet-dreaming devotee of the Shirelles.

At some point I met a young black woman in CORE. I'll call her B. She lived in a part of the neighborhood where black people with a little money had begun to buy homes. She was tall, slim, and classy. Whatever skin privileges I possessed paled before her aplomb. She taught me table manners my family didn't know existed, such as how to take a small portion from a serving platter. (*Chez moi*, you got a heaping plate of food that you could never finish.) She also brought me to church, a Baptist service. The swaying and chanting, the call-and-response, seemed very Jewish to me. During his sermon the minister pointed to the two of us and proclaimed that we were the future. I cried.

You don't usually hear about miscegenation in the civil rights movement. The image that survives is one of blacks and whites marching
hand in hand, and it's accurate as far as it goes. But there was also a
space for exploring sexual feelings, as I did with black women more
beautiful than I had any right to expect. This is very complicated stuff,
maybe too slippery to explain. I think it had to do with escaping from
racial identity, which stuck to us like a tar baby. We were trying to free
ourselves in the only way that seemed possible—through desire. As if we
could do with our bodies what we couldn't in the rest of our lives.

It would be another year before the Supreme Court struck down
laws against miscegenation. Two of my friends, an interracial couple,
had been arrested while checking in at a Washington, D.C., hotel, and
I could still recall when Chuck Berry was busted in the Midwest on
charges of "dating a white girl," as the caption under the news photo
read. I had other, even more disturbing memories. A white woman in
the project, who insisted on having a baby with a black man rather than
retreating to a "home," caused so much stress in her family that her
father collapsed on the street and died. (I saw chunks of his teeth on the
sidewalk.) So it was a tremendous act of rebellion, the most primal one
I could think of, to have interracial sex. No one tried to call me on it.
As skeptical as the black organizers at CORE may have been about the
motivations of white boys like me, they, too, believed in this potential.
Until black power made it suspect, miscegenation was a potent force
for people interested in creating change.

I remember walking home from the beach with B. It started to rain,
and she told me to hide in the bushes while she stood at the edge of the
road, presenting her long legs to the passing traffic. A carful of black
guys stopped, eager for her company. I jumped out, and, despite their
clear disappointment, they let me in. We drove through the rain, joking a
bit uneasily. We knew that a cop might stop us and demand to know
what we were doing together. But we were aware of something else as
well—a certain intensity. We were new to one another, trying to relate in
a way that our upbringing hadn't prepared us for. We had to make it up
as we went along, and for young people that's always a giddy thing.

As touching as this recollection is, I can't call it up without admitting that love wasn't all I felt toward the people in that car. I also felt
a distance that was essential to my identity. Part of me, the most shameful part, was relieved that blacks had replaced Jews as the Other. The

Holocaust was an abstract horror to me; we had no relatives in Europe that we knew of. But I was haunted by an enduring sense of danger. When I was seven or so, my family took a trip through rural Pennsylvania. Back then I wore a Star of David around my neck. We stopped for gas, and a boy approached me. He asked very politely if I would show him my horns. I was baffled. When I told my parents about it, they yanked me into the car and sped off. It was a reminder that, as normal as our lives were, it could all be ripped away.

For us, whiteness was a shelter from the storm, and I wasn't ready to give it up entirely. I was willing to fight for blacks, but not to feel like one of them. When we marched together, holding hands, I had to suppress the impulse to recoil, as if something might rub off. I prayed that the stiffness in my body wouldn't show. Over the course of the sixties, I came to understand that this wasn't just a problem for Jews like me. Every white person had a racist back alley—we were all victims of our history. In one way or another, millions of Americans my age went through this process of self-examination, whether or not they ever marched for civil rights. The current etiquette of respect is one result. I'm afraid it's the best my generation can offer, but, given the course of human history, it's no small thing.

I did what I could in the movement; that's what counts, I hope. And I received something priceless in return. All my ideas about justice sprang from what I saw and felt on the picket line. It gave me a way to fight the conviction that I was powerless to change reality. I understood that action, personal and collective, could alter even something as rooted as racial hierarchy. In the process I came to believe that taking action would shape my own destiny. I could be what I willed. It would be violent—it nearly always is. But I didn't understand that in the summer of '63. The blood took me by surprise.

I spent most of that July picketing White Castles across the Bronx. Other demonstrators occupied the interiors—sitting in. At some point, the manager of one branch locked the doors and turned on the heat. It was a sweltering day, and within an hour, several people fainted and had to be hospitalized. This should have been a warning; instead, it stiffened our resolve. The bigots who harangued us on the line were crazed extremists—no one in the Bronx really had a problem with black people working where they pleased. So I thought, until I realized during the course of the month that my neighborhood was its own racial tinderbox.

One Friday evening, we took up positions at the White Castle near my house. It was the start of a summer weekend, and people who might have been hanging out on their stoops gathered at the intersection. Soon there were hundreds, and as the night wore on, the crowd grew drunker and angrier. I saw some of my neighbors, red-faced and cursing—boys I'd sung doo-wop with, girls who'd let me cop a feel, the guy whose son had been my major knock-hockey rival. "Get the fuck off the street," he shrieked. A line of cops strained to push the mob back, but they couldn't control the incoming. Bottles flew. Boards whizzed by. It shocked me to see such venom over what was just a demand for jobs. It wasn't as if these furious people wanted to work at White Castle. What did they have to lose?

I couldn't answer that question—it would have required more empathy than I had for my neighbors. All I could think of at the time was getting away from them. But now I understand why they rioted that night. Like my parents, they had come to whiteness recently. The Italians were from Sicily, where other Italians had called their grandparents Africans. The Irish could still remember when they were portrayed in newspaper cartoons as monkeys. Only in cities like New York had these groups achieved a modicum of racial respectability. Anything that breached the boundary between them and black people was a threat to their newfound status, and the fact that this achievement was a bogus concept, a social figment, didn't make it less real. They believed in solidarity—they would rise or fall together—but I had a more middle-class view of success, even though I wasn't yet middle-class. I would make it as an individual, atomized from my origins and even my family. I was a class traitor by training and a race traitor by disposition. I fit into a future they couldn't see.

Now that I'm ensconced in my Manhattan life, I miss those people—their warmth and loyalty, so different from the neighbors I currently have. But there was another side to them, a ready viciousness, and that night it vented itself on our picket line. I didn't see it coming. I was lost in the high of protest, the rush of adrenaline mixed with righteousness. I didn't notice anything except the pumping of my heart. But suddenly I saw something in the stream of cars that cruised by, with the windows rolled down so the passengers could curse at us. One of those cars had a Confederate flag sticking out. I saw a hand pointing a gun. Then I heard a shot. All the hair on my body stood up.

Someone ahead of me on the line fell to the ground. He grabbed his face, blood dripping through his fingers. I remember his crumpled body and the sound of him screaming. He wasn't seriously injured; just shot by a BB gun. Such wounds can produce a lot of bleeding, but they don't go very deep. Still, he was surrounded by police, and an ambulance soon arrived. The crowd whooped as he was carried off—my first experience of bloodlust, the real thing.

The cops formed a gauntlet around us, and they marched us between the two lines, down the street, and away from the crowd. I staggered home, numb but exhilarated. My father was furious. He threw a pamphlet at me and announced that he had joined the National Renaissance Party. A local fruit vendor was organizing, and he'd signed up. I knew something about this group. "Congratulations," I said. "You're a Nazi." It was true—he'd joined a neo-Nazi group; my dad, the *haimischer* storm trooper. He looked at the pamphlet, mortified. It was my greatest triumph over him.

The next day I left the house, and for two weeks, I lived in a friend's basement until my father agreed to leave me alone. He licked his wounds when I returned home. But he had one more indignity to suffer. Black people were smiling at him, he groaned. He was polluted, a man who had achieved whiteness only to have his son take it from him. On some level, I think he understood how fake it all was, but by then it had become a contest between us, and he was destined to lose, because I was on the side of the new reality. He'd raised me to be better than him, and his wish had been granted.

The riot was a one-off; the neighborhood calmed down, and, though I proudly wore my CORE button whenever I walked through the project, no one dared to touch me. No one even spoke to me, but by then it didn't matter. I'd lost the last vestige of my desire to belong there. I had seen the promised land, and it wasn't just Greenwich Village. It was America-to-be, and the first mass gathering of the new nation was about to take place. This was the March on Washington for Jobs and Freedom, and all my friends were going. On August 28, I left the house at four A.M., my mother standing forlornly at the door. "Don't go near the front," she said. I wasn't sure whether she was worried about my safety or the possibility that my picture would appear in the paper. I could never tell which was worse for her: mortal danger or social shame.

I'll never forget that march, though I dozed through Martin Luther King's "I Have a Dream" speech because I was exhausted from traveling without sleep. What I remember, vividly, is the sight that greeted us as the bus passed through the white suburbs of D.C. Every store was boarded up, every window shut tight, and the streets were deserted. But once we got to the black inner city, every stoop and porch was full, and people were waving American flags. It was a stunning image, since we lefties wouldn't have done such a thing. For us, the flag was a symbol of Moloch, never to be displayed. But here was all this red, white, and blue proudly flying. It suddenly occurred to me that I was a foreigner, a spawn of the dregs of Europe who had left there because they couldn't own land or practice most professions; because they were implicitly, and sometimes explicitly, in danger. I belonged to that old world at least as much as I did to the new one where I lived. No amount of assimilation would change that. I would always be an immigrant, ungrateful to my country for rescuing me. And these black folks, with their star-spangled banners and their rock 'n' roll, they were the real Americans.

I Don't Know What This Is, but You Owe Me a Story

When the letter arrived from Columbia University, I was stunned. Not only had I been accepted at the Graduate School of Journalism, but they'd offered me a fellowship to cover the tuition. They didn't know what they were getting into.

Journalism was a very staid profession in 1965, at least as it was taught at Columbia. Subjectivity had no place in the curriculum; the truth was arrived at through a strict set of rules. But something was missing, the thing I most cared about: style. I had no intention of learning the news trade if it meant I couldn't dance at the typewriter. So I decided to treat the whole thing as a game. Writing a lead was like composing a haiku; headlines should be puns, even if that meant fudging the facts. I specialized in obituaries for myself, each more glowing than the last. It drove my professors wild, but not as much as the way I looked. Everyone else in the class wore prim dresses or trim suits, but I showed up in a lumpy jacket and chinos, with my hair spilling over my collar. I kept a cube of sugar wrapped in foil on my desk, pretending it was LSD. The faculty was very kind about all this, but there were limits. One day the dean asked me for a favor. "Richard," he said, "we're having some donors stop by today. Will you please stay off the fifth floor?"

As it turned out, I'd come to Columbia in a watershed year for transgression. The spirit of the civil rights movement, which challenged the racial hierarchy, was loosening all sorts of cultural systems as well. Every genre was changing; all aesthetic traditions were under siege. The theaters, lofts, and galleries of lower Manhattan were brimming with radical energy, and it was just a twenty-minute subway ride from school. By day I met deadlines; by night I was a denizen of the underground. I saw Beckett plays in theaters so small that you could hear the performers breathe. I watched actors charge into the audience and drag customers onstage to harangue them, and I attended readings where poets cut off the heads of chickens or tossed buckets of piss into the house. (I learned to sit in the back.) My favorite renegade troupe was the Living Theatre, a pacifist collective that had briefly been shut down by the government for refusing to pay "war taxes." I admired their politics, but it was their fleshy, writhing physicality that turned me on. They filled the room with primal emotions and invited you to express them as well, in any state of dress or undress. Taking off your clothes in the name of art was to be expected. A cellist named Charlotte Moorman made her name by playing classical music bare-breasted. No other avant-garde artist appeared so often on the front page of the *Village Voice*.

To say I was a misfit in j-school doesn't do justice to my alienation. I did what was expected of me, but always in my own way. They tried to man me up by sending me to cover the UN, but imagine a long-haired kid in 1965 soliciting diplomats for a quote. I came back without a scoop, and they soon decided to furlough me in the school's simulated newsroom, where I busied myself with the AP wire, a whirligig that spewed stories and rang bells for breaking news. Or I holed up in the library, reading up on tabloids of yore. Their sleazy energy beckoned me. I dug the combination of lurid prose and puritanical morality that made it possible to lavish attention on kinky sex while condemning it. Salvation was shamelessly combined with baseball (ANGELS IN THE OUTFIELD). Extreme-weather headlines reveled in the obvious—WHEW! and BRRR! I can't explain why I fell in love with these rags, but they inspired a new fantasy. I would be a newshound, trolling the city with a police radio in my car. I would wear a press card in my fedora, or pop the flashbulb that unleashed the chained King Kong.

I realize now that this fantasy had everything to do with the pull of the Bronx. Its passionate intensity was still in my blood. I needed to capture that vitality in my writing, to be high-end but low-down. It would happen much sooner than I thought, thanks to a literary uprising called the New Journalism. This was another hybrid of the sixties, when the most vital culture was being made in the spaces between high- and lowbrow forms. There were no rules in the New Journalism beyond the obligation to be accurate. It was a fusion of reporting and narrative writing, as real as the facts and as rich as fiction. Its appearance in the hipper magazines signaled a new mass audience with a contempt for rigid categories. This was a very sixties attitude, although I didn't understand that at the time. All I knew was that I found it stimulating. Tom Wolfe, the bad boy of New Journalism, now ran a close second to James Joyce for me. I devoured his articles and worked his style into my pieces, violating every convention my professors were trying to instill. "I don't know what this is," one of them wrote across my copy, "but you owe me a story."

In the end I learned more about proper journalistic form than I intended to, and it served me well whenever I had to organize a piece quickly. But the most important thing I discovered at Columbia was that I loved reporting. It was the perfect career for an addict of spectacle who was also an introvert. Doors to the hottest places opened; velvet ropes and police lines parted. I could flash my credentials and nearly anyone would talk to me. If I felt self-conscious about my body, I could always work the phone. It was a grand strategy for dealing with the world. When I got into journo mode I would become the man I wanted to be—aggressive, competent, smart-assed. Finally I saw a way to combine tabloid spunk with new literary possibilities. All I needed was a beat, and I sensed what it might be.

In 1965, two major forces were transforming rock 'n' roll into the art it would become. One of them was *Rubber Soul*, the album that marked the Beatles' departure from the basics toward a new, fusive style. There was a sitar on one cut, they sang in French on another, and some of the lyrics verged on ambiguity ("Isn't it good/Norwegian wood"). This album was a major step toward the potential of pop, and the fact that it fell on deaf ears in the media struck me as outrageous. Such coverage of music as there was focused on Bob Dylan, who had bona fides as a protest singer. Then, in 1965, he did something as audacious as the Beatles, though it shouldn't have been. He plugged in.

I was at one of the concerts when Dylan brought out an electric band. Die-hard folkies booed. He'd broken the golden rule of their music—it had to be played on acoustic instruments. Worse still, he'd abandoned protest for a poetic style of his own invention, one that could support songs about spite and betrayal. I identified with his refusal to be contained. I'd landed an internship at *Esquire*, a bastion of New

Journalism. I thought I'd get to write, but instead, I was put in a cubicle and told to read unsolicited manuscripts, what they called "the shit pile." After two days I stalked out of the office, shrieking the refrain from "Like a Rolling Stone," Dylan's first number-one hit and an evocation of everything I felt about the future. How did it feel to be on my own, with no direction home? It felt great.

In 1965, the pop milieu was a world in formation. It appeared on the radar of the New Journalism, but it had no real claim to chic. A new kind of nightclub called the discotheque would change that. These rooms were where the solo-dance styles of the sixties incubated—the twist, the frug, the monkey, all variations on the theme of individuality. But the class mixing was what interested me. Heiresses wiggled side-by-side with anorexic models and *machers* from the rag trade. I crashed this party, despite my obscurity, thanks to someone who came into my life because she needed a place to stay while the catheter that some quack had inserted in her womb produced an abortion. It was a common enough experience in those days. But Margaret was not the kind of guest my roommate usually brought home, if only because she was a woman and he was gay.

I'd met John during my jug-band phase in college. He was an aspiring singer and composer of folkish songs in an old-timey vein. I knew from the start that he was gay, and it intrigued me, but I also knew that he needed me to be his straight friend, and it was mostly true in those days. My homo impulses, persistent as they might be, didn't feel fundamental, and I enjoyed sex with women. John, on the other hand, was a total gay slut. We lived next door to a therapist with many unhappy homosexual patients, and John connected with his share of them. He depended on the kindness of strangers to a remarkable degree, so it seemed to me.

John took me to my first gay bar—I was there as a tourist, we agreed. It was a musty place in the Village with a sign that read, GENTLEMEN MUST FACE THE BAR. In those days, serving a drink to a homosexual was a crime in New York, and the police were paid off by the mob families that ran gay bars. The owners would be notified when the cops were about to stage a raid, and a red light would go on, signaling men dancing together to separate. I remember thinking, thank God I don't have to live like this. John's libido was certainly robust, but he was also a romantic, and he had a terrible time finding a lover who lasted. This was four years before the queer patrons of a bar called the Stonewall Inn refused to abide by the rules that made their lives an ordeal, and fought off the police. Neither John nor I was equipped at the time to draw a connection between his personal problems and the reality of oppression. It merely affirmed my belief that, while sex with men was easy to find, only women could give me love. This was precisely the conclusion that the system was intended to produce.

Margaret stayed in our place after the abortion, because she developed a serious infection. (May no woman ever have to go through this.) It was a bonding experience, and slowly John and she came to love each other. That was unexpected, given his identity, but it was no weirder than my presumptive straightness. To be a heterosexual with queer tendencies or a homo with a girlfriend wasn't so unusual in the underground culture of 1965. In that restive region, the map of sexual identities had not yet been firmly drawn. But John's sexuality, which he made no attempt to hide, wasn't exactly a professional asset. Despite my efforts to tout his music in my column, it never took off. Under the name Jonathan Kramer, he had a small role in *Midnight Cowboy*, a part in the Broadway production of *Hair* (he played Margaret Mead in a mink coat), and a scene in a Warhol extravaganza ("You're not a blonde on a bum trip," he tells Candy Darling. "You're a bum on a blonde trip"). But fame is far more fickle than talent, and this was especially true for an openly gay performer in the pre-liberation days.

I didn't go to many concerts in 1965. The songs I liked best never sounded as good live as they did on recordings. I was more drawn to the ragtag scene around underground films, those 8mm spectacles with neither plot nor production values but lots of attitude. I knew about them because, back in college, I'd run the Student Cinema Society and booked movies that could only be screened at educational institutions, which were exempt from state censorship laws. One of them was an Andy Warhol production called *Blow Job*. I didn't know what the distributor meant when he said that I could have the film at any length, but it turned out to be a loop featuring a single waist-up shot of a bare-chested man in a leather jacket, reacting while receiving fellatio. I'd placed small ads in the school paper reading, THURSDAY, 4PM, BLOW JOB, so we sold out the house, but after twenty minutes the crowd grew restless. "Where's that fat kid who sold us our tickets?" someone yelled.

(John was actually the ticket taker, but he'd retired to the men's room—for a whole hour.)

I'd come quite a way since my college years, when I ran around writing YOSSARIAN LIVES everywhere. (Boomers raised on the novel *Catch-22* will know what I mean.) But downtown was a less permissive place than the Bronx. There were many scenes I couldn't enter without someone to vouch for my hipness, and Margaret was the perfect sponsor—she seemed to know everyone who lived and made art south of 14th Street. She introduced me to a poet turned rocker, one of hundreds who had taken the trail that Dylan blazed. His name was Lou Reed. I could sniff out his pedigree: literary ambition and a grasp of rock 'n' roll, a combo I knew well. Like me, he'd grown up looking at Manhattan from across a river, longing for a way in that wasn't corrupting. He loved pop music, and it showed, giving his poetry a lean grace and his querulous voice a rough edge, much as journalism had streamlined my prose. Lou was easy to talk to, not yet the volcano of 'tude he would become. Soon I met his band, the Primitives. They would become the most important group to emerge from the New York underground, thanks to the great enabler of the vortex that sucked in people like Lou and me. I'm referring here to Andy Warhol.

In 1965, he wasn't yet a certified genius, certainly not to the other luminaries of Pop Art. If you were going to be a serious painter in those days, you had to be either butch or closeted. The art world was a decorous place for sissies, but Warhol was openly fey. Even worse for his manly cred, he was an illustrator—he'd made his mark drawing women's shoes. Yet, like many outsiders of the sixties, he was utterly disrespectful of formal boundaries. In his hands, every medium was an orthodoxy waiting to be messed with. In doing so, he shaped the cultural future. His films starring outrageous people playing themselves were a prototype of reality TV. His infinitely reproducible graphics ushered in the age of logo T-shirts and signature shower curtains. Most auspiciously for me, he invented modern disco. In 1965, these clubs were an elite, uptown sensation, but once Warhol entered the game, they became a democratic enterprise. No one ever got turned away from his events, which had a suitably pop name: the Exploding Plastic Inevitable. Giant balloons bounced around the floor, strobes pulsed, and ear-shattering music zoned you out. The latter was provided by the house band, which sounded like a cross between a dental drill and a construction site. These were my pals the Primitives. Warhol had rechristened them the Velvet Underground.

Lou Reed still wrote their songs, and John Cale provided the signature slash-and-burn riffs, but Warhol added a chanteuse who gave the group a decadent aura. She was an icy blonde named Nico. Her claim to fame had been a minor role in Fellini's *La Dolce Vita*. As for her vocal skills . . . well, I once compared her throaty alto to the sound of a moose in heat. But she radiated streetwise ennui, as did the stud who circled around the band onstage, cracking a whip. He was Gerard Malanga, God's gift from the Mezzogiorno via the Bronx. I immediately recognized him as the lucky top-man in that blow-job movie I'd shown in college. This was Warhol's greatest talent as an impresario: mixing people of different classes who had a certain self-absorption in common. In his empire of personalities, wealth and beauty didn't matter as much as spectacular narcissism. I was fascinated by this new criterion of flash. Suddenly you were a product of your own creation, a brand you willed yourself to be. And perversion was no longer a vice to be practiced in private, guiltily. It was a mark of individuality, sometimes heroic and sometimes vile, but always interesting.

When I arrived at the Exploding Plastic Inevitable, the first thing I noticed was a thin man peering over the balcony. His hair was silver and his face was pale and round. I knew who he was. Gearing up my journo persona, I sidled up to him and introduced myself, expecting to be ignored. After all, I lacked a byline that could do him any good. But Warhol made an accounting of my background, and I could tell that it passed muster. Not many people were willing to take a student seriously, especially one whose every remark said Bronx. But he was comfortable around bridge-and-tunnel people, and we sat together for quite a while, chatting and watching the set. I think he saw something of himself in my wide-eyed awkwardness.

Within a few years, I would be a regular visitor to Warhol's legendary hive, the Factory. I shied away from its most notorious denizens. Even off amphetamines, they were the nastiest people I had ever met, quite capable of tearing into anyone they deemed unworthy—including one another. Only the drag queens had any warmth. I developed quite a crush on Holly Woodlawn, who radiated the familiar vibe of Latina girls from the Bronx. But my favorite was Candy Darling, a changeling willing to risk everything, which in those days meant unsafe hormone treatments. (As a likely result, she died young of cancer.) We had several friends in common—including John and Margaret, naturally.

Unlike his minions, Andy was always welcoming to me. We'd walk around the Factory, and he'd show me the stuff he was working on. I had the impression that, under the posturing and promo, he loved making things. I came to believe it was the same kind of relief for him that writing was for me. I didn't try to do a formal Q&A—I'd seen him reduce reporters to idiots with a calculated set of put-ons. But he never ran his vacant-stare routine on me. He made me feel that I was talking to another introverted working-class guy. This was a side of him that the media knew nothing about, and it's probably why, in years to come, he would forge a bond with the young Haitian-American artist Jean-Michel Basquiat, back when this boy genius was writing graffiti on the streets. He was another ambitious outsider, like Andy and me.

I wrote up the evening at the Exploding Plastic Inevitable for my cultural criticism class. The professor was a veteran film critic named Judith Crist, as crusty as a woman who had risen in the male world of newspapering could be. I must have seemed to her like a long-haired twerp with no future in print. But she was kind enough to offer me advice: "Cut your hair and learn to spell if you want to get a job in journalism."

The faculty had every reason to worry about me. Though they inveighed against the New Journalism, even they had to admit that there was a market for it. But none of the writers in those hip magazines was under thirty. They were still rebelling against the strictures of the 1950s. To a kid like me, these conflicts were beside the point. But there was no way I could break into their ranks. I would have to find a beat that reflected my own expertise, and a venue willing to let me work it. By the time I graduated from Columbia in 1966, I had stumbled upon both. "You're bringing the whole earning curve of the class down," the career counselor at Columbia groaned when I mentioned that I would be earning twenty dollars a week. But I would have paid the editors for a chance to appear in the *Village Voice*.

In the years since I'd crossed the Bronx to find the only newsstand that would carry it, the *Voice* had doubled in circulation. By 1965, it was the hometown paper of every New Yorker who felt too hip for the *Times*—and they were legion. Hip was the new black, and the *Voice* served as a kind of social register, admitting some to the hot center and banishing others. It was a bizarre system, eminently corruptible, since no one really knew what hip meant. To me this was another way to fill a vacant self. I was determined to be part of it.

Though I would soon become the *Voice*'s first full-time rock critic, it wasn't music that got me an interview with the editor. It was a book I'd written about the new drug culture on college campuses. I'd sold an article on the subject to a national magazine aimed at students, and a publisher offered me a contract with a $750 advance. I took time off from j-school to travel around the country, interviewing young users of marijuana and their dealers, who were also their friends. This struck me as a novel arrangement, one that belied the image of demonic pushers and drug fiends. And then there was acid. In San Francisco I saw something that, as I would soon learn to say, "blew my mind." It was called the Trips Festival, and it featured loud music, a blobby extravaganza called a light show, and free-flowing LSD. In early 1966, the drug was still legal, and its advocates called these events "acid tests." I wrote about the culture they were creating, but my editor was not amused. He added a chapter called "A Guide for Worried Parents," and he changed the title I'd chosen for the book. So it wasn't called *Mr. Tambourine Man* as I'd intended (in tribute to the Dylan song), but *One in Seven: Drugs on Campus*. This was the first—but hardly the last—time an editor would stick me with a humiliating title. Whenever it happened, I felt like a pawn in a rigged game.

In this case, the game really was rigged. The magazine where my article had appeared and the publisher of my book were both CIA fronts. I didn't know that at the time, of course. I made the discovery in 1967 from a *Ramparts* magazine exposé of CIA funding in the U.S., and it came as a horrible shock. Other public figures had similarly unaware encounters with the secret government. I would discover that certain connections with sources were not due to my reportorial skills; they'd been arranged by the agency. I should have suspected that my abrupt rise wasn't entirely kosher, but at the time, I regarded it as evidence of my enormous talent. The CIA exploited gullibility nearly as avidly as they killed people.

I don't include that tainted book in my résumé, but it launched my career. Armed with it, I felt ready to land a job in journalism. I wasn't about to approach a legitimate paper, not with my sensibility. There was only one place that might let me cover pop music in a style of my own. And so, one June day, fresh out of Columbia, I ventured into the *Voice*'s cramped office on Sheridan Square. I think I was the first person to show up there with a journalism degree, and I didn't brag about it to the editor or the publisher, who shared a book-strewn room. They were classic Greenwich Village gentry—tweedy without tweed. The publisher rarely spoke, and the editor, a small man with very bright eyes, listened as I gushed on about wanting to be a rock 'n' roll critic. Finally he said, "What's that?"

"I don't know," I replied.

"Well," Dan Wolf said, "try something." And I did.

I covered a concert at Yankee Stadium called Soundblast 66. It featured a bill any rock critic would have died for: Ray Charles, the Beach Boys, the Byrds, and Stevie Wonder (back then he was *Little* Stevie Wonder). But my piece wasn't just a review; it focused on the interaction between the musicians and the fans, whose every nuance I knew well. I described fistfights in the audience, autograph hunters roaming the outfield, the bell-bottomed seventeen-year-old girl who leapt onto the field and got tackled by a flying wedge of police, the go-go dancer who complained that she'd had to bring her own costume. Everything was cast in the oh-wow style that would become my signature.

I submitted my piece and waited. When the *Voice* appeared, I approached a newsstand, trembling. There was my story, billed on the front page. Inside was a photo—captioned "the author"—that showed me as I was, a kid with the astonished innocence of someone who had no idea what it meant to pose for the press. This was the first time I'd seen my picture in a paper, and I winced. But I was being published in the weekly of my dreams. It was better than even sex with the Shirelles.

A Dork's Progress

Nineteen sixty-six was the year when I entered the media zone of Manhattan for real. I met rockers and writers whose work I cherished. I can't say that I knew them—these were relationships grounded in the intersecting worlds of culture and journalism, not to be confused with friendship—but I got close enough to form vivid impressions. It could only have happened because rock suddenly mattered, and I was the rock critic of the *Village Voice*.

I called my column "Pop Eye"—pun intended. Though music was my major beat, I covered everything from the counterculture to the revolution it spawned. But at first I didn't have that kind of access. No one knew there was such thing as a rock critic, never mind a beatnik newspaper that could generate publicity for a band. So I wrote about the scene I knew, the boys who smeared soot on their faces to look like they had mustaches, and the girl groups . . . yeah.

My first subject was the Shangri-Las, four white chicks from Queens who could work their hips while rat-combing their hair. They sang of dirtbag rebels and bikers doomed to die, in lyrics so over the top that the sound effects around their whiny voices seemed inevitable. (Of *course* there's a motorcycle crash in "The Leader of the Pack.") Their best numbers were like dialogue you might hear in a high school bathroom, the air thick with cigarette smoke.

A girl is being grilled about her new steady. "What culluh are his eyes?" her friend asks.

The girl doesn't know, because "he's always wearin' shades."

The friend has heard that he's a bad guy.

Not so, the girl insists. "He's good-bad, but he's not eee-vil."

I wrote this piece and others like it with no great expectations, so I was surprised by the reaction. There were letters praising the paper for hiring a fourteen-year-old rock critic (I did look cherubic in a messy way), and I got mash notes from boy lovers. I had no idea that I was being read by thousands of people. All I knew was that the *Voice* offered freedom, which was much more important than money to me. There was no layout to speak of, and an article could appear at pretty much any length. My copy wound around tiny ads, jumping from page to page, forward and backward, several times. Every week I'd show up on deadline night and take one of the desks that belonged to the ad takers by day. I worked until morning, when the editor arrived, grabbed my story, and proofread it on the way to the printer. The absence of interference was unheard of in journalism unless you were a writing star, but it was how the *Voice* worked in those days. This was the best way to learn style, because when the paper appeared there was no one to blame for your errors but yourself. Every awkward phrase felt like I'd dribbled piss on my jeans.

On nights when we put the paper to bed, the office was full of writers, and the gay bar below it, a lively place called the Stonewall Inn (yes, *that* Stonewall), sent peals of laughter through the windows. Every now and then I would hop across the street for a pastry at an all-night grocery called Smilers. I remember the counterman, an African immigrant with scarification on his face. He wore a paper hat and a name tag that read, HI, MY NAME IS . . . PARDEEP. In the greenish fluorescent light, he looked like Queequeg. Back in the office, struggling to find a lead, I would picture myself hurling a harpoon at the great white whale of reality.

There's some dispute about whether I was the first rock critic. It's not an issue for me, since I didn't set out to start a profession, but I was the first writer to cover the music regularly in a paper more widely read than the *Midwestern Daily* where Jane Scott had plied that beat since 1962. A small magazine called *Crawdaddy* appeared a few months before my column began. If any of its writers want to claim that they got there first, I say, *Go for it, dude!* (And I'm sure you're a dude.) Being a founder was beside the point. I was in it for the openness—there were no standards to meet. To me, a critic didn't have to get it right; he just had to notice things. My job was to write what I saw, heard, and felt about something I loved. That became a lot easier as my column caught on.

I don't know when rock 'n' roll became rock. I started using the term in 1966, though it seemed arbitrary to make a distinction between the trash of my youth and the "serious" stuff. I thought it had more to do with class than with music. Rock went to college; rock 'n' roll was a high school dropout. But there had to be a new word for songs that blasted through the traditional formula of pop, which consisted of repeated stanzas broken by a bridge—in under three minutes. I was an early proponent of the idea that rock lyrics were poetry. At the height of my influence, in 1969, I edited and annotated a collection of lyrics under the title *The Poetry of Rock*. But I took pains to argue that this aesthetic quality had been present in early rock 'n' roll as well. Buddy Holly didn't know from metaphysical verse, but he channeled its spirit when he sang, "My love is bigger than a Cadillac." R&B had its own mysterious poetry, with roots in the richness of blues. Rock was merely more overt about its pedigree. Bob Dylan had seen to that.

No songwriter has ever been so glorified by academics. They've plucked Dylan out of the sixties and repurposed him as Keats in buckskin. But at his best, he's a typical artist of his time. His most important songs are a mash-up of high and low influences; one can say the same about the work of Andy Warhol or Jean-Luc Godard. There's a reason why this hybrid vitality arose when it did. It was the mark of a generation better educated than ever before, but without the taste for fine art that could only be acquired in elite universities. As the son of a hardware-store owner, Dylan had precisely that background. He was a young man with the stomach of an adolescent, capable of digesting anything tasty. So were we all, and rock was the music of our voracious appetite.

As its prestige grew, rock appealed to the same erudite adults who sponsored other hybrid forms, such as Pop Art and the New Journalism. These people had come of age with progressive jazz, and they didn't know the first thing about Chuck Berry or doo-wop. Jazz is a music of development, but rock, at its core, is about repetition: hooks and riffs. The incessant beat, so grating to sophisticated ears, was what allowed rock to venture into exotic modes without losing its coherence. Not that I could have explained this at the time. I only knew how rock worked as a scene, but that was expertise enough. In a short time—maybe six months—my column became a must-read for seekers of the Now, which is to say, the hip.

Record ads, much bigger than the ones from local bangle shops, soon began to arrive at the paper. The editor, Dan Wolf, was pleased with my work, though he gingerly suggested that I drop the four-letter words. That was a shock—no bad language at the *Village Voice*! I should have read his remark as a sign that the paper looked at culture from a perspective more refined than mine. But I calmly replied that obscenities were part of the scene, and he never mentioned it again. I didn't think much about the contradiction between my background and the *Voice*'s readers; if I had, I would have been intimidated. But the best thing about writing is that you can hide behind it. It puzzled me when people were surprised by my (let's say modest) height. My style made me seem much taller than I was. I guess it was my version of standing on a box.

But I was still little Richie from the Bronx. When I entered a room of tall and trendy people, every muscle in my body twitched. I was sure the murmuring I heard was barely suppressed laughter. Fortunately, I'd learned from Andy Warhol how to croon "Oh, wow!" to any comment. I adopted a version of rock-critic drag that was even more distancing—a velvet cape, satin pants, and silver boots. It was how I thought a member of my profession should dress, and I was desperate to look like the real thing. Oddly enough, it worked. Before long, I was on my way to an encounter with that whirling sixties gyre of new money and brittle fame that could touch down and scoop up a schmuck like me.

A growing pack of sycophants pursued me. I had never experienced such grasping behavior, and it made me feel like I was standing on sand that could liquefy at any moment. But I couldn't resist the attention, or the novel power to put people down. You were expected to do that if you were hip. Since status was so intangible, insults were a major instrument of ranking. Dylan was a master of this craft—check out his tirade to a hapless journalist in the film *Don't Look Back*. I took my cue from him, writing that Judy Collins, a highly competent singer of artfully folky songs, could "put Jesus to sleep on the cross." I told myself that nastiness was necessary to preserve the rough-edged integrity of the music, but it had more to do with feeling like a dork in disguise. I mocked so no one would dare mock me.

In person, I was anything but aggressive, especially with the rockers I interviewed. I would sit there with an adoring expression, too shy in their presence to ask more than a few questions in a soft voice. I had no choice but to let them run the conversation, and that usually worked well. They had interesting stories to tell, tales of brutal fathers or rejection by their peers, and how music had been a way to escape from their pain. Rock was for them what writing was for me: a free, safe space. I, too, was a misfit transformed, so I could describe their feelings from inside.

Watching rockers perform left me with a longing so deep that I could only make sense of the emotion by putting it into words. It was the way I'd felt about my neighbors in the project, with their outsize sexiness. Now, that same erotic vitality was prancing and preening before me, guitars pressing on crotches so that the song went right from the groin into the audience. The music insisted on the kind of body-and-soul orgasm I had never experienced (not yet). I wanted to capture that rush. I yearned for an ecstasy so great that it would shatter my doubts about myself forever.

Dan Wolf didn't edit *Voice* writers; he counseled them. It was a therapeutic experience to meet with him. He said little but it always seemed momentous, even when it was bullshit. And he offered this diagnosis of me: "Most people escape from reality. You escape *into* it." In my case, he was right. I fled from myself by plunging into spectacles, the more extreme the better. I was hungry for any sensation that could suspend my self-consciousness. This need to lose myself was what made me a good reporter of the scene, and it turned out to be a major asset in 1966. At a time when no one knew how to judge anything new, when nothing was defined by its past or definite in its future, when the culture seemed to be floating in a boundless fluidity, journalists were the most credible authorities. I was that kind of guide to rock, though I knew hardly anything about music. All I knew was what it felt like to be in awe.

There was a small group of young reporters who understood rock the way fans did, and we quickly connected. My best friend in that crew was an Australian named Lillian Roxon. She's best known for her rock encyclopedia, but when we met in 1966, she was just a New York correspondent for the *Sydney Morning Herald*. Lillian was a major music devotee and an unlikely groupie.

I'll digress briefly to explain that term as it was understood in the sixties. A groupie was a woman who fucked the band. It was an enviable role in those days—the best groupies were legendary. I remember several of them joining forces to make casts of their favorite rock-star penises in an erect state. They called themselves the Plaster Casters, and they actually exhibited their trophies. These were fans as courtesans.

Life was hard for a woman in music journalism, especially a sometime freelancer and sometime novelist who was asthmatic and overweight, as Lillian was. She died of an asthma attack at the age of forty-one.

Because we were both earning a pittance, we shared our assets, and one of them was a talented photographer named Linda Eastman—later known as Linda McCartney. Linda and I had something in common, a love of rockers, though hers was more, let's say, corporeal. To call Linda a groupie would be to understate her allure. She was a major New York attraction for visiting musicians, and thanks to her I got to interview rock stars who had never heard of the *Village Voice*. Linda would bring me along on a shoot, and while she was setting up I would do the interview, trying to distract Prince Charming from preening for her. Then I would leave the two of them alone. That was how I met Donovan, the British folksinger turned proto-hippie. When I arrived at his hotel room, he was sitting yoga style on an ottoman between two Afghan hounds. I didn't have to fish for a lead; the author of an anti-American song with the line "As you fill your glasses with the wine of murdered Negroes" was ready for his close-up, dressed in a kaftan.

Soon I didn't need Linda Eastman to enter the hip rock hotels of New York: They knew me at the Albert and the Gramercy. I saw a lot of messy rooms, stepped around piles of half-eaten debris, learned to avoid tripping on liquor bottles. Little by little I became a fixture on the local music scene, consisting of a few clubs and, in the wee hours, when everything else was closed, the Brasserie up on Park Avenue. Our ringmaster was Danny Fields, the wry editor of a monthly fan sheet called *16*. (So many pictures of David Cassidy; so little time!) We were writers without a genre. The music industry didn't know what to make of us, and the literary world didn't notice. But because the *Voice* reached a cultivated audience, I got to cross over. I mingled with John Lindsay, New York's upper-crust mayor, who always came to the paper's Christmas party, but I also prowled the lowbrow corridors of the Brill Building.

All that remained of Tin Pan Alley by the sixties was a plaque on West 28th Street. But the Brill Building, just north of Times Square, housed more than 160 music businesses and hordes of songwriters. Carole King and Neil Diamond churned out hits there before they got to sing their own lyrics. The place was haunted by the ghosts of shysters who had bought the rights to doo-wop hits from black kids for (as it were) a song. Legend had it that one group hung the middle-aged owner of their tune out of the window until he agreed to sign over the rights. But this building was also home to publicists—a plague of them, it seemed. Many were holdouts from the days when promoting pop stars meant making them seem clean-cut. They were baffled by the new crop of bad boys with college degrees. I still remember the unfortunate woman who issued press releases under the heading "Gnus for Youze." I hated having to rely on flacks like her for story leads, probably because they reminded me of the hapless inner salesman I was trying to suppress. Even worse, they often called me "Rich, baby."

The only person I allowed to get away with that was Murray the K. The best radio DJs, and he was one, had a sheer love of hustle, and they hustled what they loved. Murray (who legally changed his birth name, Kaufman, to "the K") had an uncanny ability to insert himself into any scene. Only he would have dared to call himself the Fifth Beatle, but the Fab Four let him get away with it. To judge from the smiles in the photos they took with Murray, the Beatles loved his shtick as much as I did. "You're what's happening, baby," he would say to the latest sensation, whoever that was. He had me on his show several times, and he let me program records. I played songs that would have never gotten airtime, including "Heroin" by the Velvet Underground. This was not exactly a drug-prevention jingle. As Lou Reed droned, "It's my wife and it's my life," Murray blanched. He must have thought I would get him thrown off the radio, and after that he didn't call me baby.

Into this den of venality and vitality stepped the Brits. I was well prepared for them. I'd been to London and come home with Beatle bangs and a Victorian fireman's coat from Carnaby Street. I figured that

I'd bond with British rockers by dressing in the right gear, but I could never master the art of androgyny like a young Englishman. To them I must have looked like a Hasid in an Aubrey Beardsley print. And never mind my attempts to trade on our shared working-class roots. I was just another necessary hustler to them, and they suffered me, which is hardly the same thing as confiding. Even if they'd wanted to open up, many of them couldn't, since they were stoned, and not just on grass. It was terrible to see rockers nod on heroin, but I didn't blow their cover in print. The drug laws were so severe that the only moral response was to never rat on a junkie.

I was always relieved to find musicians who were merely manic. That's what I hoped it would be like to interview the Who. Several years before the release of *Tommy*, they were already my favorite British band (not counting the Beatles). Their songs were unlike anything in rock—acerbic, anthemic, influential in unexpected ways. I've always regarded them as the creators of the oratorical pop style that shaped groups like Pink Floyd and Queen. And their unsparing affect was a real antidote to the joviality of the Beatles. They were roughnecks as aesthetes. I was psyched to meet them.

The Who were performing at a theater in Manhattan when I got my chance. Their dressing room was backstage, at the top of a narrow open staircase that twisted around a column. As I climbed the rickety rungs I heard a familiar shriek. A cluster of girls rushed by, makeup running. One of them screamed ecstatically, "Keith sat on me!" This was Keith Moon, the most demonic of all the demon drummers in rock. Onstage he was a djinn, his arms in constant motion over his kit, slamming and crashing in what seemed like triple time. The girl he had deigned to sit upon would probably not change her clothes for days. I was ready for anything.

When I opened the door, all was quiet. The band looked sated, as if they'd just devoured a haunch of game. Only Keith seemed truly alive, but he was far beyond talking. He sat in a hyper daze as the group's leader, Pete Townshend, took my questions. The gist of his response was that he wanted his music to speak for him. I tried to egg him into discussing my favorite Who song at the time, "Substitute." This was a nasty exercise in romantic resentment, but it posed a problem for American radio for another reason: the line "I look all white, but my dad was black." That part of the lyric was missing in the U.S. version. It was the first of many times I would witness the censorship of a rock song, but this had nothing to do with sex or drugs. It was pure racial prudery—and the band had apparently colluded. When I asked Townshend about it, he sized me up, unfavorably. "Listen, mate," he said. (I'm not actually sure he said *mate*.) "Just make up my quotes."

To these musicians I was part of the machinery of fame, and they were caught between their need and their contempt for it. I had an easier time with British pop stars who performed in mod suits. They were much more willing to schmooze. I remember lunching with a Howdy Doody look-alike named Peter Noone, whose band, Herman's Hermits, did popped-up versions of music-hall ditties. I met Noone at a deli in midtown Manhattan. He stared anxiously at a mile-high sandwich and a huge bowl of pickles as we chatted. I was sure his agent had told him that he would have to suffer such delicacies in New York. I had the feeling that, to him, Jews were another unholy part of the record industry. He assured me that he loved kosher food—"So healthy," he said. I flashed him a peace sign.

I shouldn't complain about the way British rockers treated me. I had my own ambivalence. The closer they got to blues, the more they made me miss the wildness of American R&B, the showmanship and the excess. These Brits were too earnest. They had frilly shirts and hair cascading over the collar, but they were practically motionless onstage, hunched over their guitars, rarely making eye contact with the audience. This struck me as an anti-pop attitude, not so different from what I'd experienced in the folk scene, and it had something to do with masculinity. Pop is basically the domain of teenage girls—they discovered Elvis and the Beatles—but British blues was serious guy rock, meant to be played with tight, closed lips. It sounded stringent to me, reverent toward its sources (the way male culture often is) but also distant from them in a sometimes eerie way. It was strange to hear someone who sang like a sharecropper from the Delta lapse into a Midlands accent for an interview.

There was only one British performer who could sing blues without seeming suspect to me. Mick Jagger understood that rock wasn't just music; it was a gender show. He was all flounce and finery, as magnetic an androgyne as I'd ever seen, with lips and hips that made Little Richard seem butch. For about a year, I kept a picture of Mick, in full pucker, over my desk. I have a vivid memory of a concert at which he dropped from the sky in a helicopter. It was the closest I've ever come to having a Pentecostal experience. Meeting him was a whole other thing.

I had missed the famous Beatles concert at Shea Stadium in 1965, but a year later the Rolling Stones were coming to New York. I was there when they arrived at JFK airport to howls from the girly mob confined behind police lines. The Stones had been unable to find a hotel willing to risk the rabble sure to invade its lobby, so they rented a boat docked in the Hudson River, and they summoned the press on board. I was surprised to see women who were much too classy for fan mags. These were editors from the leading fashion monthlies, their perfect figures draped in tasteful versions of the mini-wear Twiggy had made hip. That was when I realized that rock had gone high-end. These ladies were fishing, desperately, for a word with a Rolling Stone. And the lads were total pros, able to satisfy any bearer of a byline the way a male escort might please a customer. I was much too shy to approach them, and I pressed myself against the wall, planning to do what I always did when I couldn't bring myself to chat up a celebrity—describe the scene.

There was plenty to write about. The Stones were dressed for the press, Mick in a bright, striped blazer, Keith Richards in red suede boots. Brian Jones, their rhythm guitarist at the time, wore a button on his fly that read SEX IS HERE TO STAY. Only the quietest member of the band, Charlie Watts, noticed me. "Don't let the photographers make you nervous," he said. "Ask your questions." I whipped out my Kodak and snapped a few shots of Brian as he put on his best sneer, and then I sidled toward Jagger. He was surrounded by women and chatting with no great enthusiasm. I had the feeling that he was standing in a suit of shining armor. I'm not surprised that he's still a brilliantly preserved version of himself, whose only giveaway is the portrait of Dorian Gray that is his face. Brian Jones might have aged into a similar creature, but in 1969, he drowned in a swimming pool. Accidentally or willingly—who can say?

I didn't get much face time with Mick that day, but when the reception ended, Charlie motioned for me to follow him. We slipped into an underground garage where a limo was waiting. A mob of fans rushed us from nowhere, shrieking, tearing at the guys. Everyone made it into the car except Brian. He was engulfed in lips and fingernails. Five girls clutched at his jacket and pants. Others flung themselves over the hood, pounding on the windows, kissing the glass. Finally Brian was rescued by the police and he climbed into the limo, impassive. So were the others. They'd seen this before, but I hadn't. I was deeply moved. These girls were expressing my own response to rock, but they were able to act on it in a way I couldn't. It was like watching a mystery cult. Suddenly I knew what my piece should be about, not just a description of the hype surrounding the Stones but a speculation on how it must feel to be a rock god. I conjured up the African deity Shango, god of thunder, and I transferred his attributes to Mick. What was it like to regard divinity as a day job? What did it feel like to stand on a stage and make thunder? I didn't have the answers, but I had the spectacle and the devotion down cold.

In the months that followed, my *Voice* column rode the wave that rock created. Only one thing was missing: money. The *Voice* paid so little that I survived mostly on cans of tuna from my parents. ("Don't give it to the goy," they said of my roommate, John.) But the paper allowed its meagerly paid writers to publish elsewhere, and I'd begun to find other venues for my work. One day I got a call from a legend of New Journalism, Clay Felker. He was the editor of *New York*, then the Sunday magazine of the city's hippest daily (by far), the *Herald Tribune*. Style was one of its major selling points, and it featured writing by the likes of Jimmy Breslin, Nora Ephron, and Tom Wolfe. Soon I was part of the magazine's stable, finally earning the uptown credentials that would give me access to major rock stars. I also gained entry to the fabled back room at Max's Kansas City, where Warhol's minions frolicked. I felt like a total snob for going there, but I couldn't resist the self-importance. Only a year earlier, I'd been a student begging to be noticed; now I was an underground media celebrity. At some point the inevitable happened: I was caricatured in an ad for pickled herring. It was part of an upscale campaign for the briny fish, featuring a character who flitted among trendy milieus. One ad was called "The Herring Maiven Goes to the Discotheque." At the edge of the sketch, amid the renderings of famous people twisting the night away, was me.

Clay Felker was a man of monumental enthusiasms, and he came up with some very unlikely assignments for his new pop expert. One of them took me to Mexico City, where John Wayne was making a movie called *The War Wagon*. I was nervous about meeting an icon whose face was its own John Ford landscape, craggy and monumental. But Wayne was infinitely more cosmopolitan than the characters he played. I thought he would let me have it for my long hair; instead he was consoling. He may have sensed the queerness under my look, because he told me that he knew what it was like to be different. His real first name was Marion, and he'd grown up being teased mercilessly about it. Was there a relationship between that childhood vulnerability and the male icon he'd become? I wondered, but I didn't pursue the point. I hadn't yet learned to ask leading questions, and I was too uncomfortable to stray from my prepared notes. He tried his best to deal with my rather cerebral topics, and I wrote an undistinguished piece about his myth, which had already been amply commented on. It missed the most interesting thing I had detected in him: his empathy. A photographer took a classic odd-couple shot of us, him in cowboy regalia and me in rock-critic drag. He was a foot taller than me, large and rugged. I was pudgy and pubescent. "We'd look funny walking down Fifth Avenue together," he quipped.

That picture ran in *Newsweek*, along with an article claiming that I'd created something new in journalism: the "pop beat." This was the kind of thing that made me feel simultaneously like a genius and a fraud. I veered between both perceptions, with no way to gauge the praise. My precocity provided an unassailable mystique, which I took full advantage of, in a benumbed state. There's another, equally absurd photograph of me. I'm on a panel at the Yale Club with several movie-industry honchos, including Jack Valenti and Darryl F. Zanuck, sitting at my side. Zanuck is puffing a cigar, trying his best to hide his contempt for this bizarre creature in a costume that made no sense to him, because he needed the kid, needed the insight that was nothing more than supposition, since who the fuck knew what it all meant? Not me. I shudder when I look at that picture, because I know how I felt. Time was moving on two tracks—professionally at breakneck speed, but emotionally not at all. I was frozen, yet careening.

Clay Felker didn't regard me as a caricature. He was the first editor I'd met who treated me like a peer. That might mean hitting on a woman I was seeing (if he was more her speed), but it also produced a comforting informality. Sometimes we met in his apartment, a large, messy duplex on the tony end of 57th Street. He was married to Pamela Tiffin, an actress so beautiful in a classic Hollywood way that, when she came down the staircase, wearing a pale blue robe trimmed in fur, my eyes went out of focus. At such moments, all doubt about my sexuality vanished. I couldn't be queer if Pamela Tiffin left me breathless. What did it matter if Mick Jagger did, too?

One day, Felker called to tell me that I didn't have to file my latest piece. The *Trib* had folded. There wasn't room in the city for a hip daily alternative to the *Times*. It would take him several years to raise the money to publish *New York* as a stand-alone weekly, and when he finally succeeded I became a contributor, migrating between that magazine and the *Voice*. I used *New York*'s expense budget to travel to places where the *Voice* would never send me. Once there, I would write about a well-known rock band for my uptown outlet and report on the scene for my downtown column. In the *Voice* I could be as polemical as I liked, and I began to develop a sense of pop as a unique aesthetic experience. It was clownish and trashy, inherently political, since it could subvert the past with lightning speed, and able to bite the hands of the industries that fed it—so I argued. This theory allowed me to tie rock to the emerging idea that mass culture could be a source of radical change. "A pop critic," I wrote, "needs his eyes, his ears . . . and an impressive German vocabulary." (I'd just discovered the Frankfurt School.)

The *Voice* was doing well enough to have its own ad campaign. "Expect the unexpected," the tagline read. But its office was oddly formal—a hip hush prevailed. *New York* had a more casual vibe. If I dropped by to bat around ideas, I was likely to run into a writer I'd imitated in j-school. The peak experience came when a man in a white suit introduced himself. This wasn't just any white *schmatta*. It was a package as distinctive as my rock-critic drag, and inside it was Tom Wolfe.

The first thing I noticed was his face. It was a shade of pink that didn't exist in the Bronx, except on a new Spalding. But the most fascinating thing, to a boy journalist like me, was his demeanor. He was engaged but remote, curious yet impenetrable—the perfect stance for a reporter, I decided right away. I was already copying so much from Wolfe—the voice that operated as a personal signature, the rhetoric meant to suit the story, the focus on those rituals of dress and jargon he called "status details." One look at him and I realized that I could never crib his look. I was far too grubby. Thank God for paisley shirts—they didn't show stains.

Tom Wolfe was very solicitous of me. He included one of my *Voice* pieces in his anthology of New Journalism, and he even agreed to give me a letter of recommendation to the American Studies program at Yale, where he'd earned a Ph.D. ("So you want to get closer to God," he snickered. I took his drift and never applied to the school.) I think his attitude toward me was part of a larger affection for men who had invented their own roles—pop-music millionaires, custom-car Michelangelos, psychedelic prophets. Eventually this fascination with the exceptional man pushed Wolfe to the right. He was a gifted picador of the liberal cultural elite, but he had no feeling for social oppression, and this prevented him from understanding the movements springing up around him. As my politics veered leftward over the course of the sixties, we drifted apart. Felker, however, remained in my life for many years. At one point I actually punched him in the stomach when he killed a story that was sympathetic to the Vietcong. But, being Clay, he reacted by inviting me to breakfast at his apartment.

Moving among famous writers didn't faze me, maybe because I didn't think of them as charismatic. I saw writing as a shelter from self-exposure. It went well with masturbation, and I was sure every author did that as a reward for producing a great paragraph. But there were some literary lions so fearsome that they might as well have been gods of the guitar to me. Norman Mailer was one. I'd sharpened my knives on his grindstone. He was my model of what a critic should be: a political thinker with a persona that challenged every orthodoxy. In college I'd devoured his collection of early essays, *Advertisements for Myself*. His style combined the swagger of a working-class bruiser with the intellectual reach of an Ivy League grad and the acuity of a radical—everything I wanted my own style to be. What I didn't want was to meet him. Mailer was renowned for his fistfights, and he'd stabbed his wife. But meet him I did, when he stopped by the paper.

As a founder of the *Voice*, Mailer was welcome there, and he would sometimes show up to poke around. He wandered through the office, chatting with writers. As he approached my desk I flashed the grin that meant I was terrified. His eyes widened and he raised his fists. This was his way of greeting a comer in the game. It was a well-known shtick, and I probably should have realized that. But all I saw was a bruiser who wanted to fight me. I was seized by confusion and panic. I fled from the office.

Yes, I was a wuss when it came to meeting my heroes. That was why I'd always shrunk away from Bob Dylan, though there were several opportunities to be introduced. I had a recurring waking nightmare in which any Dylan song about how phony most people are was really about me. At moments when I was sure my inner fraud would burst out, I heard him singing: "Something is happening, but you don't know what it is, do you, Mr. Disco?" This wasn't just a fantasy about humiliation. Dylan's lyrics posed a major challenge to my competence as a rock critic. Their meaning kept slipping out of my grasp. I should have understood that this is precisely the Dylanesque experience. The song flees from whatever it represents; it eludes definition. His great achievement in the sixties was not wisdom but dexterity. Yet I felt compelled to crack the code.

I was never tempted to search the Great Man's garbage, as one notorious fanatic did, but in my need to dredge for meaning I made one of my worst errors (and there were several doozies). I analyzed the song "All Along the Watchtower" without a lyric sheet. The words were usually printed on the back cover of albums, but I had an advance copy without a jacket. A certain line intrigued me: "Two riders were approaching and the wind began to howl." I heard it as "Two *writers* were approaching . . ." and I concluded that it was a reference to Dylan and his fellow prophet Allen Ginsberg. After the paper came out I was told by one of his associates that Dylan got a good laugh out of that.

Like many of my heroes, Dylan eventually moved rightward in his sexual politics, toward a nostalgia for patriarchal values that, I think, has rigidified his work. Ask yourself how many women artists cover his songs and you'll see what I mean. Get me stoned and, like many people my age, I will chatter on about what Dylan was and is. But the conversation usually gets around to, *Did I finally meet him?* Yes and no. Sometime during the late sixties I was invited to his dressing room before an arena concert. He sat on the edge of a table, looking like a boxer about to have his hands taped up. I, of course, had lost the ability to speak.

"I've been hearing a lot about you," Dylan drawled.

"Me too," I peeped.

I don't remember anything else about that brief conversation—the awkwardness is what sticks in my mind. I had blown it. Failed to make an impression. And, unlike Charlie Watts, he was not about to say, "Don't be nervous, ask your questions." Afterward I realized that this had been a very charged encounter. I was looking at someone with a mask of perfect insulation. At this point in his career, he was a man whose survival, creative and otherwise, depended on hiding, and he was very good at it. I was in hiding, too, for different reasons. I felt closest to myself when I got to be a fan, and that's what I became in Dylan's presence. But sympathy wasn't his strong suit. I was relieved that he didn't insult me.

It's embarrassing to admit that I met so many famous people in 1966 and didn't connect with them. This is the fate of a journalist, as I learned that year—you know everyone and no one. But it also happened because I was stiff and girded, the posture of someone in a chronic panic attack. Nothing had prepared me for life in the media zone. I felt sealed within my image, like a mummy. It would take a trip to California, where the rock scene was very different, for me to finally let myself show. Until then I wasn't really aware of the people I wrote about. They were figments of fame, and I saw them as I saw Dylan—through a glass, dorkly.

Flowers in My Hair

By 1967, I had an agent. He wasn't exactly in the William Morris league, but I wasn't looking to break the bank. All I wanted was a way to avoid dealing with negotiations, contracts, or anything that fueled the fear that I was nothing but a hustler. My agent, however, had big plans for me. He was a packager, and he had an idea that would have made my interview with John Wayne unremarkable: a TV show hosted by a boxer named Rocky Graziano—and me. *Move over, Merv Griffin*, I thought, but fortunately I didn't have to turn the deal down, because no one would buy it. I should have known then that this agent was wrong for me, but I stayed with him, partly because he was willing to finance a story far outside the kind of thing that was expected. I wanted to see what rock meant to young people behind the Iron Curtain.

I had come up with the idea after reading about Allen Ginsberg's visit to Prague, where students elected him king of the May Day Parade, a serious breach of Communist protocol. He was expelled from the country after the government seized his journal, which included descriptions of his amorous encounters with young Czech musicians. I was no stranger to fooling around with straight boys—remember, I grew up in an Italian neighborhood—but I wasn't out for sex tourism. Pop music represented a certain idea of America to kids in other countries. In Britain it meant funkiness and freedom from the propriety that confined them. But what did it signify in a place like Czechoslovakia? In order to find out, I had to convince Ginsberg to share his contacts with me.

He was eager to get together. He'd found evidence that the CIA was transporting heroin through Indochina, using the revenue to finance covert military operations. The drugs, of course, ended up in U.S. ghettos. These allegations have never been conclusively proven—though they are likely true—and in 1967 they seemed too bizarre to be credible. Ginsberg had a frenzied look on his face that I'd seen in many radicals. As a journalist I was suspicious of their obsession with American evil, and I hadn't yet come to share their rage. I told Ginsberg that I wasn't equipped to verify his information. He said it was my duty to do the story, and he was visibly disappointed when I demurred. I had the feeling that he would have been more indulgent if he'd found me fuckable. Still, he gave me what I wanted—the names of musicians in Prague.

I decided to broaden my sources by reaching out to the National Student Association, an organization that turned out to be yet another CIA front. If I'd known that at the time I wouldn't have followed up on their leads, but I would never have met the tottering old man whose job was to license Czech rockers. Yes, there was a bureaucrat in charge of pop music in that country. The government, which ran the only record label, had set out to prove that it was *modni* enough to rock, and this ancient satrap got to decide who could play the music professionally. In an office that looked like a set from *The Third Man*, he grilled me about all things Top 40. "Tell me," he said in the earnest, faintly melancholy tone I came to love in the Czechs. "What is Surfing Bird? What means 'Bird is the word'?"

The state assigned me a guide, a loyal Communist who turned out to be fairly flexible about my itinerary. But when I asked her to show me Franz Kafka's house she replied drily, "Maybe in your society you have need of such writers, but we do not." I realized that I needed to shake her, and I managed to do it by promising to send her cosmetics from the States. Soon I was hanging out with Ginsberg's pals, a contingent of musicians and their fans that gathered in the city's main square. More than once I watched the police round up these kids. They'd be back the next day, shorn of their long hair. They were criminals because they didn't have jobs and they weren't licensed to play rock. But they certainly knew the music, and they had a withering opinion of the group I was scheduled to meet, the most popular rock band in the country—pretty much the only official one.

I knew them as the Olympiks, though I've since seen them referred to as Olympic. These four guys were definitely cute enough to steal the heart of Allen Ginsberg, as they did mine, though I kept my feelings to myself. (I didn't want to be deported before I had my story.) They'd done everything in their power to look like George Harrison, down to a carefully coiffed version of his hair, and they sang gentle folk rock, mostly in English. I recall hearing them play "Sealed with a Kiss," a classic summer-romance ballad, which sounded even more wistful with a Czech accent. The group may have been a tool of the state, but they were pretty up-front about disdaining Communism. They didn't like capitalism either; they wanted a Swedish-style socialism in which the state provides for its people but leaves them alone. This was the most prevalent attitude among young people I interviewed in Prague. They always asked when America would end the war in Vietnam—and what did Coca-Cola taste like? Before I left the country I severed the leather labels on my Levi's so the Olympiks could sew them onto their locally made jeans.

The trip to Prague was the most important political experience of my life. It demolished my faith in Marxism as a system, and it made freedom seem much more concrete. Things that I took for granted were hard-won and risky here. I suppose this was the impression that the CIA and its student front hoped I'd come away with. But I also developed an attitude that would make me anathema to the U.S. intelligence community. (I love it when spies and bankers call themselves "communities.") In Prague I saw, for the first time, young people fighting a culture war against the empire that ran their lives. Within a year, Soviet tanks would move on Czechoslovakia to crush their experiment, and American students would confront troops and police in the streets. It was easy for me to see the connection between both struggles. We were all facing the military power of irrational governments convinced that they were rational. This was my first inkling of generational solidarity. Something bigger than systems and borders tied young people across the West together, and rock had a lot to do with it.

Politics was the last thing on my mind when I got back to New York. I'd come home just in time for the biggest story of 1967, at least on my beat. It was an album called *Sgt. Pepper's Lonely Hearts Club Band*, produced at a then-staggering cost of one hundred thousand dollars after four months in the studio. The result would redefine not just the Beatles but my generation. It's hard to imagine the impact of this record unless you understand the central role rock played for us. Its messages were rubrics for life, but without clear instructions; it was up to each person to put it all together, to assemble meaning and take action. So it was fitting to have, as one of the major guides, a collection of songs that broke every rule of Top 40 music, except for the sacred beat. Each number on this album was different from the next, scored with everything from animal sounds to horns, harps, and electronic rushes. Yet all of it, quite mysteriously, cohered.

Sgt. Pepper marked the moment when intellectuals fully realized that rock was an art form. So astonishing was the response that even the *New York Times*, which had never taken this stuff seriously, felt compelled to notice—and they also noticed me. I was cribbed from the underground by the Sunday Arts & Leisure section as it struggled to be hip. There was a dress code for *Times* reporters, but they exempted me because I was a freelancer. I would appear at the office in my most velveteen gear, to contemptuous (possibly envious) stares. My first assignment was to review *Sgt. Pepper*, and I'm sure they anticipated a rave. Instead I panned it. "Reeking of special effects," I wrote. "Dazzling, but ultimately fraudulent." My editor, the unflappable Sy Peck, quipped that he hadn't gotten so many letters "since we bashed the Bible." He shoved several large crates of mail my way.

I wasn't trying to pull off a contrarian stunt. I fully expected to adore *Sgt. Pepper*, since I'd loved the Beatles' two previous attempts to break out of the yeah-yeah mold. But *Rubber Soul* and *Revolver* were basically rock records; this was something else. There was no genre to describe it; the term "concept album" hadn't been invented yet. All I knew was that it didn't belong to the categories of either pop or progressive. The feeling of wonder before a truly new work is the hardest thing for a critic to express. I don't think I've ever read a review that says, "I don't know how to judge this," and I certainly never wrote such a piece, even when I should have. Instead I rejected what didn't fit my schema, so I missed what mattered most about this album, which wasn't any of its songs, but their total effect. For all its diversity, *Sgt. Pepper* is a philosophical whole, presenting a certain attitude toward identity and style. Both are mutable and self-generated—the essence of the hippie worldview.

A number of critics now think I was right to slam that record. There's a feeling that it isn't really great because it doesn't come from the gut, and I thought so too. But I changed my mind about *Sgt. Pepper* in the late seventies as I began to question the values of masculinity. It forced me to think about the relationship between macho attitudes and rigid ideas about what rock should be. As I learned to love the Beatles in their Lonely Hearts Club Band incarnation, I was really learning to love myself.

And now a confession, never before told in print. In those days before earbuds, the ideal way to listen to a record was to plant your head between the speakers and turn the volume up as high as you could bear. I did that with *Sgt. Pepper*, but one of my speakers had blown out. As a result I lost the stereo effect, which is pretty fucking important. I also missed the full force of the bass line, so it seemed even less like rock than it actually was. But I can't claim this technical lapse as an excuse. The fact is, I was an excellent skeptic, but an uneven critic. I could be right and wrong in the same piece. For example, I was an early champion of the Doors, and I praised their debut album lavishly—except for one weak cut, "Light My Fire." What can I say? Sometimes the monkey does not write *Hamlet*.

My major strength as a writer was my passion, and the rocker who aroused that feeling in me more than any other was John Lennon. Everyone had a favorite Beatle; John was mine. He had the perfect voice, with its flat accent and rough edges. I know, it's precisely the tension between rough John and smooth Paul that made the Beatles what they were. But even if he'd lived, I can't imagine Lennon going the McCartney route, writing well-tethered love songs, irresistibly melodic. John was the hungry one, aware of his personal pain but also attuned to what the sociologist Richard Sennett called "the hidden injuries of class." No one wrote as acutely as Lennon did about the battering that poverty inflicts upon young men like those I grew up with. "*They hurt you at home and they hit you at school . . .*" No one smacked us in math class, but I knew just what John Lennon meant by the bitter refrain of that song: A working-class hero was, indeed, "something to be."

It wouldn't have been hard to meet John during his New York years. We moved in concentric circles, and he mentioned the name of my column in the long list of references that make up "Give Peace a Chance." ("Rabbis and Pop Eyes . . .") After I wrote something nice about one of his records he sent me a telegram that read, "Yoko and I say thanks."

Unfortunately it was slipped under the door, and my dog chewed it up except for that line. Given my timidity, you can imagine how I felt about approaching John. That was why I never tried. But one day I got a call from a friend, a perpetual sideman who frequented music clubs where he sometimes hung out. My friend said that John wanted to meet me. I couldn't turn the invitation down.

I don't remember the precise date—my best guess is that it happened in the late seventies. It was a brisk spring afternoon. John was sitting in a van parked on Lafayette Street. All my awestruck lights flashed as I climbed inside. I felt my whole body stiffen, not a novel experience for him, I'm sure. But he was remarkably skillful at getting me to forget who he was. The look of engagement on his face was too genuine to fake. My friend had told him that I'd grown up in the Bronx, and John wanted to hear all about the place. I couldn't imagine why, since it was mainly known for its vast stretches of rubble. But those derelict streets popped with energy. Artists were working there, and my colleagues at the *Voice* were aware of the street parties that would soon give birth to hip-hop. Lennon may have heard about this nascent scene, or perhaps he was curious about the part of the city that was furthest from the grasp of visitors like him. At any rate, he was fascinated by the Bronx, and that was why he wanted to meet me. I wanted, above all, to be useful to him.

I prattled on about the history of the borough, including its development in the 1920s as a destination for the ethnic middle class. I told him about the Grand Concourse, which had been built to evoke the boulevards of Paris. I mentioned the Loew's Paradise, a movie palace with an over-the-top lobby and a marble fountain containing goldfish so fattened by popcorn that their backs stuck up above the water. All of it had been inherited by Latinos and blacks with the same dreams as I had, and access to the same route upward for the dispossessed of New York: style. John listened intently, but he didn't say a lot—or maybe his words don't seem as vivid in my memory as the feeling that I was boring him. It wouldn't have been right to whip out a tape recorder or take notes, so I have no insight into the issues that were tormenting and inspiring him. What I remember most about that meeting is how good he was at relaxing me.

When John was killed in 1980, I sank into one of my deepest depressions. I should have been used to assassinations by then, but this felt like the worst of them, because he wasn't a political figure in the conventional sense. Robert Christgau wrote the *Voice*'s obit. "Why is it always

Bobby Kennedy or John Lennon?" he pondered. "Why isn't it Richard Nixon or Paul McCartney?" His answer was a very sixties one: Those who offer hope are the ones who are killed. That was a lesson I'd learned well by the time Lennon died. But I don't want to write about my burnout right now. It won't make sense until I explain what led to it. You see, the sixties were really two eras, and the first one ended somewhere around 1966. After that it was no longer possible to maintain the rituals of irony and distance that had fostered the idea of hip as a marker of the new elite. *Hip* became hippie, and we were all "freaks."

Sometime that spring I traded my rock-critic drag for tie-dyed T-shirts and tatty jeans. That's what pretty much everyone my age wore. It was part of a larger rebellion against consumerism and the false sense of self created by mass-produced goods. Only handmade products were truly authentic, even if that meant an incongruous patch of velvet sewn onto bell-bottoms, or a shirt that someone had soaked in goat urine to make the colors stick. Beads were everywhere, a symbol of membership in one or another "tribe"—that is, a loosely arranged affinity within the Nation of the Young.

Rock was the oxygenator of this exotic planet, and I was in a unique position as a rock critic. I could move easily between the mainstream media and that shapeless amalgam known as the underground press. It consisted of local, mostly radical newspapers, that reported what the dailies, with their wealthy, politically ambitious owners and their dependence on large-scale advertising, would not. These scrappy weeklies were much less literary than the publications I wrote for, but they produced a vivid account of the era, its values and its manias. Today's "alternative" papers are the descendants of the underground press, and like many remnants of the sixties, they preserve the aura of the original without much of the radicalism. To their young writers, the sixties must seem like an Oz-like existence—and they were.

I had been present at the creation, as a nomadic college student taking refuge in the oasis of the Village, and the counterculture was an expansion of that scene, so I felt very much at home. The shyness that had burdened me dissipated, since everyone looked weird and anyone could join the welcoming herd. With my long hair and hippie haberdashery I was part of a vast youth culture in which the barriers between journalists and their subjects were porous. I could hang out with rockers and engage them on a meaningful level, with no press agent in sight. Through these encounters I discovered the self I never knew. It's the self I still possess.

When I think of those years I picture a sheet of ice melting from the surface down, growing wet and warm in the sun. That was the impact of this new era. I grew more trusting, and I learned that when you trust people you can relax. So I relaxed, maybe too much. But first things first. It began with a trip to California during that uncanny season called the Summer of Love.

In 1967, London was heroin and New York was speed. But San Francisco was all about psychedelics. The postman would offer to share the joint he was puffing on, his long hair flapping under the official cap. Pungent odors emanated from every doorway in the district where young people had settled by the thousands, an area near Golden Gate Park named for the intersection of two ordinary streets—Haight and Ashbury.

I never found out how the Haight, as the neighborhood was called, acquired its mystique. I figured it had something to do with the Merry Pranksters, the crew of acid explorers, led by Ken Kesey, that Tom Wolfe wrote about. The Pranksters were architects of hippie style. Swirl-covered buses like the one they traveled in were a common sight, as was their other major innovation, mass celebrations that featured LSD. In 1966, when I was reporting on the new drug culture for my ill-fated book, I'd witnessed one of these Acid Tests, as they were called. When I returned to San Francisco a year later LSD was illegal, but it was easy to come by, and certain manufacturers, such as the legendary Owsley, were treated like rock stars. The result was a stoned, sensate community, something I'd never imagined even in my wildest fantasies about what was blowing in the wind.

I wasn't very hip to the San Francisco scene when I arrived. All I knew was what I'd seen on TV. There was lots of coverage, little of it knowledgeable. The reporters were outsiders, and their attitude was fascination mixed with dread, a combination I hated. (I still remembered the "Guide For Worried Parents" that the publisher inserted into my drug book.) But nothing since the Beatles had produced such a media frenzy, and I was sure I could do a better job than these pros at describing it. Only problem was, I didn't smoke grass. Though I'd tried it in college, I was convinced that if I got high again I would turn into Norman Bates. But there was no way I could understand the hippies without sharing their signature experience. So I bought a nickel bag in New York—approximately enough for two joints. Being stoned was less unsettling than I feared. I stuffed myself with Sara Lee cheesecake and got lost in a song, but there were no major changes. My intellect was intact, and I could still take notes, though they might climb the side of the page. Once I realized that I could function on grass, I felt ready to head west.

I arrived with the mental baggage of a New Yorker, sheathed in cynicism and highly suspicious of anything that claimed to be mystical. In that respect I wasn't so different from the lefties who created the alternative culture of San Francisco. Their attitude toward the ragtag army of young longhairs in their midst was both welcoming and skeptical. On the one hand, these kids shared the values of the left, including collectivism, environmentalism, and an obsession with consensus. But they had no politics in the usual sense. They were hardly intellectual, and most of them mistrusted reason. This was profoundly unsettling to the old guard, as it was to me. I didn't know whether to mock the hippies or protect them, especially since many were high schoolers, the lowest of the low. They had no money and no homes. They moved among de facto crash pads, occupied the sidewalks, or camped in the temperate groves of Golden Gate Park. That was where I'd been told to go if I wanted to meet the real thing. So I checked out of my motel, determined to live like a denizen of the scene—in the open air.

It was late spring. A warm mist wafted over the cypress trees; music mingled with the caw of seagulls; salt and incense were in the air. Food simply appeared, and I wandered from group to group chowing down. When I was tired I plopped on the side of someone's sleeping bag. I had come expecting to be drenched in sex, but it was harder to come by than I expected. Free love didn't mean you could just walk up to a chick and whip out your love wand. You had to connect on a level that seemed mysterious to me. I hadn't yet come to appreciate the beauty in a woman with downy legs. It took getting used to, as did trusting in that vague sensation of compatibility known as "the vibe." The consolation was that my body type mattered less than the color my karma produced in someone's mood ring. Within a day or two I managed to hook up, though I'd never had sex in a park and I couldn't help worrying about the cops. I wasn't sure my partner was on the pill, and it didn't reassure me to see her douche afterward with water from a canteen.

At first I was appalled by all this. The hippies seemed so blockheaded, so forced in their mellowness, blowing bubbles or handing me the gift of a small rubber dinosaur. I could tell from their disregard for money that they were securely middle class, while I came from a background where dropping out meant only one thing: poverty. What I saw looked dangerous and, even worse, indulgent. But the naïveté was irresistible. It brought out the Holden Caulfield in me. I wanted to be their catcher in the rye.

I quickly learned to honor the astrological metaphysics that functioned as a greeting. "What sign are you?" I was asked many times, and when I replied, the response was, invariably, "I knew it." After a while I stopped thinking of this as silly; it was just another code, like the peace-sign salute. I was beginning to fall under the spell of the scene, with its remarkable capacity to calm my anxieties. Everything that mattered in my life—the clawing for fame, the fending off of sycophants, the constant risk of being put on or put down—all of it dropped away. Every now and then I'd catch myself, take a step back, and think, *what the fuck am I doing in this place?* Me, the Herring Maiven, a wunderkind of the written word, nodding to the sound of a (not very well-played) drum, seriously contemplating losing my dignity with a woman in a dress that had recently been a bedspread. But out here I was just an ordinary dude, which was precisely what I wanted. I yearned to let go of the struggle, to strip off my Manhattan identity like winter clothing until, naked (or maybe in just my underwear), I would live as a desiring animal in the wide open of the California dream.

I didn't realize it then, but this line of thinking would soon spread across the whole grid of my generation. It was the great temptation of the sixties, the ghost of Rousseau that haunted every Freudian my age. What lay beneath the layers of repression? Suddenly it seemed possible to know, not through a lengthy course of psychoanalysis but simply by being here now. The Oedipus complex—fuck that! In the words of the Incest Liberation Front (a West Coast group of the sixties), "Sex before eight, or else it's too late." If neurosis was the price we paid for civilization, maybe the only way to be healthy was to be uncivilized.

I veered between embracing what I saw and bristling with contempt for it. Finally I decided that I was on vacation, and that nothing I did here would matter once I got back to New York. That was how I gave myself permission to wade, if not plunge, into the hot tub of desire that was all around me. Everything seemed inchoate, unstructured, accepting. Any combination worked: hetero, homo, bi, the categories lost their grip. Gender was (ideally) fungible, race was (officially) irrelevant, class was . . . what's that? Never mind that these distinctions were still lurking under the long hair and jeans. I was sick of living in a world where the social order was all too obvious. That's why the hippies were so appealing to people like me. They represented liberation from reality.

Out here in the land of the unrooted I left all my connections behind, among them the woman who would soon become my wife. I had to be mobile; that was my excuse for traveling without her, but actually I needed a break from everything in my life. Though I wanted to marry Judith, the idea of being truly intimate with a woman frightened me at the age of twenty-three. It helped that monogamy wasn't part of the deal—like many sixties couples, we were free to explore. But cleaving, as my parents had, for better and for worse, seemed so . . . Levitical. Before it could happen I had to understand who I was. San Francisco was perfect for the purpose, and so was the music that came from there. It felt as wild as British blues were restrained. There was none of the ornate eroticism of the Rolling Stones. The musicians were sexy in an ordinary way, and their sets seemed shapeless, though not aimless, to me. This was rock gone elastic.

The best bands played for free in Golden Gate Park. It felt a little like the folk-music gatherings I'd joined in Washington Square, except that there was no turf to fight for here, no standard of purity to defend. The competition among college students from Queens over who could sing like a native Appalachian was as irrelevant as a medieval debate about the nature of angels. The only offense was ambition. This, I was told more often than I liked, was an ego trip. A game. A curse that could only be explained when I admitted that I was from New York. Then I would receive a look of pity, a hug, and perhaps an exhortation to trip. I became so anxious about being plied with LSD that I refused to drink out of any bottle that wasn't sealed.

Lots of people told me that the only way to appreciate hippie culture was to drop acid, but I was convinced that it could be explained by the right theory. I had several, ranging from the fashionable postlinear ideas of Marshall McLuhan to a homegrown historicism in which the hippies were an incarnation of the revolutionaries of 1848. In a way they were, just as they echoed the mystical beliefs of the American Transcendentalists, but they were also a manifestation of something timeless and universal. By suppressing the vaunted "reality principle," LSD created patterns of thought and visual styles that pulsed like the glowing abstractions in stained-glass windows or Tibetan mandalas. It struck me that there was a reason why these disparate mystical traditions produced the same patterns as your average tie-dye. They all evoked the deep structure of consciousness, the interplay of neurons. That was what acid had in common with Buddhist and Hindu meditation; it unlocked perceptions blocked by the organizing power of reason. But unlike those other practices, it did so instantly. The passion for shortcuts, which had always been present in America—Tocqueville noticed it in 1832—was the real enabler of LSD.

It wasn't until I actually took acid that I encountered the part of me I was searching for, the self I'd denied. It had little to do with my sexuality. Desire, which felt so central to my being, now seemed like only the surface. On LSD, I accessed my subconscious, and it contained not only monsters and immense depths of love but the evidence that I had something in common with all living things. That was a big relief, because I'd always felt trapped in my uniqueness. Certain artworks—the Black Paintings of Goya, the late portraits by Rembrandt, the Paleolithic drawings on the walls of a grotto in France—have had a similar effect on me; the sense of connection, across time, with a consciousness beyond my personality. Which is not the same thing as feeling the presence of God. Acid didn't change my atheism, but it was the source of whatever spiritual feelings persist in me. Like the kids I'd been skeptical about, I found the hippie within.

Still, I'm unwilling to give up the idea that drugs have a social dimension. Every high, no matter how personal, is also collective; our associations, even in an altered state, are guided by the culture around us. Kids who drop acid today don't have the same experience that the hippies of the sixties did, because they don't have the same wide-open sensibility. Of course, some things about the psychedelic scene seemed ridiculous even when I was stoned. There's no other way to describe the mantra I heard often in the Haight: "Dog is God spelled backwards." Or the anthem of the Summer of Love, warbled by an L.A.

folkie who had reinvented himself in a floor-length robe, Donovan style. This song would draw perhaps fifty thousand kids to a city ill equipped to handle them.

> *For those who come to San Francisco*
> *Be sure to wear some flowers in your hair*

Don't bring cash, just your stash—and get ready for a giant "love-in" there. Well, the love-in lasted until it became apparent that the kids wandering around stoned and senseless were so many sitting ducks. Dope dealers and bruisers looking for sex descended on them, resulting in rapes and an influx of heroin. It was presented by the media as proof that the land of commodification was the only safe place; beyond lay dragons. It took less than a year for the festival to turn ugly. But at first it actually seemed that a new society was emerging, based on the life force—eros in the broadest sense. Every institution could be transformed by the creative potential of ecstasy, even the media.

A new newspaper had appeared in town, consisting of type that curled around the pages like paisley. It was called *The Oracle*, and as far as I could tell it was completely illegible. The covers lacked coherence; they usually consisted of mystical symbols superimposed on images of various gurus. From watching people read this paper I realized that you were supposed to let it resonate with the vibe in your mind. I tried and failed—linearity was my karma. I'd been trained to take notes, obsessively and accurately. But I didn't know how to report my feelings. That would have violated the Tom Wolfe rulebook, which I still carried in my mind. When I look at my piece about the San Francisco rock scene of '67, what strikes me is that none of the changes I was going through made it into print. Instead, I dutifully described the music: "jug band scraping against jazz." I noted the right word for a great group: "heavy." I reported on the rivalry with L.A. without taking sides, though I shared the contempt every musician I interviewed expressed for the sprawling Babylon to the south. The counterculture here defined itself by being everything Los Angeles was not. A member of the Quicksilver Messenger Service summed up the local attitude when he told me that "L.A. hurts our eyes." But he had to go there to record.

The studio was the great Satan of these rockers. From band after band I heard about the importance of playing live. The thing that made

San Francisco music special was its tangibility. But that was only possible because the scene hadn't yet been industrialized; it was still a communal rite. The best musicians didn't just play for the people, they *were* the people, and you couldn't pick them out from other hippies on the street. I had a dire feeling that all of this was temporary, as underground cultures always are. But I didn't say so—not yet. I was here to celebrate, and to stand guard.

I wasn't the only catcher in the rye. There was a band of renegade activists who called themselves the Diggers, after a group of radical British agrarians in the seventeenth century. The mission of the new Diggers was to feed hippie strays, whose numbers were growing by the day. They invented slogans that have since become the stuff of retro Day-Glo posters: "Do your own thing" and "Today is the first day of the rest of your life." These people were determined to remain anonymous, and in the spirit of transgression each of them was named George Metesky. It was a cryptic reference to a notorious criminal of my childhood, the so-called Mad Bomber. I made my way to the Digger Free Store, and there I met the group's leader, Emmett Grogan. I took out my notebook and asked him to spell his name (a reflex from j-school), and he complied. I didn't realize that by publishing a piece that revealed his real identity I was effectively outing him. After it appeared he phoned me in a rage. No one was supposed to know who the Diggers actually were. "But I told you I was a reporter," I said. He spat out a comment that made me feel like I'd finally succeeded in fitting in: "We thought you were faking. You looked like a runaway." Then he threatened to throw acid in my face, and he didn't mean LSD. "You know too much," he snarled.

I thought about calling the police, but in the end I let his threat pass, and he never carried it out. Years later Grogan wrote a memoir under his real name. Well, I thought, he's got a right to blow his own cover, and I don't blame him. Not many people who spent their productive years in the service of the counterculture were left with much to sell except their names and memories.

I've left out the most enduring part of the San Francisco scene, which happened indoors, where, for a modest admission, you could spend a long evening at the city's two major rock venues. I shuffled between the Fillmore and the Avalon (the latter run by a company called the Family

Dog). Mesmerized by deafening blasts of sound, I would sink into a trance and forget that I was a fucked-up New Yorker.

These concerts had an added attraction that couldn't be seen in the park—endlessly mutable light shows. Dyed liquid, manipulated between two glass slides, produced pulsing globulous shapes, squids of the mind. It was a new art form, as were the posters that advertised the concerts. Readable they were not, since they featured lettering in elusive patterns that seemed to be a combination of Art Nouveau, faux-Aztec, and Hindi script. I would stare at these strange things, trying to decipher the names of the bands appearing that weekend. Moby Grape, Chocolate Watchband, Sopwith Camel (originally an old biplane)—it was all part of a code, allegedly comprehensible only through the fluid logic of LSD. But it was also a scheme for building a new society. This was an unexpected outcome of the feeling I'd had when I marched for civil rights. It wasn't just about race; it was about existence. The future was a product of will.

The best San Francisco bands were composed of migrants from every part of America where it was hard to be a hippie, which is to say most of the country. Many of these performers had been the nerds and sluts of their high schools, and they came here the way I took the subway to the Village with my sandals in a paper bag. But as the scene ripened it attracted less alienated types. With one call to their label I reached the most professional local band, the Jefferson Airplane. They'd already been featured in a *Newsweek* story, and one of their songs, the bolero-based "White Rabbit," had became an anthem of what was being called acid rock. The Airplane were more cosmopolitan than the other musicians I'd met, ambitious and polished to a sheen. We had a sensible chat, with no druggie behavior, and we posed for pictures. (I have a shot of Grace Slick standing beside me, though like much of my rock memorabilia it's stuck to something else.) But the encounter didn't reveal much about what made the youth culture of this city so rich. I needed to connect with the real, hairy thing. So I returned to the park, where I met a child of God from Brooklyn and his "old lady," who had baptized herself Thistle. They offered me the tarry end of a joint and we chatted until sunset, when they casually mentioned a crash pad where they were heading. I was sure to meet musicians there.

Today the Victorians in the Haight have been spiffed to an asset-rich patina. But back then they were ramshackle buildings, often unpainted and splintery, and the house on Ashbury was typical. Anyone could wander in, and I did, messing my hair to look like I belonged. But I still bore the edgy signs of a Bronx native, and my accent lacked that stoner drawl. Someone asked if I was a narc. There was a strange belief that an undercover cop had to identify himself when confronted, so when I said no they believed me. No one demanded to know what I was doing here. It didn't take a press card to get in.

I wandered through rooms furnished in mattresses. People were milling about or sleeping something off, and a pot of mush was simmering—yellow lentils coagulating. I turned down a plate of ricey glop, and the bread looked like it might shred my gums. It would have been easy to find sex, but I was looking for the band that owned the place. I asked everyone I could where they were. Finally someone pointed to a tall, lanky dude whose straight hair fell nearly to the belt of his jeans. He had the most incredible baby face and a body that reminded me of a willow tree. This was Bob Weir, rhythm guitarist of the Grateful Dead, and he had pretty much the same effect as Pamela Tiffin had on me. Bob epitomized what I found hot in hippie men, a fluidity that challenged masculinity. But I was not about to broach the subject of sexuality—his or mine. Instead I asked him about the threat of commercialization. This was a major topic among musicians here: whether the large advances that record companies were dangling would corrupt the scene. "If the industry is gonna want us," Weir said, "they're gonna take us the way we are. Then, if the money comes in, it'll be a stone gas."

I didn't share his optimism, but as it turned out most San Francisco bands had complete freedom in the studio—the record companies didn't want to intrude on the vibe. For the Dead, Weir told me, this meant making albums that sounded as close as possible to the way they played live. That was their signature, and it's why they represent a certain attitude toward music so effectively. I've never fully understood the Deadhead phenomenon, but I suspect that it has more to do with the ambience of freedom they created than with their skill. At their best the Dead did a rollicking update of Western swing, but to me their songs were a habitat for wandering. As for Weir, he buffed up and butched up after the sixties ended, but back then, up close, he was a model of the new, less locked-and-loaded attitude that I found wondrous to behold in men.

I later discovered that this crash pad was known as the Grateful Dead house, and that the band stayed there when they weren't on the road. I was free to stay as long as I liked, and I didn't need the auspices of a sexy photographer to meet the band. At any moment Jerry Garcia might saunter by, smiling through his curly beard. But the most memorable part of my visit came when someone tapped me on the shoulder. I couldn't quite place him, but he looked like the guy I'd met at Tom's house in my college days, the guy she kept as a stud. His hair was longer than I remembered, tied back in a ponytail, and a drooping mustache made his lips look thicker. But he had the same up-for-anything grin. I didn't want to bring up the association with sex for room and board that came to mind when I thought of him. Maybe he'd found more gainful employment since those days—there was an infinite demand for lanky musicians out here.

"How are you?" I stammered, and then I realized that I'd never found out his name. "*Who* are you?"

He smiled broadly. "Right now I'm Groovy."

There were hundreds of Groovies in the Haight, probably several in this house. But I didn't object.

"I've been reading your stuff," he said. "Nice . . . but . . . "

"What?"

"You'd be a better critic if you dropped acid."

I went into a rant about how I could dig the music without taking drugs; after all, it was an expression of Emersonian ideals, which had themselves emerged from, ultimately, Kant.

"Okay," he said warily. Then he pulled out a spliff and handed it to me. "Breathe deeply," he whispered in my ear. I did—and coughed. It was stronger than the grass I was used to, possibly because it had been soaked in hash oil. He urged me on, and I took another puff. After a while I felt my eyelids close, but I could still see.

"Yeah," he murmured. "Let it flow."

He led me to the mattress by the window, where the sunlight was streaming in. I watched it flicker across the ceiling and crystallize in the panes of glass. He strummed a few chords on his guitar and began to hum. Time passed—I don't remember how much time. I was too enchanted by his voice.

"I'll show you," he said. "I'll get you there."

In the days that followed, I absorbed Groovy's circle of friends by a kind of osmosis. Among them was a schizophrenic cartoonist named Rory Hayes, who drew teddy bears with auras in gnarly landscapes. How did he live, I wondered, since he seemed too fragile to function? I was told that a group of cartoonists cared for him, and that was how I became aware of another art form germinating in San Francisco, a new kind of comic book, rife with sex and drugs. I quickly became hooked on these comix, as they were called. They came in a wide variety of styles, from pulpy realism to psychedelic abstractions featuring Mr. Peanut. My favorite characters were a crew of stoners called The Fabulous Furry Freak Brothers, the creation of Gilbert Shelton. But the most fascinating comix artist to me was Justin Green, whose intensely autobiographical work included a strip about his father succumbing in a hospital bed while berating him for his wicked ways. This was a long way from Casper the Friendly Ghost.

I didn't actually meet these artists until 1969, when I was given carte blanche by Bantam Books to edit a paperback magazine called *US*. Unlike today's celebrity rag of the same name, this was a collection of countercultural writing that featured, among other things, the poetry of Jim Morrison, early feminist writing by Ellen Willis, and graphics by underground cartoonists. The most famous of them was R. (for Robert) Crumb. He was rail thin, even more wary than me, and, like other introverted men I'd met, he had a robust Jewish woman in his life. I approached Crumb about publishing him in my magazine, and he let me have one of his sketchbooks. I selected a portfolio of work, including a drawing of Jesus crucified on telephone lines. The publisher was pissed. I was told that the image got a whole line of Bantam books banned from Woolworth stores. *US* lasted for only three issues.

I didn't regret running those sketches. Crumb was the most important visual artist of the counterculture, as serious an explorer of the crannies of consciousness as Dylan was. His skill at rendering lifted his work out of its time, as did the primal sex fantasies he portrayed, some of which verged on what would now be considered child porn. Even if you didn't share his wet dreams, their relationship to your own was so vivid, their candor so intimate, that you could only gape in glee. The dominant feeling in these cartoons was delight, though they trafficked in all sorts of stereotypes, racial and otherwise. It felt like a minstrel show without the power relations. Everyone was the butt of the joke, and so the libido was free to play. This was a major theme in sixties culture—infusing the forbidden with new meaning—and it's directly related to tripping, images of which abound in Crumb. I still own some of his sketches, and they're quite disturbing. One of them shows a man, presumably on acid, with a lightning bolt splitting his head in two. When I look at it today I don't just see a bummer. I see the ripping open of consciousness, which is the story of my youth, and it wasn't always pleasant. Crumb captured the dominant mood of the time, the duality of ecstasy and horror.

Meeting Crumb and his fellow cartoonists was further proof of what I'd noticed in New York. So much was possible once you grabbed hold of a degraded form like comic books; so much quality was hidden within it, waiting to be mined. All sorts of innovations could appear when the boundaries between high and low art were smashed. And in California this process was taking place where the traditions that dominated the East Coast barely had a toehold. At any moment you might see something that should have existed only in a trip—perhaps a hot-dog stand shaped like a hot dog. The popular, drenched in an absurd innocence, *was* culture. The music, the posters, the light shows, and the comix all expressed the texture of daily life. In New York, this communalism was missing. Bohemians existed as a special order in an indifferent city, and every transgressive act was performed with one eye on the media. But out here there were no experts on the trendy. It felt like freedom to me.

If you want to understand the difference this chaotic spirit made, compare the music of the Velvet Underground, which sounds highly considered even when improvised, and the sonic mash-ups of Frank Zappa, which blaze in all directions. The Velvets are cosmopolitans; their songs work as well in Paris as in New York. But Zappa's compositions are site specific. They flame with the spirit of California in the sixties. Not that he was part of the hippie scene. He shunned San Francisco, and he lived in a rather ordinary house in a desert town. I visited him there once. I recall a small recording studio in the basement, and a child called Moon Unit scrambling around my feet. (The name didn't faze me; I knew babies called Ocean and Sprout.) Zappa was venomous about the record industry, and the feeling was more or less mutual. His albums were over the line even in that lineless time, with brazenly disrupted melodies and lyrics beyond the enigmatic. But, though his pieces were as tightly erudite as the Grateful Dead's were meandering, Zappa shared with them a sense of abandon that was pure West Coast. In New York you worked hard to achieve this feeling. Out here it was as breathable as a contact high.

Despite my dabbles in hip living, I was far from sloughing off my personality. I would relax to a certain point, and then I'd flash on committing some infantile error, such as drooling. I realized that this intense defensiveness was the reason why I was drawn to Groovy. He seemed to live without doubt, and I kept thinking of what he'd said to me at the Grateful Dead house: "I'll get you there."

That was why I tagged along with Groovy and two of his friends on a trip to Lake Tahoe. I suspected that this expedition would culminate in dropping acid, and I remained uncertain until the moment when I decided to swallow the tab of acetate that he offered with a grin. I was on vacation from my vacation, with someone I trusted, so . . . what the fuck! Half an hour, and nothing. Maybe I was so uptight that not even LSD could subvert my ego. "Nothing's happening," I groaned. And then I got hungry.

Acid is supposed to diminish your appetite. A hamburger will look like what it is—charred flesh. A section of orange can feel like a feast. But the drug didn't have that effect on me. I was famished. Ravenous. And I realized that I'd felt that way from a very early age. Someone offered me a hard candy. I started to unwrap it, but the crinkling was like loud static, and when I popped the candy into my mouth and chomped down, it felt like shards of broken glass. I spat it out. There was nothing to do but suffer. I decided that I would always be hungry, never satisfied. This was my karma.

Gradually the hunger faded. I don't know how, but I clambered up a tree (something that seems impossible, since I'm afraid of heights), and I sat on a high branch, looking down at the lake. The bark was vibrating. I realized that it was alive. Wood was more than just a product, and so was I; more than the sum of my neuroses. I was human, no more or less. Groovy and his friends, with their forest of hair—they were animals like me. I watched them crowd into a small boat that had mysteriously appeared on the bank. They urged me to join them. I held back. I was sure they would attack me, but I was cold and beginning to shiver. I needed the warmth of their bodies more than my defenses. So I climbed down from the tree and stumbled into the boat. The water swirled around us, prismatized, like the colors in an abalone shell. It wasn't a hallucination. The play of light actually produced all these shades in the water; it was my mind that assembled them into blue. Acid disrupts the ability to organize stimuli into functional patterns. But it reveals reality.

That night we ended up in a casino. I have an enduring image of us sitting on the floor, still stoned, while gamblers stepped around and over us. At some point, Groovy reached into his back pocket and pulled out a picture of a little girl. It was his daughter from a previous marriage. I tried to reconcile the image of him as a father with my memory of his qualities as a stud. Just then he put his arm around me. The smell of his sweat was faintly nauseating. I began to shiver. It wasn't just a latent-homosexual panic but something more primal, the fear of vanishing into the body of another person. If he'd been a woman I might have been able to discharge my terror in an erection. As it was, I sat there shaking until he took his arm away.

"It's okay," he whispered. "You're safe."

When I got back to San Francisco my skin was itching badly. I realized that I could no longer live without a shower, so I got a motel room. I also called Judith. She arrived the next day, and I began fielding calls from publicists. One of them made an impression on me, probably because he wore very tight pants. This was my first encounter with a music-industry type known as the company freak.

These go-betweens were hired by baffled record labels to serve as liaisons with the cryptic music scene. It was a job for hippies willing to put in the time, and it mainly consisted of scouting for promising unsigned bands. It also involved relating to rock critics, who were more numerous by that time. My new friend wanted me to meet two typical San Francisco bands—that's how he described them. I realized that I had only interviewed musicians who were well-known, so I accepted his invitation, and the next day he picked up Judith and me and drove us to a strange place called Daly City.

I'd heard of this suburban development because it was the subject of a mocking folk song by Malvina Reynolds, called "Little Boxes." The homes looked alike, and they were made of what the song called "ticky tacky." We pulled up to a house like all the others. The front door was ajar, and inside we were greeted by a farrago of hair and guitars. That was how I met Quicksilver Messenger Service and Big Brother and the Holding Company. They hadn't released any records yet, so I'd never heard of them. In the corner I noticed a rather chubby woman holding a baby close to her chest. Someone introduced us to Janis Joplin. I'd never heard her sing—no one outside the local scene had—but she looked like someone who could belt the blues.

While I busied myself with the other musicians, Judith and Janis shared a joint. They talked about growing up pudgy, about their alienation and pain. I talked to Janis as well, though much less personally; I was interested mostly in quotable lines for a story. More to the point, we all grokked, to use the sci-fi term that meant communing. I took notes, naturally, but when I looked at them later they were circles and curves. I retained enough to produce a piece that ended with the words I'd blurted as we all left the house in Daly City. I watched a vanful of musicians careen away, long hair flying from every window. "We shouldn't be interviewed," I shouted after them. "We should be friends."

Weird Scenes in the Gold Mine

I was still having acid flashes when I got back to New York. It wasn't unusual that summer to see young people roaming the streets in an advanced state of distraction, and I didn't want to look like that. But it took several days to banish the perception that the wood in my floor was a living thing. Trees pulsed before my eyes, and, yes, I wanted to hug them. I'd become a hippie trapped in the body of a hard-driving, working-class Jew, not an easy fit.

The only thing that tethered me to reality was journalism. Writing had always served to cohere me, and now it came in very handy. I filed a celebratory piece about the local hippie scene, with no mention of my acid trip. I didn't want to describe the feelings it had awakened in me. I was sick of reading about finding God in a flower, and there was nothing admirable about melting in the California sun. New York didn't reward such states of being, so I kept myself out of the article. But I couldn't keep reality at bay, and I was haunted by the feeling that there was a bigger story than flower power out there, something that would shock the counterculture away from its beautiful aspirations. The onslaught of rape and hard drugs in the Haight was part of it, but the real impediment to building a society of love was the war in Vietnam.

There were already close to half a million American soldiers there, but the hippies I'd hung out with believed that the violence would end on its own once people dropped acid and expanded their consciousness. It was still possible in certain drumming circles to speak of summoning the Aquarian Age, and the Beatles were chanting, "All you need is love."

The deranging experience of combat was as foreign as Communism to these kids. Either they were too young for the draft or they managed to evade it one way or another. It wasn't hard for children of the middle class to do that—a note from a sympathetic shrink was usually enough—but the boys I'd grown up with in the project were shoveled into the military, and some of them would never come home. At the *Voice* I got letters from soldiers in Vietnam, often with peace signs on the envelopes, letting me know how much rock music meant to them, how it was all that kept them alive. The knowledge that I was safe and free to pursue my career while those guys were in mortal danger left me with a gnawing sense of guilt. It was clear that, at some point, I would have to write about Vietnam. But the antiwar movement was still largely a campus phenomenon, and I wasn't a student anymore. The counterculture was my area of expertise, and my shelter from the firestorm.

By 1967 the music industry had mastered the art of appealing to writers like me. Record executives wore their own version of the hippie look: a requisite Nehru jacket with a discreet string of beads. Publicists would flash a peace sign at the end of a pitch. At the major labels, there were rooms set aside for previews of albums not yet released. I remember being invited to one of those special private concerts. The president of the company, which specialized in rock with vaguely folkie credentials, greeted me personally. He ushered me into a sound-baffled chamber with huge speakers and plush chairs. He pointed to a butterfly-shaped box on the table, and then he left the room. Inside the box was a small pipe and a block of hashish. The music started. I sank into a chair and lit up. It was much harder than payola to resist freebie drugs.

I was beginning to feel apprehensive about where rock was headed. Some of the musicians I'd met in San Francisco were being offered advances of $100,000, the equivalent of about $700,000 today. Still, I told myself that Bob Weir was right: as long as the bands controlled the product, money wouldn't change anything. After all, the lyrics were as subversive as ever. Sexual references and allusions to drugs were no problem as long as the message was couched in code. If all else failed, the band could deny that the double meanings were actually double. (I was particularly amused by the Byrds' insistence that their song "Eight Miles High" was merely about their trip to London.) Code words for marijuana were constantly being invented, and as long as the FCC was happy, the record labels looked the other way.

I, too, was riding high. *Life* magazine had commissioned me to write an essay on rock lyrics, to accompany a set of pictures of the top bands. You could tell that these photos were psychedelic because they were shot with wide-angle lenses. (Heavy!) The words didn't really matter, so my anxiety about the Time-Life house style was unneeded. My piece appeared pretty much as I'd written it, but the title got changed. My valiant attempt at cultural synthesis was now called "Wiggy Words That Feed the Mind." The loss of control was devastating; I fell into another media-inspired depression, and it led me to conclude that I had to back away from the mainstream, not just in the assignments I took but in the things I wrote about. Acid rock was getting all the attention it needed. The real story was how the music actually got made. Notwithstanding the San Francisco attitude about playing live, in the new era that *Sgt. Pepper* had created, the recording studio was where the real action was.

If you're not interested in the men who turned Neumann mikes, Pultec equalizers, and eight-track tapes into an instrument, you can skip the rest of this section and go right to the stuff about celebrities. But any backstory of pop music in the sixties has to acknowledge the key role that producers played. They did everything from arranging and mixing to discovering acts. John Hammond had a major impact on rock by signing Bob Dylan and Bruce Springsteen. The Beatles could never have realized their sonic fantasies without George Martin. And then there were the girl-group classics created by Phil Spector. His Wall of Sound was as close as rock 'n' roll got to being Wagnerian. His production of "You've Lost That Loving Feeling," with the Righteous Brothers, is impossible not to sing in the shower. But Spector's greatest masterpiece was "River Deep, Mountain High," with vocals by Tina Turner. She was still under the suasion of her husband Ike when the song was recorded, but Spector banished him from the studio, and he virtually imprisoned Tina, putting her through so many takes that she quipped about singing the same lines five hundred thousand times.

I remember watching one of the many studio sessions for this song in 1966. When I arrived at around ten P.M., Tina was perched on a high stool, sipping tea. She was a rather uncertain presence, far from the icon she would become. Spector sat behind a glass partition, hunched over the recording console, bringing bits of her vocalizing up and down as snippets of the arrangement surged by. He was easy to mistake for a wiry nerd. After an almost wordless greeting he barely noticed me, and he didn't seem very focused on Tina. He kept asking her to redo clusters of bars, and she complied, her hands cupping the mike. I could imagine how difficult that must have been, since she was singing only phrases, like an actor reciting a line of dialogue for a certain shot. I've always thought that the emotional valence in Turner's voice could only be captured in a flowing take, but Spector saw it as an element in a larger composition. He was essentially sampling her live.

This was my first glimpse of a studio master at work, and I didn't know how to read his attitude. To me it seemed like indifference. I wondered whether he'd felt that way about the girl groups he recorded as a teenager; after all, he'd married one of the Ronettes. I thought it was sexy to manipulate a woman's voice, to set it like a jewel, but it was also eerie to watch, and the fact that Turner was a black woman being styled by a white man made it even more discomforting. I told myself that it was just the usual way performers were handled by men who made an art of processing "talent." This was not the only time when I would assuage my conscience by deciding that I was only witnessing professionalism. They went at it for hours; when I left at three A.M. they were still working on the same stanza. I didn't hear the bridge until the record came out.

At some point, even the Grateful Dead lost their optimism about making a recording. "We just don't have the same fire in the studio," Bob Weir has admitted. But some producers knew how to stoke the flame. One of them—my favorite of the bunch—was Jerry Wexler. He played a central role in the fortunes of soul music and its greatest singer, Aretha Franklin. She'd begun as a gospel performer, but once she was signed by Columbia Records she found herself snared by the classic strategy of whitening up a black voice for the crossover market. That meant adding strings. For Aretha it was a disaster, like a thick coating of pomade. Her career languished until her contract was bought by Atlantic, where Wexler paired her with R&B-savvy sidemen. He knew how black music should sound the way I knew how to write a story.

Wexler started out as a writer and editor for the trade weekly *Billboard*. During his time there, in the forties, he convinced his colleagues to change the term for black music from "race records" to rhythm and blues. He became a partner in Atlantic Records thanks to its founder, Ahmet Ertegun. They were old friends. As young men, Wexler told me, the two of them would prowl the music dens of Harlem, and in the wee hours, stoned and sated, they would ride downtown on the Fifth Avenue bus, which still had an open top deck. (In those years, only hipsters and jazz buffs smoked pot.) By 1967 they were very rich. Ertegun was a snazzy socialite, but Wexler stayed pure street. That was probably why, though I met them both, I bonded with Jerry.

With his gruff accent and unruly beard, he reminded me of Allen Ginsberg sans lotus position. I spent a very fruitful afternoon at his home in Long Island. He said he was going to teach me about rock 'n' roll. I listened intently as he played record after record from his collection, pointing out details I'd missed in very knowing though hardly academic terms. Finally he pulled out an album by a performer from the postwar era named Mama Yancey. I'd never heard of her, but everything I loved in rock 'n' roll was in her style. I was hearing classic blues overlaid with boogie-woogie, the great matrix of rock 'n' roll. Jerry's demonstration was probably a sales pitch, since Mama Yancey's old discs were being reissued by Atlantic. But he got me to see the power in her technique—it was animate—and he walked me through her rhythmic riffs with great patience. In the end there was no payoff for him, since I never wrote about her. But it was the most important music lesson I ever had, and it made me even more uneasy about the relationship between black blues and its brocaded British heirs.

If I'd been more honest with myself I might have admitted that I needed the racial mediation that groups like the Rolling Stones provided. James Brown, who had the most unregenerately black sound of the sixties, made me uncomfortable, though I never understood why. Now I do. He lacked the signifiers of whiteness that made a black artist like Jimi Hendrix palatable to ears like mine. Brown's refusal to adapt those signs is part of what made him a great performer. But to me he was a fairly threatening mystery, and I never tried to interview him.

Wexler, I think, understood the commercial paradox of admiring black music until the point when it became really black. His fortune depended on walking that line. But he was pessimistic about the future of R&B, even in its crossover form. He predicted that rhythm tracks would soon be synthesized, and that tonality would become utterly precise, killing the imperfection that was central to soul music. "No more backbeats," he said sadly, referring to the rhythms that circulated under and around the main one. Of course he couldn't have imagined that technology would open up the liberating possibilities of sampling. But he was right about perfect notes and processed voices. Pop singing today, especially by black women, is typically either an orgasmic purr or an anthemic roar, the swoops and flights flawlessly shaped. Performance is often a gloss on prerecorded tracks, and it has to be, since no one could duplicate the sound live. To me it feels as stylized as the moans and cries in a porn film added after the fact. This is nothing new, I guess. Devotees of classic blues complained about the amplified sound of R&B, and I'm sure Mick Jagger's rendition of Robert Johnson songs (e.g., "Love in Vain") sounded just as flat to Wexler as dubstep does to me. I think he took so much trouble with my education because he thought I could stem the standardizing tide. Of course, neither of us could have steered the beast we were riding, he on its broad back and me on its swinging tail.

In 1967, rock became a billion-dollar baby, and I added a section to my column about the machinations of the recording industry. I called it "Weird Scenes in the Gold Mine," a phrase I'd borrowed from the Doors song "The End." The beast had begun its feast, Cuisinarting everything it couldn't digest. But there were still outposts of local musical sensibility. I never got to see the studios in Muscle Shoals or Memphis, but I did make it to Detroit, where the greatest factory of black music was located. This was Motown, the only major black-owned record label in the sixties, and also the only major black company in entertainment. The label's founder, Berry Gordy, had plucked a lot of his acts from the city's housing projects. This gave Motown a rich connection with the doo-wop and girl-group traditions, apparent in the funkiness under its sleek sound. But its presentation of the female body was more conservative than in most black acts—the singers wore gowns, and they were likelier to sway than to shake their booties. These elaborate moves were assembled in one of the many tiny rooms where the Motown sound was made. It was the oddest operation I'd ever come across.

When I got out of the cab on Grand Boulevard I thought I was on the wrong street. All I could see was a row of small private houses. But there was a whole finishing school inside, including a choreography room, a costume department (where the Supremes were given their prom-night look), and of course the recording studios, all contained in a series of connected basement spaces. It was warrenlike—there was a rumor that Motown used a hole in the ceiling as an echo chamber. I never got to see that, but during my visit I watched Harvey Fuqua, a veteran producer, work the studio console while the Four Tops recorded a song. I think it was "Seven Rooms of Gloom," but I may be confusing that title with the cramped feeling of the place. When I recall my visit to Motown I see creaky floors and narrow passageways. It reminded me of the writers' floor at the *Voice*.

I figured it was only a matter of time before Motown closed up shop in Detroit and moved to L.A. (It did, in 1972.) All the major labels had offices there, and the city offered state-of-the-art studios. It was where you had to go in order to meet the new crop of producers, who were young, hip, and sometimes part of the band. The most eccentric of them was Brian Wilson, the genius behind the Beach Boys.

They weren't exactly darlings of the rock press. Their songs were considered simple-minded and certainly not blues based—hence, not manly enough to be serious rock. But I loved the Beach Boys, even in their earliest incarnation as architects of surf music. To my ears, their car-crazed optimism was the realization of Chuck Berry's American dream. I don't think you can beat "Fun, fun, fun (till your daddy takes the T-bird away)" when it comes to the poetics of hedonism. This was a fantasy, of course, and a banal one at that. But then Brian Wilson dropped acid and began to create remarkable elegiac songs, with barbershop harmonies gone psychedelic. I watched the Beach Boys' evolution with awe.

"Good Vibrations," their mega-hit of 1966, was as complex as anything the Beatles thought up a year later on *Sgt. Pepper*. It had a multiple melody and a musical palette that included one of the first uses in rock of the theremin, an electronic instrument whose spooky sound had mainly appeared in horror films. When you play Beach Boys tunes from that era it's hard to believe that the arrangements weren't MIDI-generated, but of course such programs didn't exist then. Wilson used the recording technology of the time to maximum effect, but he also played with found sounds. To apply a critical term I didn't know at the time, he was a rock *auteur*.

In the fall of 1967 I wrote a piece for the *Times* on the Beach Boys' latest album, *Smiley Smile*. I was struck by its fragile melodies and their relationship to sacred music; those familiar ride-the-curl voices, now "hushed with wonder," reminded me of the Fauré *Requiem*, but they were utterly American. I was listening to proof of my belief that pop could produce a mass culture that was at once accessible and profound.

I don't think my editor at the *Times* bought the Fauré comparison, but he agreed to pay my expenses so I could travel west, and I guess Brian Wilson was impressed by my piece, because he invited me to his home in Bel Air. Judith came along, and we stayed at L.A.'s hippest hotel, the Chateau Marmont, with its Spanish-colonial lobby and windows that actually opened. Our room had a view of Laurel Canyon, but if we craned our necks we could see the Sunset Strip. It was quite a contrast—on one side verdant slopes and on the other a barren avenue with bill-boards the size of drive-in movie screens. Everything about L.A. seemed incongruous to me, so the interview with Brian fit right in.

His wife, Marilyn, answered the door. One look at her and I could tell that she was another strong Jewish woman with an introverted artist for a husband. Pointing to a limo sitting on the lawn, she said, wearily, "He's hiding." I'd heard about that car—it had once belonged to John Lennon, and Brian bought it as a totem of the group toward which he felt the most competitive. He was determined to beat the Beatles at their elevated game, so he'd teamed up with Van Dyke Parks, a member of the L.A. pop avant-garde whose style encompassed everything from Stephen Foster to blank verse. To this remarkable range Parks added a wry affection for the Disneyesque. The open harmonies and quirky touches of the Beach Boys brought out the whimsy of his lyrics, as in:

> *I know that you'll feel better*
> *When you send us in your letter*
> *And tell us the name of your . . . favorite vegetable*

Little of what Parks wrote made linear sense, but his lyrics were enchant-ing, and I championed his solo album, *Song Cycle*. That was when I real-ized how far my critical taste could stray from the judgment of the record racks. The album was a flop—even rock had its limits when it came to free-form obscurity.

Parks co-authored the most legendary sixties record that never was (although a version of it did appear in 2004). This was *Smile*, Brian Wilson's uncompleted "teenage symphony to God." I can only imagine what that work would have been like if he had ever finished it. But he blew deadline after deadline, and the final product, *Smiley Smile*, was a truncated version of what he intended. The most ambitious piece—a suite based on the four elements: earth, wind, fire, and water—was missing. Later I would hear that Brian had destroyed the master tapes. A fire had broken out not far from the recording studio, and he became convinced that the music would cause things to burst into flame. This was the story that made the rounds, but it seems that he didn't actually trash the masters; he only said he had, perhaps to avoid admitting that he was uneasy about the work. At the time I accepted his original explanation, because it sounded like something he was capable of.

Brian's emotional state, which was fragile to begin with, had deteriorated under the pressure from his record label. It must have seemed to him that he would never again be able to produce a hit. I didn't know anything about that when we met; he kept the details hidden from me. But his instability was evident, and, I think, directly related to his audacity as a producer. He was capable of creating moment of sheer tonal whimsey, pellucid choral interludes ("Wind Chimes"), and cartoony riffs as twisted as the stuff in comix. (Give "Fall Breaks and Back to Winter," aka "W. Woodpecker Symphony" a listen and you'll hear the origins of Animal Collective.)

I've read monographs on the Beach Boys that describe Wilson as a self-conscious artist, fully aware of musical history. That wasn't my impression. He came across as a typical rock autodidact, deeply insecure about his creative instincts, terrified that the songs he was working on were too arty to sell. As a result of this ambivalence, he never realized his full potential as a composer. In the light of electronica and minimalism, you can see how advanced his ideas were, but they remain bursts of inspiration from a mind that couldn't mobilize itself into a whole. This was the major tragedy of rock in the sixties. It set out to shatter the boundaries of high and mass culture, but there was a line, invisible yet rigid, between violating musical conventions and making truly popular music. Anyone who couldn't walk that line was doomed to a respectful rejection, and a few albums with disappointing sales usually meant silence. The market was a fickle mistress. (What else is new?) You needed a strong ego to read the public's taste, and an even stronger one to resist it. Dylan succeeded because he was supremely willful, and the Beatles would have succeeded at anything. But the California performers I admired—and sometimes loved—were deeply insecure. They yearned for fame, as only needy people can, but they also wanted to make art, and when both of those impulses couldn't be achieved they recoiled in a ball of frantic confusion.

I walked over to the limo where Brian's wife, Marilyn, said he'd be waiting. The windows were tinted brown. Down it rolled, and there was Brian, eyeing me with suspicion. I flashed him my biggest grin. "Meet you in the tent," he said warily.

I don't remember the piano in a sandbox, but I do remember the tent that stood in his living room. It had rugs, an oil lamp, and a hookah, or maybe it was just a joint. We got stoned; I'm certain of that. I pressed him to agree that his music resembled Fauré's—I wanted to prove my point to the *Times*. He looked like I had pulled a knife on him. "I never heard of that guy," he muttered. I switched gears, asking about those dazzling harmonies. Where did they come from? "Barbershop," he replied. Yes, of course, the traditional heartland style, but hadn't barbershop originally been a black form? And what about Chuck Berry? Wasn't Brian actually producing a grand synthesis of racial pop styles? I was tempted to point this out, but then I remembered that another reporter had been careless enough to ask about the black roots of his music. Brian's response, as the reporter related it to me, was: "We're white and we sing white."

The Beach Boys were mostly a family affair, and the Wilson boys were sons of the great migration west from Oklahoma to escape the Dust Bowl. So the author of "Fun, Fun, Fun" was a spawn of *The Grapes of Wrath*, the first generation in his clan to take security for granted. It struck me as moving, even poignant, that Brian had crafted the icon of the blithe surfer, since he was a chubby introvert who never went near a board, preferring the safety of his room. But I understood his fixation. Surfers were the Apollos of SoCal. When I saw them on the beach, perfectly tanned, or when I watched them twirling in the waves, I grasped the transcendental element in surf music. It was all about freedom from the rules of life, the whole of your being concentrated in the act of shooting the tube. For several years after that trip to L.A. I subscribed to *Surfer* magazine, and I practiced the Atlantic Ocean version of the sport, though only with my body and on rather tame waves. With my voice muffled by the water I would shout a line from "Surf City." To me, this was the ultimate fantasy of plenty: "two girls for every boy," except I sang it as "Two girls for every *goy*."

Fortunately, Brian has survived the schizoid tendencies that seemed close to the surface when I met him. He's still performing and writing songs. But it was his emotional battle and the intersection of that struggle with the acid-dosed aesthetic of the sixties that produced his most astonishing music. He was hardly the only rocker torn between the warring gods of art and popularity—merely the most erratic. He needed critical validation even as he rejected it. I suspect that was why, at the end of our rather inconclusive chat, he invited me to join the band for a photo shoot in Palm Springs. Judith and Marilyn came along for the ride, and quite a ride it was.

When I think of that weekend I flash on Brian running around the desert with his wife trying to corral him, shouting, "Pick up your pants." He was high; so was I. (We'd stopped along the way to pick up some weed from one of the Byrds.) We ate lunch at a coffee shop that was playing Muzak versions of Beach Boys songs. Then we hopped on a funicular that took us from the desert to a mountaintop, where the baked sand changed to snow. Everyone rolled around in it, including Dennis Wilson, who, not a half hour earlier, had been frolicking among the cacti. At some point during that excursion, Dennis hit on Judith. He was too stoned to succeed—she claims. I wouldn't have objected. It was the sixties; possessiveness was a cardinal sin. And winning the admiration of a Beach Boy was a dream come true for her. She'd grown up in a household where playing Hindemith on the stereo was prime-time entertainment, but she was a secret Beach Boys fan, just like me.

By the end of the day I'd forgotten why we were in Palm Springs. But I can still picture Dennis's face as I saw it at night, in the green neon glow that suffused the porch of our motel. It made me feel like I was trapped inside a lime Life Saver. Southern California lighting in those days was a bad trip in itself, and the tikis that graced many courtyards put me in mind of umbrella drinks. But for Dennis this emerald excess was just another jewel in the pleasure dome. With his well-shaped jaw and sandy hair, he was the all-American member of the group, the only Wilson brother who wasn't chubby and, as far as I know, the only Beach Boy who had actually ridden a wave.

Dennis had a soulful side, but it was hidden behind a well-developed set of sybaritic impulses. He never made it past the age of thirty-nine. In

1983, after a day of heavy drinking, he drowned while swimming in a marina. It wasn't exactly a shock. I still hadn't forgotten the trip from Palm Springs back to L.A., with Dennis at the wheel. "Whoa!" he said, clearly still high. "The road is doing these weird things." I thought, If I survive this I promise never to do drugs again.

The piece I produced for the *Times* was decorous enough to suit my editors. I had learned to leave the viscera out of my copy after they censored my description of Diana Ross farting during our interview. ("Ooh," she said, "my tummy is upset." I thought this was a wonderful moment of self-revelation, but it didn't suit the paper's definition of news "fit to print.") Once I filed the Beach Boys story, I had several days to kill before my flight home. I dreaded spending them alone. Judith had already left, and L.A. is a place where isolation can feel like death. At least in New York the odor of car exhaust is masked by garbage, but out here it mixed with tropical blossoms, giving me the impression that I was entering a room-deodorized gas chamber. But one of L.A.'s distinctive charms for a pro like me was the chance to party at homes of the media elite. Though I preferred the ambience of a crash pad in San Francisco, I couldn't resist the invitation to cocktails chez Hugh Hefner.

I remember more about the driveway, which seemed miles long, than I do about the house, except that it looked unlived-in, like a movie set. I don't know which wife Hef was on, but I recall catching sight of him surrounded by women so slick in their beauty that I could have varnished a car with it. He was the only VIP in the room; everyone else wore the expression of serenity masking envy that I associate with Hollywood. I suppose he had set up the guest list so that no one outranked him, certainly not me. I considered schmoozing up a *Playboy* editor for an assignment. They paid better than any magazine I wrote for, but I didn't think anyone actually read the articles, and I wasn't interested in competing with a centerfold. (It wasn't the sexism but the processed quality of these images that appalled me.) So I retreated to the grounds, which included a menagerie with all sorts of animals. The wildlife followed me as I strolled along, monkeys in the bushes and even fish in the stream that ran through an artificial grotto. They were hoping for a handout. I'd never been stalked like that, and it was an eerie feeling. But it struck me as a metaphor for my role in the music industry. There was no escaping the procession waiting to eat from my hand, and I was addicted to the feeding frenzy.

It was a troubling thought, and I buried it in a Mexican dinner, one of my main consolations in L.A. I felt incapable of grasping whatever made this city the metropole it was. The money was here, and so were studios of all sorts, but most of what the city produced didn't seem homegrown. The local bands I'd heard were as artificially psychedelic as the flaming Polynesian fakes that were everywhere. There was no funk. Black styles were barely relevant to the scene, and without that scaffold everything just . . . flowed. If I'd been able to stretch myself I might have understood that L.A. offered a harmonic blend of folk rock and mellow jazz, which would blend with the more rough-edged San Francisco sound to dominate pop in the late sixties. The city also hosted a music milieu that I knew nothing about, until I got to meet some of the local singer-songwriters. They were bohemians without the New York defensiveness and the encrustations of chic. Thanks to them I discovered an alternative sensibility, different from the one in San Francisco but no less distinctive. The mood I'd mistaken for terminal mellowness was actually acuity.

I owe my initiation into the real rock culture of L.A. to a transplanted New Yorker who worked as a publicist and talent scout. When he called, inviting me to drop by his house, I assumed he was just another company freak, but I had learned by then that those people were often excellent judges of quality. And I was intrigued by the name of his street, which I remember as Blue Jay Way. I may be confusing that with the title of a Beatles song, though to me every byway in Laurel Canyon should have been called Blue Jay Way. I took a cab up the slopes, which seemed to my urban eye like a fragrant jungle. Music wafted from every door, along with the smell of weed. This was the lane where Billy James lived.

Billy was an amateur in the original sense—he worked the rock scene with a loving touch. He shared his house with a teenage son—I recall a sign on the kid's room that read, WARNING! A SENSITIVE SOUL LIVES WITHIN. Many of Billy's discoveries used his place as a mail drop and crash pad. They were not quite ready for prime time, but very talented. I remember a lovely woman who'd grown up in perhaps the ugliest stretch of California, the stagnant Salton Sea. She wrote ballads about empty landscape and hardscrabble dreams, so poignant that I doubted she would get very far, even with a name like Penny Nichols, which she'd been born with. Thanks to the Internet I know that she now directs a retreat for singers and songwriters, and she looks like a vagabond troubadour who made a life—no small accomplishment. In 1967, there were many music strays in L.A, as gentle as the hippies of the Haight but more knowing. Most of them never hit the big time, and this is a city that has never honored obscurity.

I had much more faith in another of Billy's clients, who would become the essential singer-songwriter of L.A. mellowness, Jackson Browne. Under his studied casualness he was a savvy dude, but as an Angeleno of the Aquarian Age he knew how to hide his ambition behind a sublime vibe. To a New Yorker like me, it was like watching the suave alien in *The Day the Earth Stood Still*. Jackson was lean and chiseled without being done up, and he radiated worldliness. I remember hearing him talk to a woman on the phone, clearly someone much older. He called her by her first name and acted like a trusted advisor, giving romantic advice about dealing with her new boyfriend. Billy told me later that she was Jackson's mother. I'd never heard someone address a parent with such blithe intimacy. He was an incarnation of the laid-back polish I could never achieve—I was all edge, and still am. I will always associate his song "Take It Easy" with my California fantasies of no-stress sexuality.

> *We may lose and we may win*
> *Though we will never be here again*
> *So open up, I'm climbing in*

My most vivid memory of Jackson is the offhanded way he greeted his friends. "Taj Mahal, on the ball," I heard him say to one of the few black musicians in the local rock scene, another of Billy's clients. "Jackson Browne, back in town!" Taj replied. I don't know why this exchange still stays with me, except that it's the essence of L.A. style in the sixties, a wry imperfection, like the imprecise notes that make a solo personal. On subsequent visits I would notice the same quality in the L.A. comedy scene. I had a brief affair with a wealthy woman who'd given up her class privileges to become a social worker (though she hadn't given up her BMW). She'd bought a house in Venice, which was still blessedly shabby, and she opened it to a group of young creative types, one of whom was Harry Shearer. Even then he had a gift for irony without the hostile edge that New York stand-up specialized in. The same was true of Richard Pryor; for all his subversiveness, he never lost his affection for the absurdity of human beings. Nor did Lily Tomlin, or Cheech and Chong. Randy Newman has this same sly humanism. By now it's been upgraded into a whole meta sensibility, like the city itself, but back in the sixties L.A. demanded *not* to be taken seriously, which was the most serious thing about it.

I'm sure Billy James hoped I'd write about his roster, and that was fortuitous, since he tipped me off to a local band he had recently brought to Elektra Records. Their name was an homage to Aldous Huxley's book about his experiences with LSD, *The Doors of Perception*. This was all I knew at the time about the Doors.

Billy took me to the Whisky A Go Go, the premier rock club on the Strip. I feared that, with a name like that, the floor show would feature girls in high boots and miniskirts dancing in cages. There was a romantic mystique around these babes—check out the ballad by Gordon Lightfoot: "Only a go-go girl in love/With someone who didn't care. . ." The girls were there, twirling behind bars on a platform above the stage. It was not a very big room, and that stage was tiny, as I recall. We were so close to the musicians that I could see the bulge in the singer's leather pants. Jim Morrison gripped the mike, black hair curling around his angelic face. I knew right away that he would be a major rock star.

Morrison had a feral intensity, riveting to behold. But his persona was shaped by a shrewd sense of theater, and he sang with the measured ranting of a beat poet. The musicians backing him up—I was most struck by keyboardist Ray Manzarek, who looked like a groovy schoolteacher in his round glasses and neatly long hair—had devised a sound that was both tight and trancey. The slash-and-burn of rock might have fought Morrison's wildness, but this style seemed to incite it. "We may look cool," Manzarek would tell me when I interviewed him, "but we are really evil, insidious cats behind Jim. We instigate the violence in him. A lot of times he doesn't feel particularly angry, but the music just drives him to it."

The set I saw at the Whisky was stunning, and the first thing I did when I got back to my hotel was to pound out a piece about the

Doors for the *Voice*. When I returned to New York an advance copy of their debut album was waiting. I've already mentioned my blooper about "Light My Fire," but I praised the record as a whole, and as a result I had easy access to the band. Within a year of watching them perform at the Whisky I was back in L.A., on assignment from *New York* to interview Morrison. I got to watch him slither down the Strip in a snakeskin jacket, oblivious to the teenyboppers fluttering around him. I also spent an afternoon riding around with him in a little red sports car, with his girlfriend at the wheel. I noticed that she did the driving. It was further evidence that fragile male rockers needed the support of strong women. That was an emotional necessity for these guys, who courted collapse. I don't think I was introduced to Jim's "old lady" by her name, or maybe I've forgotten it, but I do remember that she was an ad exec, not an easy career for a woman circa *Mad Men*. She had invented a very successful concept for Alka-Seltzer. The product was a remedy for "the blahs," a condition that fell short of illness but merited medication. The term, she told me, had come to her while tripping.

Morrison was wearing a slept-in pullover and the requisite leather pants. He turned up the radio and fiddled with the bass control as the DJ announced one of his songs. This was the first time he'd heard himself on the air, and I wasn't sure whether he looked happy or anxious—he pulled his lumpy hat down over his eyes. We were headed for one of his favorite spots, an ashram called the Garden of Self-Realization. Gandhi's ashes were reputed to be there. (This was the L.A. equivalent of pieces of the true cross.) We plopped down on the lawn, beside a stucco arch with a cupola sprayed gold. I pulled out a tape recorder, but I put it down too far from him. When I played back the tape most of what I heard was the sound of Jim's fingernails scratching nervously at the dirt. Fortunately I also took notes, and the quotes that follow come from the piece I wrote. Years later I was astonished to hear bits of that interview used as dialogue in Oliver Stone's dubious film *The Doors*. You wouldn't know from this movie that Morrison ever had an intelligent idea in his head.

"When you started, did you anticipate your image?" I asked him.

"Nah. It just sort of happened . . . unconsciously. See, it used to be I'd just stand still and sing. Now I . . . uh . . . exaggerate a little bit."

He shot me his famous half smile. "I'm beginning to think it's easier to scare people than to make them laugh."

He didn't hold much back, except the circumstances of his birth. "I don't remember it," he said drolly. "Maybe I was having one of my blackouts." Like Brian Wilson he'd had a rough relationship with his father, an admiral who moved the family around—Jim still lived with friends or in motels. I learned about his fondness for alcohol (which, in those days, was not something hip people bragged about). But mostly we talked about his ambitions as an artist, how he wanted to combine the charisma of Elvis with the power of incanted poetry. "See, singing has all the things I like. It's involved with writing and music. There's a lot of acting. And it has this other thing—a physical element, a sense of the immediate. When I sing I create characters."

He wasn't exactly an intellectual, but he had a feeling for philosophical concepts in an art-school kind of way. What I remember most about him is that he radiated neediness, but that was nothing unusual in a California rocker. Far more striking was his imagination, erratic but sophisticated. I came away thinking that he was a serious artist, piecing together myths he'd gleaned from various readings. His mentor, the San Francisco beat poet Michael McClure, had taken in this SoCal stray. There's a relationship between Morrison's fixation on the phallus and McClure's play *The Beard*, which got the actors arrested. (I've forgotten most of it, but I remember the moment when Jean Harlow describes Billy the Kid's dick as "a piece of meat hanging from a bag of meat.") Jim studied acting at film school and spent his down time in the Venice creative scene. Manzarek was the one who thought of setting his poems to music. His songs, his verse, his persona—all of it was a pastiche held together by his desire to create a role that could bring his warring impulses together. In our interview he was pretentious and revealing at the same time, as in this aperçu, meant to be quoted, I'm sure: "A game is a closed field, a ring of death with . . . uh . . . sex at the center. Performing is the only game I've got, so I guess it's my life."

He had read about the figure of the shaman and its function in primitive societies, and he wanted to bring that power to rock by combining visionary lyrics with a physical ritual. His aim was to unleash the subconscious. "The shaman," he said, "was a man who would intoxicate himself. See, he was probably already an . . . uh . . . unusual individual. And he would put himself into a trance by dancing, whirling around, drinking, taking drugs—however. Then he would go on a mental travel and . . . uh . . . describe his journey to the rest of the tribe."

Morrison was dead serious about this agenda. Say what you will about the bombastic quality of his lyrics, but they were remarkable in a hard-rock context. Not even Bob Dylan dared to write a song about incest.

> *Father . . . I want to kill you*
> *Mother . . . I want to . . .*
> [Insert shrieking here.]

I've emphasized Morrison's artistic ambition because that's usually the part left out of his hagiography. But I realized, as I often did when talking with rockers known for their sizzle, that this was another border-line personality. The conflict between fame and aesthetics would be especially hard for him to deal with, because he wasn't just known for his songs, as, say, Dylan was. Morrison was most famous for his voice and body, especially his crotch, which he unveiled during a concert in an act of drunken spite that got him arrested and made him even more notorious. I knew instantly, when I read about the incident, that it was a gesture of rage at the audience for failing to take his message about reaching into the subconscious seriously. "Break on through to the other side," he would bellow. But he was swallowed up by the spectacle he thought he could shape. When I met him, before he lost what there was of his balance, he could still speak hopefully about his mission. As in this observation about the relationship between rock and play: "Play is not the same thing as a game. A game involves rules, but play is an open event. Actors play—also musicians. And you dig watching someone play, because that's the way human beings are supposed to be . . . free." If I had to sum up Morrison's achievement I'd say that he combined rock with Method acting. He performed himself.

There's a video of me interviewing him. (You can locate the clip online.) It was one of several programs on rock that I hosted for PBS, mostly on speed, since I was terrified about appearing on TV. That may be why I look so spacey, though I can't account for the puff-sleeved flower shirt I wore. Morrison, bearded by then, looked great, and he made a very smart prediction about the future of rock. He said it would be created by just one person working a machine. This is basically what electronica is today. He was, as I've said, a fitful but perceptive artist. All the more reason why he freaked out before his appearance on *The Ed*

Sullivan Show. This was an obligatory ritual for famous rockers, had been ever since Elvis Presley's performance, famously shot from the waist up. It was a tradition on that program to censor lyrics that were too sexual. Even the notorious Rolling Stones had caved, changing a key line in one of their best songs from spending the night to "spending some time together." When it came to "Light My Fire," the Doors were faced with a double whammy. "Girl, we couldn't get much higher" could refer to sex, drugs, or (most likely) both.

I was present at that broadcast, standing backstage with the group. A deal had been struck—the Doors would leave the offensive line out of the song when they sang it on the air. It was a small price to pay for shamanizing the nation. But then they caught sight of the set. It was a series of doors—big ones, little ones, fancy and plain ones, but doors! This was an egregious insult for a band that had named themselves after a meditative book on psychedelics. Jim threatened not to go on. A conference followed, and a decision was made. He would sing the forbidden line—and he did, snarling, "Girl, we couldn't get much *HIGH-ER*." I caught the livid look on Sullivan's face. The Doors were never invited back.

That incident raised my respect for Jim, though he'd always had my sympathy. I never saw his legendary aggression. He was gentle and vulnerable around me. But I did get to witness one of his drunken outbursts. It happened at a recording session. Morrison had envisioned an album called *The Celebration of the Lizard*, a twenty-four-minute "drama" he'd been working on. The band was in the studio. The producer, an earnest longhair named Paul Rothchild, sat at the console. Jim arrived wearing his favorite snakeskin jacket. He had brought the notebook in which he wrote his verses. That wasn't unusual—no one knew in advance what words he would be singing. Morrison would enter a glass-enclosed booth to record the vocals while the band played behind him. This is why the Doors sound so spontaneous on their albums. They were.

I could tell from Jim's wobbly posture, and from his girlfriend's dire expression, that he was plastered. In fact, he guzzled from a bottle of brandy. "I'm the square of the Western hemisphere," he boomed. "Man . . . whenever someone said something groovy it'd blow my mind. You like people?" he grunted at me. "I hate 'em. Screw 'em—I don't need 'em. Oh, I need 'em . . . to grow potatoes."

He was teetering and belching. "Hafta break it in," he said, fingering his jacket, which crinkled like tinfoil. His girlfriend tried to distract him by mentioning a Mexican wedding shirt he'd commissioned from a custom tailor. "We have to get you measured," she said.

Jim bolted backward, his eyes large with fear. "Uh-uh. I don't like to be measured."

"Oh, Jim," she muttered. "We're not gonna measure *all* of you. Just your . . . shoulders."

By that point in my career I had learned to take notes in the dark or without looking at the page, holding a pad discreetly on my knee. As Morrison ranted I scribbled it all down in an ersatz shorthand only I could read, and I wrote about that recording session, including the moment when Rothchild summoned Jim to the glass booth. The plan was to put him where he wouldn't interfere. The other musicians were really pissed, but they had learned to work around him when he was like this. They were Apollonians to his Dionysus—so Jim had told me. He would constantly prod them to "get into the Dionysus thing," but they would stare at him blankly and say something like, "Oh, yeah, right, Jim." Now they hunched over their instruments, trying to ignore him as he entered the vocal booth. He fit himself with earphones and began to sing in breathy grunts. The words were too slurred to be recorded, and the musicians were trying to play over them, but his voice intruded, bigger and blacker than ever. Finally the producer turned off the sound. Jim looked like a silent-movie version of himself, a pungent but necessary prop. Suddenly he burst out of the glass chamber, sweat drunk. "If I had an ax," he slurred, "man, I'd kill everybody . . . 'cept . . . uh . . . my friends."

There he stood, a lizard-skinned titan in a helpless fit. As useless as he had probably felt when he was a child. Every attempt he'd made to escape from that sense of insignificance, of dreaded obscurity before a rejecting father, surfaced in this tantrum. His girlfriend sank back in her seat and gave herself over to a cosmic case of the blahs.

I've already said that Morrison reminded me of Brian Wilson, but there were other West Coast rock stars who had the same effect. The greatest of them were terribly fragile. The more emotive they were onstage, the more insecure they seemed up close. In New York we were better at hiding our vulnerability, but showing that side was easier out here, perhaps because it was part of the culture of honesty that made the local scene so ridiculous—and appealing. I certainly was surprised by the readiness with which these rockers confided their doubts to me. There were no publicists to intervene; no time limit or subjects off-limits. They didn't present me with a fake mystique, and I didn't have to be shy around them. I began to feel something I'd never let myself experience as a reporter; I started to care for the people I wrote about, and I struggled to balance the need to make a story out of their lives with the desire to represent them in all their complexity. I was learning to drop the stylization that my role required, to break on through to the other side. But there were unintended consequences. As I watched these performers sink under the churning currents of fame, with no ego strength to buoy them, it heightened the sense of helplessness that would eventually overwhelm me.

Rock stars in those days were expected to be priests in a rite of fucked-upness, and it reinforced their most self-destructive impulses. Madness was its own reward, and the crazier and more volatile they got, the greater the fascination it produced. I suppose that's always been the case in show business, the worship and devouring of vulnerable personalities; it explains the cult of Judy Garland, and of Marilyn Monroe, both of whom ended up drugged and dead. But in the counterculture, where love was the watchword, it seemed especially painful to witness this emotional cannibalism. The luckiest stars were buffered by lovers, loyal managers, or members of the band who formed a protective phalanx. But often a forced tolerance prevailed, because, after all, these freaks were bringing home the soy bacon. A vicious indifference hid under the insistence that dangerous, sometimes fatal behavior was simply "doing your thing."

Well, I got to do my thing in California, for better and for worse. But I'm getting ahead of myself yet again. I keep wanting to jump the sequence in which these events occurred, probably because that's the way I remember them. I know who I hung out with in L.A, but I'm not sure about the order of these encounters. Maybe it doesn't matter; why should I presume to be a fact checker of my own mind, when the most accurate way to describe it is as a light show of pulsing shapes that suggest the image of people who exist only as images anyway, since most of them died long ago—and long before their time. My most vivid memory is the feeling that everything out here was fungible. At any moment the earth might shake and it would all be swept away. Dennis Wilson's words still resonate within me when I think of California in 1967: *Whoa! The road is doing these weird things.*

The Summer of My Discontent

I didn't just bliss out in the Summer of Love. I got married. All sorts of living arrangements were possible in the sixties, from group sex to shacking up, as it was still called then. But Judith and I both wanted—and no doubt needed—something more permanent.

We'd met when I was in j-school at Columbia and she was a student at Barnard College. We bonded despite her yowling Siamese cat, but our families didn't. If you raise an upwardly mobile child, as my folks did, your in-laws will probably be classier than you, and her parents were certainly that. Her mother was a talented painter, and her father was the rascal descendant of a British rabbinic family. Judith was raised to be an intellectual, but she had a secret passion for rock 'n' roll. It corresponded to a hidden sense of herself as a voluptuous woman, and that zaftig hottie emerged during the five years when we were together, to my delight.

Our wedding celebration was held at the Cheetah, a large midtown discotheque with thousands of flickering lightbulbs. Murray the K hosted, the Velvet Underground played, and the bride wore a nightgown. (I was hoping she would wear her paper sari to go with my silver boots.) A few weeks later, we had a proper Jewish ceremony for the parents—this time Judith wore a minidress. When the rabbi was late, she stormed out of the bride's room, shouting, "When the fuck is this going to happen?" I stomped on the glass that the groom is supposed to break, out of anxiety that I wouldn't succeed. Our honeymoon was a trip to the event that inaugurated the tradition of rock festivals, Monterey Pop.

First marriages are often auditions, especially when they happen at a young age. My best understanding is that Judith and I grew each other up. Thanks to my career, we had remarkable adventures together. She was the best editor I ever had, and she managed to drag me out of despair about writing more than once by insisting that blocks were creative opportunities, urges toward change. She was right about many things except my ability to stay committed. My love for her felt real, and the sex was so good that it allowed me to quell the drawn-and-quartered feeling of my conflicting drives. The problem was my inability to let her—or anyone—all the way in. I saw myself as a fragile balloon, pendulous with liquid, that would burst if penetrated, splattering its murky water on the freshly waxed floor. It took many years and a long struggle, with some false starts and painful turns, to break through this terror of intimacy, but at the age of twenty-three it was buried so deeply that I wasn't even aware of it. I was a jumble of desires and equally urgent fears. Still, there were times when everything seemed like it was right where it should be. I remember the morning we spent in Monterey before the opening concert. Monarch butterflies filled the air, and Judith was radiant with self-possession, her insecurities banished in the California dreaming.

When we got to the festival I realized right away that this was no love-in for nomads like the kids I'd met in Golden Gate Park. Though the tickets were cheap—a mere $3.50 for an evening show, as I recall—the crowd was anything but common. These were members of a new aristocracy, courtly and enlightened, wearing costumes of fine fabric in shimmering hues. Watching them promenade through the craft market, a woodsy version of the pushcarts I'd grown up with, I felt a bit like Otis Redding must have when he performed at Monterey. (He was the major representative of soul music; Motown was nowhere on the lineup.) Glimpsing the audience, Otis allowed himself a gently cynical quip: "This is the love crowd, right?" No R&B singer could achieve the perfect lack of edge, the casual insularity, that these people displayed. I was witnessing the birth of a new class pretending to be classless, and it was imperial at the core. The descendants of this bangled illuminati now dine on free-range meat and artisanal cheese. They colonize neighborhoods, driving out the poor and turning slums into Potemkin villages of art. You know these hipsters by the tilt of their fedoras, but their ancestors flashed peace signs.

Somewhere in the crowd I caught a glimpse of Brian Jones in a fur-trimmed-robe sort of thing. I introduced myself, sure that he would remember our encounter on that yacht during the Rolling Stones' first American tour—after all, I'd been part of the rescue party that saved him from a pack of wild fans. But he looked past me and ambled away. We'd met as journalist and subject, which meant we were strangers. I should have known that, but I always felt hurt when it became apparent. I licked my wounds and proceeded to the press gate, where I identified myself. The credentialer was skeptical. "You're the third Richard Goldstein we've had today," she groaned.

I was flattered, but I needed access, so I yanked out my press card to prove who I was. As a journalist I could enter the restricted area behind the stage. I joined the scrum of performers and their roadies hanging out there. I'd arrived in the aftermath of an argument between Jimi Hendrix and Pete Townshend of the Who over which of their bands would go on first. This was an important issue, since both were hard-rock acts. According to Townshend, they solved the problem with a coin toss, but the buzz backstage was that Hendrix lost the dispute because he was less famous. (That would change after his performance at Monterey.) I caught a glimpse of Hendrix huddling with his sidemen, thin British gents who could have played footmen to a libertine lord in a costume drama. It looked like they had a plan. I had a feeling that it had something to do with smashing guitars.

That was the Who's signature shtick. Townshend would throw his ax into the amps during the climax of their most belligerent song, "My Generation" ("Things they do look awful c-c-cold/I hope I die before I get old"). Then Keith Moon would knock over his drum kit as smoke enveloped the band. Busting up equipment seemed risky to me, but it epitomized the Who's crypto-punk image, though it also obscured their musical gifts. I think of them as the fathers of anthemic rock and, in a broad sense, all the genres that emanate from metal. As for Hendrix, he redrew the borders of pop by melting blue notes and reshaping them into elastic sonic sculptures. His revision of "The Star Spangled Banner," complete with bombing sounds and snippets of "Taps," is the most astonishing statement in sixties music about the violent and ecstatic dream life of America. Hendrix was the John Coltrane of the wah-wah pedal, but it took me some time to grasp that. At first his playing seemed too disconnected from melody, too chaotic. As I've already confessed, I came to rock as an English major.

I understood why Hendrix was focused on the Who. He had a history of topping his betters. As a rookie rocker he'd outflashed Little Richard in that singer's own band. (He got fired for that.) Now he decided to outdestructo the Who. Hendrix would smash his guitar and then ignite it, tossing the flaming thing into the audience. The moment has been captured in countless video clips, but I saw it happen. I was sitting just below the stage, and I ducked the incoming. Robert Christgau, who was sitting near me, made a World Series catch, grabbing the remains of the charred instrument. He kept it in his East Village apartment until a subtenant lost it.

I "interviewed" Hendrix not long before he died in 1970. The occasion, I recall, had something to do with the opening of his recording studio in Greenwich Village, but it may have happened earlier than that. What sticks in my memory is the way he looked. Hendrix was stupefied, his shirt stained with what looked like caked puke. I listened to him mumbling for several minutes before leaving as graciously as I could. There was no publicist to make excuses or even wipe him up. I was tempted to put that meeting into print, but by then I had lost my distance from the musicians I wrote about. I'd learned to honor the feeling of empathy that they often aroused in me. There were two kinds of rock stars, it seemed: the survivors, such as Dylan and Jagger, who hid behind their personas, and those whose precarious egos marked them for ritual self-destruction. No way would I perform the journalistic equivalent of that nasty spectacle by blowing Jimi's cover. I was horrified but not surprised when he choked to death on his vomit.

By the time of my encounter with Hendrix I had lost my cynicism about why performers were willing to behave in such self-abasing ways before a reporter taking notes. But at first I thought of it as a kind of show. They wanted to give me something that would make good copy. It was part of the symbiotic relationship between celebrities and the press, and it meant that I could write about whatever went down without worrying about hurt feelings. An interview might be superficial, but my readers expected insights into the personalities of those they adored. In order to meet this need I had to be basically hypocritical, sympathetic during the meeting but merciless at the typewriter. I would scour my notes for intimate details that could be shaped into a character analysis. I still cringe when I remember these invasions of privacy. The most unforgivable one followed a chat with Leonard Cohen in a shabby hotel room near Times Square. He kvetched for nearly an hour. Finally he excused himself to take a pee, and I could hear him through the thin walls, relieving himself in short bursts. Who knows—maybe he had a finicky prostate. But I used that detail to portray him as a man so neurotic that he couldn't even piss decisively. Several years later I was traveling to a panel discussion with some countercultural writers when the van had a flat. We got out while the tire was changed. One of the men paced in the road, dying to take a leak, but he wouldn't do it. Finally he gave me a hesitant look. "No one will piss in front of you," he said. I got a laugh out of that, but it stuck in my throat.

I realized pretty quickly that it was impossible to turn a real person into story form, but if you're going to be a New Journalist, using the techniques of fiction in the service of reality, you have to be prepared to mold a life, with all of its complexity, into a well-shaped narrative. A good reporter can make readers think they've met a person even though they're merely encountering a protagonist. Only when I got involved with rockers as they actually were could I create true impressions of them, and that was far more difficult than rendering a journalistic sketch. Forging an ethic I could live with was a slow process, and my time in California with Brian Wilson and Jim Morrison was the start of it. I decided never again to treat my subjects like haunches of beef ready for carving. Though it was hard to convey the true texture of their conflicts, it seemed essential to my role as a chronicler of the new, fragile art form that was rock. Of course, I limited my scruples to performers I saw as artists; otherwise I wasted them for fun and profit.

Yet, try as I might to be faithful to the spirit of the music, there was always something to remind me of the gap between authenticity and artifice that was such a central issue for me during the sixties. Rock, for all its power to stir and transgress, to shake and rattle the establishment, was also show business. At Monterey I was constantly reminded of that fact. Since I was sitting in one of the front rows I could see what was going on in the wings. As techies prepared the stage for the Who, I watched them carrying sacks with something inside. I deduced that the bundles contained chunks of dry ice, which could create—or at least enhance—the smoke when the group kicked over the amps at the end of their set. Looking closely at Townshend's guitar, I thought I saw seams. Did that mean the instrument could split apart neatly when he smashed it? I wasn't sure, but I decided on the spot that the Who's famous rite of destruction was a fake. At one point perhaps it had been real, but now it was something the audience expected. It looked fabulous, but dangerous it was not. Whenever I hear the famous poignant refrain from *Tommy*— "See me . . . feel me . . . touch me . . . heal me"—I picture that seamed guitar. Maybe the Who were so good at critiquing the pop-star spectacle because they themselves were a show.

I think it was while watching their set that I realized what this festival was really about. It was the dawn of the New Age, for sure, but not of its stated intentions. I'd seen the potential of rock to subvert the order; also its capacity to subvert the subversion. This was a music whose reach depended on mass consumption, and that produced a contradiction. How can you have a revolution that hinges on turning a profit? The question nagged at me as I realized why this crowd was different from the hoi polloi in the Haight. I was sitting in some sort of VIP section. It looked like the entire hip contingent of the music industry was there. Unlike the performers lingering backstage, who had no idea who I was, these *machers* were eager to connect with me. I flashed back to my stroll through the grounds of Hugh Hefner's house, when I was stalked by the exotic animals in his menagerie. Any sign that I belonged on the business side of the music business horrified me, probably because I feared that I did belong there.

In New York it was easy to believe I had nothing in common with the hit mongers, because their attempt to be cool was so transparent. But out here I couldn't detect the difference between an "under-assistant West Coast promo man," as the Stones had dubbed such disposable types, and . . . well, a hard-working hippie like me. (At twenty-three I was already on antacids.) It's hard to convey in retrospect why I was so anxious about where I fit. Cultural commerce is so extensive and entrenched today that it seems naïve to fret about the consequences, and no critic of any popular form will get very far by taking a stand against marketing. But that wasn't the case in the sixties, especially when it came to music. In the Summer of Love it seemed possible to create a culture based on tangibility, a hands-on, person-to-person sensibility that would displace the system that organized human beings into consumer groups. I'm not talking about a guerrilla form like street art, but a well-organized and mass-distributed movement with creativity at its core. That's what the counterculture meant to me, and the bursts of love and hope I'd felt hanging out in the Haight, dropping acid with Groovy, meeting rock stars who were making music from the issues in their lives—the intensity of these encounters had a profound effect. I was no longer just the chronicler of a hot new scene; I was a crusader in the eternal struggle between light and darkness, the real thing and hype.

It's not unusual for a young man to love music so much that he thinks it stands for truth and beauty. But I was in a position to instill that passion in a large audience of my peers, so I thought. I would only gradually understand that rock critics have little power to shape popular taste. Everything depends on the audience—and the agents of stylization are always waiting in the wings. I should have known that, since I was in a position to see it firsthand. The broader the appeal of a new sensibility, the more conventional it eventually becomes, and commerce rapidly accelerates this process. But rock proposed a different model. It was blunter about the relationship between freedom and desire, between sexual and political repression, than any mass form that had come before it. I believed that the channeling of erotic energy was the means by which the system controlled us. Rock was all about breaking through that block, and therefore it had the capacity to smash the order. If money still circulated around it, at least it could express an alternative to the world as it was, and in doing so provide a paradigm for a new way of life. Such was the importance I placed on pop culture that I saw it as the key to social change. So, yes, I thought of rock as a revolutionary force.

I would soon find a potent ally in the émigré philosopher Herbert Marcuse. White-haired and vigorous, he gave lectures to halls packed with students, offering a critique of the system that focused on its capacity to unleash carefully manipulated forms of pleasure, creating a stunted eroticism and an impoverished being he called "one-dimensional man." Marcuse was the most countercultural of the Old School Marxists, and Marx was a thinker whose ideas had to be liberated from Communism as it actually existed—that was what people like me believed. It was a thorny project, but a crucial one for radical democrats, and Marcuse was an important part of it. I was especially drawn to his concept of "erotic labor," which I took to mean insisting on work that enlists your deepest passions. It's painful to think that this idea may seem like pure fantasy to many young people caught in the struggle to plug into a career or staggering under student debt. I owe my good fortune to the fact that in the prime of my youth there was room enough in the economy to find jobs that enlisted my deepest instincts, or to invent those jobs. This wasn't a matter of working in some office with yoga mats on the premises, and it wasn't just about making art. Lots of people found the pleasures of erotic labor in political organizing. This was about work as an act of love. Marcuse made me see that when work is love it can be liberating.

I also shared with him a faith in the revolutionary potential of art. At its purest, it had the capacity to alter our perceptions of reality, and so it was a more reliable source of consciousness expansion than LSD. The question that both inspired and haunted me was whether the strategies of art could be applied to popular culture. The answer, if there was one, lay in the combination of freedom and commerce, of music and community, that was rock. It was up to critics to protect its potential. My job was to be a champion of the sound that would remake society.

Looking back on the intensity with which I embraced this mission I realize that it wasn't just a commitment. It was a way to resolve the conflict between the hustler and the artist within me. Many people in my generation felt, I think, that rock was an agent of refusing to accept our assigned fate, which was to fit the mold of success. A political movement would soon emerge from this rebellion, one I became deeply involved in. But in 1967 it had yet to gel. There was still a gulf between hippies and the hardcore left, and students were just beginning to feel their power. Music was the thing everyone had in common, and the way to build a social agenda was to form a community of fans who understood that the "four-chord music anyone can play" (my favorite definition of rock 'n' roll) was now a model for an alternative identity.

This was why I couldn't just go with the flow at Monterey, though it was the most extraordinary rock lineup I'd ever seen, ranging over three days. I felt the auspiciousness of the occasion, and, flush with angst and aspiration, I found every reflex of the audience meaningful. Naturally I was disappointed. The crowd acclaimed everything in a state of indiscriminate delight. The most rancid schmaltz and the most militant antiwar sentiments received the same standing ovation. When the audience rose as one for Ravi Shankar, master of the sitar, I understood that few people had the faintest idea what raga music was about. In the film *Monterey Pop* the crowd is totally with him, leaping to its feet at the end of his piece. But the movie doesn't show that he also got an ovation for tuning up. Poor guy, I thought; to represent an ancient musical tradition in an arena where all that matters is that it sounds trippy. I pondered the interview I'd done with the young white bluesman Paul Butterfield. I'd asked what he thought of the microtonalities produced by the sitar. "I get raga," he replied. "All ghetto music is the same."

What, finally, was the real thing? The question may be irrelevant now, given the triumph of the hyper-real, but in 1967 it demanded to be answered, and I remember quite clearly what the real thing meant to me. It was the feeling I had at Monterey when all my misgivings were swept aside by a band that was unknown outside San Francisco. The sidemen were thin and long-haired, à la mode, but the lead singer was a rather squat woman with a not-so-hot complexion and very messy hair. It took me a few minutes to realize that I'd seen her before. She was the woman Judith and I had met at that house in Daly City. I'd also met the members of her band, but I'd forgotten its name. Now I heard it announced. They were Big Brother and the Holding Company, and she was Janis Joplin.

I'd never seen them perform; not many people in that audience had. The sidemen seemed completely focused on Janis, cradling her with their riffs and coaxing her vocal flights. From the first notes her voice stunned me with its primal drive. And her songs were all about the contradictions of desire. Why is love like a ball and chain? She posed that question with aching frustration and sputtering rage, cut with an assertion that, yes, this is me, inside and out—take my heart if it turns you on. This was every reason I had for never trusting anyone, the great fear of helpless devotion that lurks beneath paranoia. But she was willing to acknowledge her vulnerability and able to face the terrifying prospect of emotional dependence. I was many years away from letting myself go the way Janis did in her songs. Hearing her for the first time was like meeting my most guarded self. Her voice was the liquid inside the balloon that I struggled to prevent from spilling out. I understood the connection between rock and the inexpressible demanding to be made overt. This was the power I had seen in Jim Morrison's performances, the thing that made sixties music a singular art, daring the market to set a price on it.

Of course, the market did, with astonishing speed. But for a little while I could give myself to the belief that this woman wailing onstage had a direct line to my emotions and the possibilities for creating a new world that lay within me. I suppose this feeling of intimacy with a great artist is the grand show-business illusion, but I'd never experienced it before, and neither, I suspect, had anyone who saw that performance, not in quite the same way. I knew instantly that Janis would be a big star, someone I would have to write about in my column. But I didn't imagine that she would also bring me as close as I ever came in the rock world to loving someone.

I got back to New York as the first heat wave of July was smothering the city. Within a few days the sex and drugs and rock 'n' roll, even the rush of seeing Janis perform for the first time, all seemed like a fantasy of being abducted by aliens from an advanced planet. The hot and crowded streets of Manhattan didn't invite openness as California had. It was either *Fuck you!* or *Fuck me!*—business as usual.

Only the hair on young men had changed, longer by a foot since I'd left town, so it seemed to me. Tie-dyes and sandals were everywhere, along with peasant shirts with strips of embroidery, produced by old Ukrainian tailors baffled by their new clientele. But it was the arrival of mass-produced psychedelia that really pissed me off. An ad in the *Voice*, placed by a pair of local light-show producers, declared their availability for "discotheques, fashion shows, industrial shows, commercials and bar mitzvahs." Was it the bluntness of this pitch that made it seem so New York, or was there something about the city that repelled utopian experiments like the ones I'd seen in the Haight? Generations of radicals had found a home here in the general indifference to extreme behavior, but the counterculture was too big to fade into the urban parade. Hip was a vanguard that had caught on, and it was porous to the point of incoherence. In California, the threat was violence and tour buses, but here it was the swarm that the scene had become. Long-haired kids descended on Greenwich Village. I would see them in the parks, scrounging for communion and spare change. I decided that isolation was the real consciousness here, the ideal mode for working and consuming.

My college friend Joel had risked his life as a civil rights worker in Louisiana, where he'd come under fire from the Klan. Now he was living communally, tilling the land in the Catskill Mountains, not far from the Borscht Belt resorts where his parents had scarfed gefilte fish. For Joel, leaving the city was the only way to maintain the hippie ideal against the urban corruptions of commerce and chic. The soil was its own romance, as it had been for centuries of radical utopians. It was where the transformation of consciousness could take root, Joel explained in a voice that seemed unnaturally serene. I was skeptical but intrigued, since he was a pretty rigorous guy. The commune he described was more structured than the crash pads I'd stayed in, with duties assigned and decisions made by consensus. I decided to check it out.

In college Joel had favored preppy chinos, but when we met he was wearing a work shirt and overalls. In the back seat of his truck, his college girlfriend, whom I remembered for her loose hair and pendulous earrings, greeted me with a sturdy hug. I didn't recall her birth name, but now she was Stardust, her face scoured with grit, her smile still radiant. I stayed with their "family" for several days before I finally made my excuses. It was wearying to watch them vote on who would go to town for milk (since they didn't have a cow). I wasn't tempted by their diet of parsnip stews, and the women were too tired at night for anything but nodding off to the Grateful Dead. I soon realized that I was hooked on pavement and novelty, on streets that sizzled with activity, and on the ambivalence that the city inspired. There was no solace for me here.

Still, I gave my friends their best shot by writing about them. I left my doubts out of the piece, not just as a favor to Joel but also because I wanted such projects to succeed. The idea of collective living intrigued me, and by the end of the sixties, I was part of a commune. The results were very mixed. I can only say in retrospect that, narcissism and possessiveness being what they are, communes based on the hippie model—which involved affinity and little else—have a short life span. The ones that endure are grounded in strongly held beliefs, not just a general injunction to do your thing or a quest for family. But that was the whole problem with the counterculture. There was no will to form institutions that could transmit values, only a feeling that everything worth learning could be comprehended in an instant or immediately felt. "Nothing you can know that can't be known," the Beatles sang to us. "It's easy."

The absence of boundaries was liberating to some, but for others it would produce a yearning for the most authoritarian forms of devotion. I could see this coming long before Charles Manson or the Peoples Temple because I covered the most egregious spiritual leaders of the sixties, who always presented a vivid spectacle. I was invited to attend a press event for the man who had guided the Beatles to enlightenment though a practice called Transcendental Meditation. He was known as the Maharishi Mahesh Yogi, a set of honorific titles that obscured his ordinary Indian roots. After his anointing by the Fab Four he attracted the attention of the hippest of the hip. When I met him in a flower-decked room at the Plaza Hotel, he was represented by the same firm that handled publicity for the Ringling Bros. circus. Cradling a hyacinth bud in one hand and gesturing with the other, he explained that the poor were that way because they were lazy, and they were lazy because they lacked self-knowledge. Wealth was a sign of inner harmony, and there was no reason to share it. "Like a tree in the middle of a garden," he intoned, "should we be liberal and allow the water to flow to other trees, or should we drink ourselves and be green?" But isn't that selfish? someone asked. He replied with the lacquered smile of an airline steward. "Be absolutely selfish. That is the only way to bring peace, and if one doesn't have peace, how is one to help others attain it?" Mitt Romney couldn't have said it better.

The Maharishi's message was the most odious thing I had ever heard, and it disgusted me to think that it appealed to the Beatles. (It still attracts affluent aesthetes who think they're too spiritual for Scientology.) Were the Beatles so freaked out by fame that any exotic claptrap seemed wise to them, or were they searching for a way to enjoy their fortune without guilt? It didn't matter. To me, they lacked the bullshit detector that is absolutely necessary to guide yourself through early and abrupt success, and this was nearly as bad as selling out. I should have been more sympathetic, since I was grappling fitfully with the same issues. All that saved me from the gurus was a thorough skepticism about authority. But I was convinced that the music scene in New York was threaded through with charlatans. The only way to escape them was to devote my column to what remained of the underground.

I took shelter in the Downtown poetry scene, where I met a group of young writers who were attempting to extend the ideas of Frank O'Hara into the hip scene. I admired their determination to write highly personal poems that couldn't be set to music, their respect for the magic of mere words, and the sustenance they found in each other. They congregated at a venerable radical church, St. Mark's-in-the-Bouwerie. This was the scene that had produced Lou Reed and would soon spawn Patti Smith. I wanted to publicize these people, but there was only so much I could add to what was written about poetry. The same was true for experimental theater; it was too avant-garde for the mainstream, and so it wasn't part of my beat. I was doomed to chase the elusive ideal of a radicalism that could also be popular. But New York was not San Francisco. Self-inflation was what the big city offered, in abundance, and that was what I often ended up writing about, in the most withering prose I could summon. Nothing was as ripe for plucking as a young French import named Antoine.

His is not a name that will ever grace a street in Paris. After the sixties he faded into the ether of Eurotrash, but for a year or so he was the hottest thing in post-yé-yé pop. Antoine had mastered an ersatz genre called *le protest*, and his greatest hit was a rant about saying what you think and doing as you please. I can't convey the feeling of this lyric in English, but it managed to insult both rock poetics and the French chanson. I couldn't resist covering his arrival in New York, courtesy of Warner Bros. Records. He was a classic nerd, with hair that curled too neatly around his ears and a bemused look on his face. The best quote I got was from an electrical worker who asked, with practiced disdain, "Who the hell is he?" Still, Antoine had his admirers, among them Andy Warhol, who had probably been paid by the Warner label to "host" him. This was surely why Warhol had decided to give him a screen test. I was shocked, since I still thought of Andy as making something sacred called art. But I was watching the low end of his enterprise, an early example of the marriage between chic and shlock, and I had a part to play in the mix. Nobody cared if I unleashed my venom in print. It didn't matter what I thought of it; only *that* I thought of it. Say what you want and do what you can—just like Antoine.

Why was I drawn to pseudo-events like this? The answer had less to do with covering things that made good copy than with my fascination for fakes and failures. It was like watching a cripple and feeling good about your flabby legs. There was an Antoine within me—that's what I believed—and I had to be careful or he would burst out in a song and dance. *Very* careful. A local news show wanted me to review rock concerts. When I pointed out that these concerts often lasted past midnight, while I would have to be on TV at eleven P.M., the producer shrugged and said, "So leave early." I flashed on a musician getting electrocuted onstage (this would actually happen to several rockers) as I blithely praised his playing on-air. I turned the gig down, another chance to break into the big time rejected because of the agita I felt at moments like that.

My agent accused me of feeling guilty about making real money. I knew he was right—the Oedipal fear of besting my father welled within me. But I also needed to preserve my self, or what was left of it. The connection between writing and my emotions, which had been such a solace in my life, would be lost behind the flattening demands of television. I would end up as a velvet-caped exotic, canceled after a season, no doubt. I would never be the writer I wanted to be. My talent, such as it was, depended on connecting with my passions, and TV was the enemy of real emotions. In those stunted days before the Internet, every entry into the mass media demanded stylization, the thing I dreaded most. It was a betrayal of erotic labor and an argument for clinging to the *Village Voice*, though it paid bubkes. Like many of its writers, I needed the freedom to make my own mistakes in the name of sincerity. My agent was undeterred. He took me to lunch, and, over dessert, he chirped, "Don't say anything—just think about this." Then he revealed that he'd heard from a music publishing company. (Libel laws prevent me from naming it here.) I'd be paid $25,000—a very significant sum in 1967—to give a few lectures at their conferences. But that was just the pretext; it was understood that I would favor their artists in my column. In other words, payola! I excused myself, and in the toilet I barfed up the food.

There would be other, nearly as repugnant offers. In 1968, the Hollywood producer Otto Preminger took me to lunch and asked whether I was interested in writing the book for a musical he wanted to bring to Broadway. It would be called *I Protest*, and the opening scene, as he described it with glistening eyes, would feature students marching down the aisle, carrying signs, to the heroic strains of Beethoven. This time I managed to avoid a trip to the toilet, but, needless to say, I never got back to Preminger.

By then I'd stopped returning my agent's calls. But I couldn't shake the feeling that I was caught on a hook, lured by the glitter of a bauble bobbing in the sunlight. I reacted by railing against hype. No hustle escaped my wrath, and when I wasn't venting I proclaimed a generational uprising, an intifada of the kids. But the more I fulminated, the greater the demand for me. I thought I was protecting myself by refusing big money, but the attention was much harder to resist. Why was I making all these pronouncements about youth culture, swinging wildly? I asked myself that question many times, until I recalled an incident from when I was maybe seven. A child had run away, and I said I'd seen him. Suddenly I was surrounded by police and by the anguished mother pleading for details. I can still see her face as it became clear that I'd lied. I longed for the spotlight. Everything threatening dissolved in its magic beams; I was special after all. I remember how thrilling it was to be famous in the housing project, even for a moment—and how ashamed I was to need that.

A ball of terrified fury, sustained by charcoal pills for chronic indigestion, I chose my friends from outside the pop milieu, and only when stoned with them could I briefly relax. Sex? I had more than I deserved, considering how jittery I was. But the idea that I might have an affair, or even a close friendship, with a rock star seemed more fanciful than even the offers my agent had dangled before me. Just as I was sinking into the routine of interviewing people who were afraid of being unmasked by me; just as I was resigned to feeling riven; just as I felt my style grow heavy with alliterations that passed for passion; just then I got a call from the bass player of Big Brother and the Holding Company. He hadn't forgotten the time we'd spent together at that house in Daly City. The band was about to embark on its first tour of the Northeast. Would I like to join them in Philadelphia? In the words of my favorite literary character, Molly Bloom: *Yes I said yes I will Yes.*

Even when she was a certified superstar, Janis was far more accessible than her equivalent would be today. You might see her mingling with the audience before a set, and you could probably worm your way backstage if you tried. I didn't have to carry a press card. I just caught up with the band. In those days, an emerging group like Big Brother and the Holding Company would play in venues that were often old theaters, sometimes with the seats ripped out so people could mill around. In Philadelphia they performed in a huge converted garage. Their sets were long and rarely rehearsed. It was an exhausting ordeal, with little to keep the musicians grounded except one another. The guys who made up Janis's band were very good at creating an umbra of warmth, even in a strange dressing room. They kept a close eye on her, much as one might watch an insecure sister diving off the high board. They weren't doing it because she was their rainmaker. They cared for her—it was obvious and it moved me. Unlike the members of the Doors, who had a simmering contempt for Jim Morrison and his bouts of drunken release, these musicians respected Janis's need to be intoxicated. They didn't drink, but they also didn't judge.

Her fragility was hard to miss up close, but before a performance it was especially intense. Waiting to go on in Philadelphia, she stalked around the dressing room, her fingers drumming on a tabletop. "Oh, shit," she said, looking out at the crowd. "We'll never be able to get into those kids. Want to see death? Take a look out there." The crowd was an undifferentiated herd of hippies—the usual. I had the sense that she was like this at every show. She looked like she was trying to jump out óf her skin. For someone as self-conscious as Janis, stepping onstage must have been a very charged sensation.

She reached for her trademark, a bottle of Southern Comfort. In those days it had a lower proof than most alcoholic concoctions, but she could guzzle an uncanny amount of the stuff. "I don't drink anything on the rocks," she told me. "Cold is bad for my throat. So it's always straight or in tea. I usually get about a pint and a half down when I'm performing. Any more, I start to nod out."

As a nice Jewish boy I'd never seen anyone drink like that, and it was hardly the drug of choice for a hippie. But liquor is famous for its disinhibiting effect on shy people, and, as countless alcoholic writers will attest, it can loosen up the associative parts of the imagination, as can other drugs with hazardous side effects. Some musicians are lucky enough to get there from the act of performing itself, but many do their best work in an altered state. I cringe when media wags gloat over a performer's overdose. They demand greatness, but they won't accept what it takes to achieve it. In the sixties this puritanical reflex was suspended; unfortunately, it was replaced by a reluctance to intervene no matter how self-destructive the behavior. In that respect Janis was a typical victim of the decade's worst sin: indifference to consequences. But as long as she remained attached to her band, she was safe.

No one makes great art out of contentment with the world, and Janis had the requisite rough youth in Texas. She was the town slut, a victim of the nasty collusion between sex and contempt for women who crave it. No need to go into detail about her biography; it's pretty well-known—her time in Austin, where she was part of the boho music scene that seeded the San Francisco sound; her journey west with Chet Helms, who would run one of the city's two major music venues, the Avalon Ballroom; her appearance at the legendary Trips Festival. "We were just interested in being beatniks then," she told me. "Now we've got responsibilities, and I guess you could say . . . ambitions."

Too much attention is paid to the flash of great sixties rockers and their larger-than-life lives; not enough to their craft. If you listen beyond her famous shrieking you'll realize that every note Janis sang was shaped. She was a serious student of blues, especially the music of Bessie Smith, the great stylist of the 1930s. Janis's greatest achievement—and it influenced the entire range of rock vocalizing back then—was to blend Bessie Smith's expressiveness with the drive of Otis Redding. "See, Bessie, she sang big open notes in very simple phrasing," Janis explained to me. "But you can't fall back on that in front of a rock band. I mean, you can't sing loose and easy with a big throbbing amplifier and drums behind you. The beat pushes you on. So I started singing rhythmically, and now I'm learning from Otis how to push a song instead of just sliding over it."

Sexual politics didn't come up in our conversations, but her articulation of desire and frustration was certainly something a proto-feminist could identify with. And she had more than booze in common with Jim Morrison. Both were "erotic politicians," to use his phrase. They were dedicated to the idea of music as an intoxicant of liberation. I would call that the best instinct of the sixties—the Whitmanesque urge to sing the body electric. But Morrison's allure depended on a certain distance. I never felt close to him, not when I heard him sing or when I met him. With Janis I had the feeling that I knew her issues intimately.

There was an edge of doubt to her performance of herself, and I understood it well. That was how I'd felt as a kid and how I felt years later as a media sensation. It was easy to see the writhing and swaying of her body as a woman in the throes of orgasm, but orgasm contains so many emotions that complicate the question of ecstasy. The sexual spectacle she made of herself was clearly the effect she intended, but it wasn't the only thing she wanted. Validation, degradation, possibly cessation— all of that was in her voice. Thinking of her now, I can't help wishing that she'd grown up in a place like Queens, where she would have had friends who didn't regard her as a tramp just because of her sexual appetite. If she'd been part of a scene with kids who had creative compulsions like hers (kids like, well, me) she might have had the strength to resist her fate. What I'm trying to say is that I wish I could have saved her. She is one of the ghosts that haunt my memory of the sixties, the ones I cared for who died before their time.

Janis was the most self-conscious performer I'd ever met, about her shape, her breasts, and especially her hair. She made Morrison's fragility seem puny and my own body issues trifling. I didn't know about her bisexuality (an attribute of Bessie Smith as well), and I didn't mention mine, though it was surely part of the reason why we clicked. As for heroin, I never saw any telltale signs in her. But I was acutely aware of how hard she found it to connect with men. Being an emblem of unleashed female emotion hardly helped with the dudes who made up her core audience. "I never end up with a guy on these tours," she groused. "I mean, you saw me dancing out there between sets. All these guys were standing around, panting in the corner. Finally I had to say to one of them, 'Well, do you wanna dance or not?' and he comes on waving his arms around like a fucking bat. Now, why do things like that always happen?" She sighed. "They're all afraid of me. Shit."

Just as she was bemoaning her fate, a man in a fur suit sauntered into the dressing room. His name was Gary the Gorilla, and he'd been hired by the club to stoke the crowd. Janis offered him her bottle, and he pulled off his ape head to chug from it. Then he unzipped his belly and passed his paws around. Suddenly she leapt into his lap, and she sat there buzzed and contented until it was time to go on. I watched her empty her guts into song after song, howling need and frustration, stomping out the beat and the pain. "Ball and Chain" was her signature number, and she regarded it as the hardest of her songs. "I have to really get inside my head, every time I do it," she said. "Because it's about feeling things. There's this big hole in the song that's mine, and I have to fill it. So I do. And it really tires me out. But it's so groovy when you know that the audience really wants you. They yell back at you, call your name, and like that."

When the set was over and the band bounded into the dressing room, sweaty with the sizzle of playing, I watched Janis throw herself at Gary the Gorilla, who was waiting patiently. I have a vivid memory of her nuzzling his furry chest, burying herself in his faux-hairy folds, and opening another bottle.

I saw Janis several times after that tour. Once I accompanied her to a party celebrating her new contract with Columbia Records, which came with an enormous advance. Her annual income would soon top $1 million in today's dollars, and in New York nothing draws the glitterati like new money. Amid the glad hands, Janis gazed at herself uneasily in a mirror. She shook out her hair only to confront an elegant woman out of *Harper's Bazaar*, who covered up her drink and hissed, "Do you mind?" To which Janis replied, "Fuck off, baby." It was a show of bravado, but later I caught her pouting into that mirror. "Face it," she muttered. "You've got ratty hair." At that point, of course, her hair had become a style millions of young women imitated, but to her it was still what it had been in Texas, a symbol of her otherness.

We never had a date or anything like that, but I did take her to the Jewish dairy restaurant Ratner's. It was right near two major downtown rock venues, the Fillmore East and the Anderson, and after a concert the place was full of hippies stoned on music and whatever they could score. Ancient waiters delivered blintzes and tea with hands shaking so badly that most of the liquid was in the dish under the cup. I expected a mob scene when we walked in, but everyone was zombie-faced. She loved the ambience, and we stayed for hours. I remember strolling with her at dawn, the sky glowing dark blue over damp and empty streets. It was the kind of early morning that makes New York look like a movie set. We kissed lightly. It was more than a buddy peck and less than an invitation. I was way too shy to ask what was on her mind. But I left with a feeling more gripping than even sexual arousal. I realized how deeply I cared for her.

I hardly ever had sexual fantasies about the rock stars I wrote about. (Exceptions: Bob Weir and Dion, the Shangri-Las and the Shirelles, a few others I'm too embarrassed to mention.) The romance of meeting musicians was too ethereal to be truly erotic, and I could never cast them in obscene scenarios, any more than I could have lusted for Mickey Mantle, the baseball hero of my youth. But friendship seemed at least abstractly possible, and I don't think I ever did an interview without hoping that it would result in a personal connection. For a number of reasons—my introverted nature or the arbitrary quality of these encounters—it rarely happened. That was one of the many ironies of my life in the sixties. Openness was almost a fetish back then, yet I felt more isolated than ever. With Janis I sensed a warmth based on a certain recognition. We shared a knowledge of self-doubt, a sense of ourselves that would make us outcasts even when we reached the hot center. Most people are grotesque, but not many know it, and those who walk around with that awareness as a steady undertone recognize each other. On that basis I think we connected.

Over the next few years I lost touch with Janis, and then she was dead. I can easily imagine the struggle she must have waged to do her thing again and again on ever more impersonal stages, to enact the spectacle of need that she was known for while maintaining the tangibility of her art, which involved a self-exposure so intense that it impelled everyone in the audience to do the same. That was the essential rock experience of my youth, and she will always represent it. For me, Janis was the promise of the sixties—and the tragedy.

I Was a Teenage Marcel Proust

The essay was called "Learning from the Beatles," and the author was the eminent literary critic Richard Poirier. I perused it anxiously—maybe he'd proven once and for all that a bona fide thinker could understand the Fab Four better than a fan like me. Sure enough, I found myself criticized by Poirier for my negative review of *Sgt. Pepper*. I felt immensely flattered to be bashed in the *Partisan Review*, but I shouldn't have been surprised. Rock had entered the realm of high discourse, and my work was being noticed, at least in passing, by the literati. Nineteen sixty-seven was when intellectuals began to move among people like me. I wanted in.

I'd always thought of intellectuals as the Real Thing—classy but open, a bulwark against political brutality, the guardians of humanism; they wrote books with words you had to look up, and they read journals without pictures of celebrities on the cover. I regarded these "little magazines" as an alternative to the predations of the slicks, and I was determined to break into their pages. But I had mixed feelings about the new attitude toward rock. On the one hand, it affirmed my belief that hierarchies of taste were bullshit. But I thought the anything-is-art sensibility was bullshit, too. Pop culture had its own standards, and many older critics had no idea what they might be. They gobbled up whatever seemed vital, like the voracious guests at a Luis Buñuel dinner party. Poirier was among the most discerning of his kind, and he made a pretty good case for *Sgt. Pepper,* but I remember feeling that he'd missed the larger point about the Beatles. They were merely the most visible sign of a counterculture that the academy hadn't yet noticed. Where were the learned essays on underground comix, psychedelic posters, or any pop music that wasn't made by JohnPaulGeorge&Ringo? I thought I saw an opening.

But I no longer had a patent on rock criticism. There was a lot of competition, not just from young writers, which I expected, but also from well-credentialed scholars, some of them far less honorable than Poirier. A professor named Albert Goldman would make a career, and a lot of money, out of attacking rock icons. But that was later in the decade. At first he went with the flow, and in 1967 he wrote a piece for *New American Review* on "The Emergence of Rock." It was a lush setting of conventional wisdom, perfectly pitched to people who didn't understand the music but desperately wanted to. I remember Goldman's description of Doors guitarist Robbie Krieger: "He opens up visions of an artificial bird singing in the gardens of a Byzantine emperor." Not even at my most pompous could I have written such gilded prose. I resented Goldman—he was another cat eating out of my bowl—but I also hated his knee-jerk response to youth culture, and I couldn't bear the fact that we were often confused with each other because of our similar names. I preferred being mistaken for Al Goldstein, the bad-boy publisher of a weekly sex paper called *Screw*.

To the extent that I had real ideas about pop culture, they were much more radical than what I wrote about rock. I was fascinated by supermarkets and private swimming pools. I didn't grow up around such emblems of suburban banality, and they aroused a wondrous feeling in me. So did anything Disney. I cherished a small plastic statue of Mickey Mouse. It was blue, its baby's head and cute belly protruding over a body that seemed all hands and feet. This was a very complex piece, calling up unconscious associations with the infantile, and it was sensuous to the touch. Also mass-produced, and about as ordinary a souvenir as you could buy. If I could find a way to describe my feelings for that blue Mickey I might produce a new kind of criticism, one that had less to do with my crusades against the music industry than with the possibility that show business was an arena in which our deepest desires were exercised. Any major pop phenomenon captured a social moment, which meant that you could read the hidden currents of the present in entertainment. That simple word was very complicated.

But I didn't have the intellectual chops for such a project at the age of twenty-three, or the ability to focus for more than the time it took to meet a weekly deadline. And even if I acquired those skills, where would I publish? The demand for my work only applied to my expertise on youth culture, not to my views on frozen food and sitcoms. My greedy heart soared when I received a commission from the *American Scholar*. The subject was rock lyrics, but I figured that I could broaden my base once I published there. This journal had been founded by Ralph Waldo Emerson—I was, like, *so* impressed. It didn't occur to me that by 1967 it was a sclerotic remnant of itself, running safe pieces for settled minds. In the course of my career I would often find myself called upon to juice up high-toned periodicals that had sunk into a well-worn rut, only for the editors to discover that my writing was too vulgar. Something like that happened at the *American Scholar*. After struggling to fit the sensibility of rock into the very different tradition of written poetry, I ended up with a jumble of ideas papered over with sparkling prose. "Felicitous" was the word the editors used in the letter I received in response—but no thanks.

The revelation that I fit into neither the academy nor the mainstream caused the most severe of my media depressions, and it got even worse when a publisher looking to branch out from textbooks offered to print a collection of my articles. There was one problem: they didn't want to use the word *rock* in the title. They worried that the book would be displayed in the geology section. By then I was used to such outrageous reasoning, and frankly I was lucky that the anthology ended up being called *Goldstein's Greatest Hits* instead of the title I preferred: *A Rock Cosmology*. But that didn't answer the question nagging at me. Where did I belong?

The answer was the *Village Voice*. It was the only place where I was welcome to pursue my version of a hybrid sensibility. Fortunately, this was a profitable fit. The new flexibility, the growing interest in radical ideas, and the slippery question of who and what was hip all drew readers to the vivid journalism that was practiced at the paper. And by 1967, the audience was much larger than the ragtag tribes of hippies in the parks. In addition to the Nehru-collared art-and-party crowd, there were a quarter of a million students in the city, as well as God knows how many unhappy souls in the advertising and communications industries. This was our readership, and it now numbered around 150,000, an astonishing circulation for a bohemian weekly. We were no longer an underground paper; we were a journal of perception on a deadline—and the field itself was now a hot literary form.

From the perch that was my column I railed against hype. The word didn't just apply to the marketing of entertainment. It signified any kind of undue promotion, such as the media hype surrounding the war in Vietnam. I regarded this scourge as a virus that had inserted itself into the marrow of even the most radical culture. Hype was everywhere, and there was no way to cure the disease—I think I knew that, but it was such a handy target, and it lent itself to a hyper style. If I was going to publicize the evils of publicity, I had to be fierce and flashy, to load up on metaphors and alliteration. Deep down I suspected that flash was all I had.

Plastic! That was my epithet of choice. It didn't refer to the shape-shifting substance, but to the attitude produced by marketing strategies so supple that they could transform any idea into a product. By now young people have devised a whole set of defenses to deal with the machinations of commerce, or else they don't think it's an issue. But in 1967 we did. There were many attempts to set up an alternative entrepreneurial system, and it worked pretty well as far as it went. But only some things could be handmade, and only so many artisans had the talent and patience to create filigree jewelry or tie-dyes. For most kids, especially those who didn't live in major cities, everything that signified a hip identity, from bell-bottoms to protest music, was mass-produced. There had to be a word for all that ersatz stuff. It was *plastic*.

Today, plastic is the stuff of life, and it's hard to believe that the p-word was once an indictment. But in 1967, when tribes weren't yet market niches and rock festivals weren't festooned with corporate logos, the phenomenon we called "hip capitalism" was new. It presented itself as doing more than pushing product. *Consciousness* was the buzzword, and the narrative was about using the system in order to subvert it. But it seemed to me that the artist was always the one who ended up subverted. And publicity was what made the transition from authenticity to plastic seem as inevitable as the season or the tides. Hence, the need to fight the power that was hype.

But it wasn't so easy. Hip New York was an engine of promo and profit, and I was an enabler despite my efforts to resist making a buck from it. New records arrived at my home at the rate of several dozen a week. Most of them had white labels that said "not for resale." I sold them anyway, for a pittance, but I couldn't imagine that someday a white label on vinyl from the sixties would spike its value on eBay, only because of its rarity. Nor could I have guessed that a complete run of Fillmore posters would be worth a fortune. I owned such a set—Bill Graham, who ran the Fillmore, gave it to me—and I glued the posters onto the walls of my apartment. They livened up the corridors, but when I moved I couldn't get them off the walls. Another missed opportunity to cash in, but at the time I didn't believe in clinging to possessions. If it's beautiful, hang it up. But don't hang on.

It was much easier to let go of possessions than to free myself from the tightening grip of hype. I felt like I was stuck to a tar baby; the more I struggled against it, the more it stuck. I had no one to mentor me—no writer had ever occupied a position quite like mine—but a few performers were willing to share their wisdom. One of them was Paul Simon. I met him in 1966, not long after my column began. He hadn't yet developed the acuity that shows in his most memorable songs (and there are many). In those days he was still making heartfelt folk rock, and his lyrics seemed portentous to me even as they mocked portentousness. But he knew all about the music business, since he and Art Garfunkel had started out as a rock 'n' roll duo called Tom and Jerry. And he was echt New York, someone who knew how to find a good, cheap Chinese restaurant on the Upper West Side.

That was where we got together, up a flight of linoleum-covered stairs. I was struck by how much he looked like me. We were two short Jewish guys who'd let their hair grow for other than religious reasons, two outer-borough kids who'd turned a love of rock 'n' roll into a career. We could sense each other's lives from the way we scooped up pork fried rice and chomped on egg rolls. (All New York Jews of our generation know that Chinese food is exempt from the kosher laws.) I understood immediately that Paul was not one of the fragile souls he sang about. He was a pro, a veteran of the payola era, and he talked about the record industry as if it was just a conduit for his music—no big deal, ignore the hustle and make your own way. The conversation was too personal for me to write about without making myself the story, which I was still loath to do. But it was one of the few times when I left an interview feeling reassured. Paul would still remember me a year after that dinner, when I ran into him backstage at Monterey Pop; there's a photo of him chatting with Judith and me. I wish I'd kept his advice in mind as I descended into the maelstrom of promo that was the rock explosion. I would have saved myself a lot of tsuris. But there was no bridge over troubled water for me. Just the leaking boat of my ego.

I was haunted by the specter of the Monkees, the faux-Beatles act that had been put together in Hollywood and thrust into the prime-time spotlight. Their songs were pseudo-countercultural, irresistibly catchy, and bouncy to the beat. As musicians they weren't untalented, but they *were* merchandise—and they were huge on TV. I thought of groups like them as the rock equivalent of the robotic false messiah in *Metropolis*. But pop culture was more complex than that. It sponsored the revolutionary and the trite with the same that's-entertainment attitude. The raw and the cooked were two sides of a shtick to the producers of chat shows, which thrived on celebrity freaks. These were entertainers who knew how to dress and act the part of misfits. Not that they were necessarily faking it. The problem for me as a critic was distinguishing between Monkee wannabes and artists who had wrung a vision from their torment. Both could be successful.

How to parse the relationship between Johnny Carson, the essence of mainstream, and his frequent guest, a tall, gangly freak named Tiny Tim? With his giant nose and dishrag hair, he was the ugliest man in pop music. Carson made jokes about him entering the Miss America pageant representing Death Valley. But Tiny Tim had put everything that didn't show on his body into his voice. He sang in an ungainly falsetto, accompanying himself on a ukulele, and his repertoire consisted of old-time tunes such as "Tiptoe through the Tulips." These relics of a forgotten innocence were keys to the kingdom where he yearned to reside.

His real name was Herbert Buckingham Khaury, and he'd grown up in a stretch of upper Manhattan where it wasn't cool for a guy to wear makeup. The other kids called him "Crazy Herbie." He was the scapegoat every working-class neighborhood needs, which meant that he endured a hail of abuse. But he lived for his old records, and he gravitated toward any theater that showed films from the thirties or even the twenties. "I had to be alone in the dark," he told me, "because then I could feel like I was alone with the performers, feeling their voices inside me." It was a lot like the way I'd felt about great writers when I was a boy—their voices were inside me, too—and I understood why he had put so much energy into creating an alter ego. In that persona he was a wind chime vibrating to the breezes of memory. It was touching to watch this lug transform himself into such a wistful creature. Like a great clown, he could cast his audience into a realm of childlike purity. The same quality made him one of the first camp superstars, because, in the end, his delicate pose of androgyny skirted failure.

That may explain why his first gig was at Hubert's Flea Circus in the old Times Square, where, for a nickel, you could see a parade of performing freaks among the trained insects doing tricks. Tim also worked the subways for pocket cash. But his favorite dive was a bar in the Village where, as he put it, "the ladies liked each other." He must have seemed like just another gender bender in cosmetics to them. But he wasn't trying to be a woman, he explained. He wanted to imbibe the feminine aura. In makeup, he said, "I feel that I'm in a garden of paradise, alone with beautiful ladies. They are the essence of my soul."

I wasn't sure whether he was giving me sincerity or feeding me good copy, and I decided that it was both. His act was a pretense, but it had been born of real suffering, and I wondered what would happen once the ordeal was replaced by stardom. Especially since he was straight; straight as a yardstick and just as inflexible. Sex, for him—and he would only spell the word—was something that must be redeemed in marriage, and he couldn't get married until he saw a sign from heaven. Meanwhile, he told me, "I try never to be alone with a beautiful woman, because then the devil in me becomes dangerous." In short, he was destined to play Las Vegas.

That was where I saw him in 1967. It was my first trip there, and I felt like I was in a ring of hell reserved for pop critics. The entrance to Caesar's Palace, with its 150 feet of floodlit fountains and its garden of pseudo-classical statues, was beyond even my mother's decorative schemes. A Cinerama billboard proclaimed Tiny Tim's name in letters seven feet high. What was a denizen of the flea circus and the dyke bar doing in this feather-and-pastie fantasia? As soon as I unpacked, I headed for the Circus Maximus room to find out.

I stood in the wings among the showgirls grabbing a smoke while he warmed up. There was no trace of the fey troubadour he played onstage. He was more like a baseball player, trotting in place and swatting the air with his hands—*here comes the windup and then the pitch . . . a wicked spitball*. The look on his face took me by surprise. It was intent and thoroughly butch. So there was a jock inside him, cohabiting with the angelic faerie. How would this marriage of convenience fare in the face of fame? I was always looking for the story that hadn't been told, the part left out of the press bio, and now I sensed what it was. I'd heard reports about parties in his hotel room, bacchanals where he rolled in rich desserts ordered from room service. Yes, he would admit to me, he'd had a few drunken bouts, spent too much money, and, yes, he'd slipped a few times and given himself to women. But then he had to "cut the cancer out." It sounded like the rap of a married man who cheats and then consults a priest. But this was someone who had devised an elaborate system of fantasies to cushion him from life. What would happen to the tenuous balance between art and desperation once the freak succeeded? It was a question I would ask myself many times; in fact, it was a theme of my writing on rock stars. In Tiny Tim I saw an extreme version of the answer.

He was so fragile that, on the road, his manager roomed with him. But I demanded to be alone with my subject—that was always my condition for doing an interview, and I usually got my way. At the appointed hour I knocked on the door of his chamber. "Hel-lo, Mr. Goldstein," I heard Tiny Tim say in that familiar warble, and I walked in. It was the day after his first performance, and I expected to see breakfast dishes and other signs of late rising. But I didn't count on tray after tray of cakes and puddings, a number of them overturned on the carpet. He still had smears of cream on his chest and face—or maybe he was wearing one hell of a foundation. "I've always wanted to do this," he said sheepishly, pointing to the mess. I didn't ask him to elaborate.

By then I'd learned a lot about the fragility of icons, and I didn't want to collude in his misery. So I filed a piece that described the state of his room but not my misgivings about his fate. My apprehension was well taken. His star faded with the sixties—not even a wedding witnessed by Johnny Carson on *The Tonight Show* could restore it. But he continued performing long afterward, despite suffering a heart attack onstage, until finally, at another gig, he had a coronary that would be fatal. He wasn't the first performer, and I doubt he'll be the last, whose existence depended so heavily on the ratification of fame that he would die in the service of show business.

*

Tiny Tim was a good example of how the New Journalism, with its semi-literary credentials, worked in tandem with the culture's taste for the freaky. The appetite for extreme and enigmatic behavior was what kept writers like me in business. We were explorers on the frontier of the new. But it wasn't just the lively prose or the ability to personalize our stories that made us indispensable; it was our eagerness to interpret what we saw. Whether we used the first person or the objective voice, we weren't wedded to any concept of neutrality—neutrality was a lie. I had no doubt about it, since I'd witnessed protest marches that bore no relationship to what was described in the press, which seldom conveyed in any detail the brutality of the police. I concluded that the only reliable reporting would come from engaged individuals free of the constraints of institutional style. The New Journalism now meant more to me than using fictional techniques; it was about actively participating in the event—the correspondent as witness and truth teller. Walt Whitman had written the code I swore by: "I am the man. I suffered. I was there."

In the sixties, reporting still had a virile image. The mystique of tough guys pounding on old typewriters and drinking themselves noble persisted even in an era of white-suited wags and j-school pros. And journalism was, for all its compromises, an enemy of entrenched power. It was the rock music of the written word, and for many intellectuals a way to kick out the jams. I suspect that was why Norman Mailer ventured into my profession.

It began with his account of an antiwar march in 1967. Thousands of protesters tried to levitate the Pentagon by ohming and chanting. Mailer was there, and his narrative of the event, *Armies of the Night,* became his greatest success. It won a Pulitzer Prize and a National Book Award, a remarkable twofer. Despite our difficult meeting at the *Village Voice* office, when I'd fled from his raised fists, he was still my primo literary hero. But there was a problem. He had dropped, from a great height, onto the street where I lived. And so I saw him in a different way.

We ran into each other from time to time at social events. Smiles were exchanged, but I didn't want to connect with him. It wasn't his legendary belligerence that put me off—I had learned not to take it seriously. It was the sense of privilege and insulation that hung over his shoulders like an ermine cape. By then I'd gained quite a lot of knowledge about what it meant to be trapped in a role. Or maybe it was just that as I got closer to the writers I idolized, they seemed more like competitors. In any case, everything I'd admired about Mailer's style as a student—its radical candor and erudite intensity—now felt inappropriate. The image of the bad-boy genius, which he'd worked so hard to create, now collided with the subject he was writing about. I would feel that way about many hip intellectuals when they tackled youth culture. They didn't understand how the values of my generation were different from theirs, and they fell back on reflexes that had once been rebellious but were now reflexive. And when an ego as big as Mailer's tackled a phenomenon as remote from his daily life as the antiwar movement was, the result was a show of pure Me.

Armies of the Night is about a great American writer and media sensation going through changes, but the event it describes was about the struggle to end an unjust war. Ordinary kids were more important than Mailer in that battle, and far less insulated from the violence that ensued. He would eventually try to compensate for his elevated status by casting himself as a character called Aquarius. In this guise he could fully express his commitment to the new sensibility of the sixties. It met my standard of engagement, but its effect was to make his own experience more important than the action, and his persona the most fascinating thing of all. As artful as his journalism was, it seemed like a violation of the countercultural ethos that I'd come to share. We kids saw politics as a collective activity, something we did together. Radicals in Mailer's generation had struggled to maintain their individuality, but we fought to maintain community. These were very different battles, and they made Mailer's project suspect. It was all signature, and I learned little from it except for the example it offered of the kind of writer I didn't want to be.

The honorific term for people like Mailer was "public intellectual." They took positions, signed petitions, and wrote passionate works of dissent. But they didn't shy away from self-promotion; like everyone in the sixties, they went for it big-time. From my position at the crossroads of culture and hype, this was an unsettling discovery. It meant that intellectuals were now part of the celebrity culture. Those who knew how to use the mass media, such as Mailer and Warhol, Gore Vidal and Truman Capote, had joined the spectacle and TV expanded the star system exponentially, so that it included anyone deemed exotic. In the fifties, it was Beat poets, and homosexuals sitting behind potted plants. But in 1967 the hip thing for a chat show with blue-chip pretensions was to have a professor as a guest. These weren't run-of-the-tenure-mill types. They had to have an outsize sense of their importance, a blind confidence in their ideas, and a conviction that they could single-handedly alter the course of history. Most important, they had to have a skill that wasn't supposed to exist in the academy. They had to be entertaining.

The *maiven* who benefited most from this opening was Marshall McLuhan, a James Joyce scholar turned media savant. Gabbing with Dick Cavett or savoring a cameo role in a Woody Allen film, McLuhan was the perfect gnomic oracle, ever ready to make a point no one could firmly grasp. He epitomized the style of fluid thinking that was trendy at the time. Anything that sounded compelling could be—just might be—true. As in McLuhan's fame-blazing slogan "The medium is the message." This was a very reductive update of Walter Benjamin, the German cultural philosopher of the 1930s who argued that the mass production of images had changed the nature of perception. Benjamin was a Marxist mystic who didn't know from quips, but McLuhan had none of those limitations. His knack for cryptic assertions—New York is obsolete; movie stars will soon cease to exist—propelled him into prime time.

The fact that no one outside media-studies courses reads McLuhan today says something about the quality of his thinking. He produced a buckshot of ideas that usually hit only the vicinity of its targets. Yes, TV was a "cool" medium, as he proclaimed, but cool was the style of the time; today TV is a "hot" medium and we live in the age of Snooki. Yes, TV was turning the world into a "global village" (his phrase), but each new tool of communication, as it spreads, globalizes experience; today the Internet is having much the same effect. Any novel mass medium will produce the shifts McLuhan described, and television was still relatively new when he wrote. What he did get right was the importance of inventing a role. Like me, he had devised a new one—the media guru—and in 1967, that was enough to make you wise.

I didn't merit a private audience with the Wizard of Ozzie and Harriet. I was told by McLuhan's publicist that he "only does sit-downs with national media." I settled for one of his press conferences. It was a bit like interviewing the Maharishi, minus the garlands. McLuhan dispensed edicts, and we wrote them down. After about an hour of this ritual I decided that it was a shuck (the word we used for a scam). I wrote a piece that described him as a cross between Madison Avenue and

Harvard Square, a "para-philosopher" who specialized in "concept barbs," like the slogans in commercials. His ideas about TV were really about the triumph of advertising and the incursion of its techniques into the realm of theory. This was yet another hype.

But my real beef with McLuhan had to do with rock. My generation hadn't been shaped by TV, as he claimed. It was a distant second to music in terms of influence. So his ideas about us were wrong on the face because, like most of his peers, he ignored our primary form of expression. I don't think he ever wrote a word about rock; it didn't interest him, probably because its technological properties were just a small part of what made it special. As for hippies, at the press conference I attended he called them "despicable, revolting people." Only someone who was oblivious to youth culture could have concluded that what made us distinct was the medium we grew up with. Television was nothing mysterious to me; what didn't make sense was the way people in power acted. But there were a lot of baffled elders out there, and they needed a guide. As a cautionary tale I kept, pinned to the wall above my desk, a quote from the *Herald Tribune* proclaiming McLuhan "the most important thinker since Newton, Darwin, Freud, Einstein, and Pavlov." Why not since Dick Cavett?

In this climate of radical status flux, Clay Felker had an audacious idea. He wanted to send me to Saigon. "The Pop War!" he proclaimed, with a stop-the-presses look in his eye. As usual, he was right about the story. Felker had a real gift for matching writers with subjects, and going to Vietnam would have been a great career move for me. But there was no way that the experience would be as benign as his last bizarre assignment, which involved John Wayne. I pictured myself threading through the night town of Saigon, entering whorehouses and interviewing men my age who were traumatized by a war that I, and many of them, abhorred. Most of these guys were working-class. How could I move among them with my ponytail pulled up under a helmet? Wouldn't it be clear that I was exempt from the draft? And how had I carried that off? A set of providentially fallen arches? No. I'd used something more effective—and unmentionable. I had "queered out."

That's what it was called in the project, and it was worse than even admitting that you had a tiny dick. But when my student deferment expired and I was summoned by the draft board, I considered all my options. I'd gotten a shrink to write a letter. When I saw the diagnosis—"schizoid tendencies"—I knew it wouldn't fly. Schizoids could make very efficient killing machines. No way was I going to fight in this war. I was prepared to leave the country if I had to, and I'd already lined up a job at the *Toronto Star*. But I didn't want to live in a sensible place like Canada. There was only one other recourse. I checked the box that said "homosexual feelings"—some phrase like that. I girded myself for the moment when the doctor saw it. Surely a siren would go off and I would end up standing naked while a circle of men spat at me. But I did have those . . . feelings, which is what I told the white-coated man who placed me behind a screen and asked a few questions in an even tone. Had I had sex with a man? Yes. (Back in the Bronx, with that boy who picked me up in his Pontiac with the Madonna on the dashboard.) Had I enjoyed it? *Joy* wasn't the right word to describe my confused feelings, but I nodded yes, and that was that. I would never have to share the shameful secret if I didn't care to. But it made going to Vietnam as a reporter seem like the height of hypocrisy. Of all the reasons why I was in a privileged position, toting a notebook rather than a gun, my uncertain sexuality seemed like the most unconscionable. It felt like a betrayal of the kids I'd grown up with. So I turned the assignment down, leaving the story of the "pop war" to someone more securely straight.

I suppose I should say something conclusive about my relationship to gay culture in the mid-sixties, but I didn't have one. I had a friendship with a gay man, my roommate John, and an ample yearning toward certain guys, but no sexual connections with them. Even at the *Voice*, which had hired homosexuals during the fifties, when such a thing was unheard of in the media, the queers kept a low profile. As for the music scene, forget it. For all its florid androgyny, rock was a very macho milieu, and even critics I knew to be bisexual didn't send those signals in their writing—nor did I. It wasn't just discretion or cowardice; I honestly didn't feel gay. But there was one exception to my heteronormativity. I dug drag queens.

I had met Holly Woodlawn and Candy Darling at the Factory. It was one of the first media-savvy scenes where camping was a truly public act, and where sexual personae of all sorts were part of the mix. I guess most transgender kids today would regard the sense of incipient failure that Holly and Candy displayed as the essence of oppression. In the films

Warhol made with them, they could never get the man of their dreams—usually Joe Dallesandro, the outer-boroughs hustler as superstar—and they seemed always a shriek away from falling apart. This aura of incipient breakdown is why they were so fascinating to me. I don't think it had much to do with my uncertain sexuality. It was more like a metaphor for my class anxieties, my inability to master the codes that marked someone as affluent, or even middle-class. I was much more sensitive about my Bronxitude than I was about anything else, and in order to hide my roots I wore a costume so flamboyantly hippie-dippy that it was beyond class. In effect, I was a drag queen in rock gear.

If I'd had the need to integrate my sexuality into the rest of my life, I might have come out as whatever I was. But I didn't feel incomplete or inauthentic with women, and the cost would have been considerable in 1967, not just for a rock critic. Gay writers were expected to be bitchy, fragile, or geniuses, and I was none of those things. Instead, I went with the orthodoxy of the time and told myself that everyone was basically bisexual. It was hip to be androgynous, and I could convince myself that the fantasy I savored, of Mick Jagger in net stockings and pumps, was some sort of tribute to British style. In California I'd heard musicians talk about a "gay-off" as a kind of adventure in ecotourism; it had no implications for one's identity. There were queers all around me, but they faded into the hippie parade. Whatever happened in gay bars—which were all run by the mafia in New York—decorousness was the dominant public code, especially among the homosexual elite.

Several important gay men took an interest in me in the sixties, but I didn't respond to their overtures. It wasn't just homosexual panic. I saw all gay men in Manhattan as rich, and I was afraid of rich people. I remember an invitation to the home of Henry Geldzahler, a renowned museum curator and a leading proponent of Pop Art. He was openly gay, an exceptional stance at the time. Over the course of a lengthy conversation I could feel him sizing me up. Perhaps he saw a certain potential in me, or maybe he just liked my type. I couldn't tell, but it freaked me out, and I shrank from his gaze. I was sure someone like Geldzahler wanted only one thing: to be fucked dumb by me. I had the feeling that I was being slotted into the role of working-class stud, the mold I thought gay culture assigned to guys from housing projects. But that wasn't me. Nor did I fit the other gay stereotype, that of the suave sophisticate. I was neither a butch vulgarian nor a fey aesthete. I was just an uncertain commoner, and that meant there would be no future for me in gay life, even if I'd wanted to be part of it.

After this incident I confided in John. We weren't living together, but we were still close friends, and he had nearly as great a stake in my heterosexuality as I did. (He wasn't the only gay man with whom I would play the role of an accepting straight friend.) John said it was all about training. I could deal with the problem of class by mastering the codes of conduct in my new milieu—after all, he was the son of a ward heeler, and now he was messing with upscale guys. "Sure," I told him. "You're fucking them." My anxiety went much deeper than my proletarian roots, but he convinced me that all I needed was a crash course in etiquette. I would have to learn verbs like *to dine* and *to summer*—and, puh-*leaz*, he groaned, say Long Island, not Lung-island.

And so I set out to conquer my fear of the haves. My first stop was a soirée at the home of New York's senior senator, the very honorable Jacob Javits. I wasn't just there for basic training. I knew it would give my father *nachas* (earned pleasure of the sort you get from a successful child) to know that I was being invited to meet the most powerful Jew in American politics. Every year my father sent Javits a Hanukkah card, on the chance that the senator would see this greeting from a fellow Yid and intervene to wrest a promotion at the post office. Needless to say, he never got a reply. But maybe I could have a word with Javits on his behalf, he said bashfully. I promised I would, but I knew such things weren't done—my father understood even less than I did about how to behave in tony circles. I stood in the corner of the senator's elegant parlor as soigné people sauntered by. Mrs. Marion Javits, who was very much the socialite, approached me. I looked into her perfectly shaped eyes and explained in some detail who I was, thinking there must be fifty thousand Goldsteins in the New York phone book. "Oh," she said, "I *know* who you are." Then she floated off. I realized that journalists who appeared at salons were expected to be seen but not heard. I had a lot to learn.

Fortunately for me, the rules were changing fast. In a smug and stable time, there's a logic to what passes for couth, just as there is for wisdom. But in a Lewis Carroll wonderland all you can trust is your reactions, and journalism is an art of the first impression. Immediacy is its major virtue, and this authority of the quick take was a major reason why serious writers attempted reportage. Though I still felt unworthy in their midst, the way I had around Italian guys in the project, now I had a secret weapon. The cool kids of Manhattan wanted a guide to the new hip action. This was a service I could provide, and they were seeking me out. Even Susan Sontag wanted to meet me. Me, Little Richie from the projects.

Sontag was one of the few people over the age of thirty whom I trusted. She understood the power of pop culture, and she was far more knowing than other intellectuals about things like pornography and camp. Her privileging of the sensual surface over interpretation, and her occasional nods to rock, made a major impression on me. It was true, as Sontag wrote, that a song by the Supremes was as complex as a piece by Bach, at least when it came to the canon that Motown artists drew from. Just the fact that pop music *had* a canon was an idea I never thought I'd see articulated by a prestigious critic. I was more in awe of her than I'd been of even Norman Mailer. And there was no danger that she would want to box me.

Imagine how I felt when she appeared, out of the West Side ether, at a café near Lincoln Center. She flashed the wry but engagé look she showed in photos, and soon we were chatting away. I wish I could recall that conversation, but my mind draws a blank, a sign that I was very nervous. The only thing I remember—quite clearly—was what she said about my work. She told me that her young son, now the writer David Rieff, had hipped her to my column. And then she said, twinkling a bit, that I was "a teenage Marcel Proust."

I didn't know it then, but backhanded compliments were typical of Sontag's personal style. She was constantly hustled for endorsements, which she reserved for work that met her rigorous standards. European authors obscure to me—I didn't know there *were* poets in Romania— won her loyalty, but she was wary of supporting writing she didn't truly believe in, even by her friends. So she found a way to compose a blurb that was an art form in itself. I remember one such comment about a novel by a friend of mine, and hers. "A revolutionary down," Sontag wrote, "but do we deserve an up?" At the time when we met, I had no feeling for the drollery that passed for hedging your bets in Manhattan. I'd read enough Proust to know that I was no teenage version of him. All I could do was wince at that pat on the back. As a cartographer of the new culture, Sontag was supposed to know better than to call a novice a genius. Another hero had turned out to have feet of irony.

But why did she want to meet me? I think it had to do with something I didn't believe I had—a sensibility. Rock wasn't really her thing. She didn't seem desperate to unearth the mysteries of the Beatles. The word *heavy* was not in her vocabulary. But she couldn't be the premier critic of now-culture without understanding rock, and that wasn't as easy as, say, grasping the meaning of films, since there was a whole body of work about what the French had convinced us to call *cinema*. But once she confronted pop music in all its vulgar energy, she was lost in a world without her finely honed standards, and for a critic that's a pretty scary place. I was someone who lived and breathed pop. I seethed to its beat. This was probably what made me interesting to her.

Fortunately I never needed a favor from Sontag, except for the time I asked her for a letter of introduction so I could report from revolutionary Cuba. She wasn't keen on it, and the way she said so was to point out that the money the Castro government would spend on me could be better dispensed to the poor. Even I got the drift of that brush-off. But we remained in touch over the years, and I did my best to provide experiences that I sensed she needed. In 1975, on her first night out after her surgery for breast cancer, I took her to a place called the Loft, the most exciting downtown disco, the kind of utopian space where all the races and sexualities shook their booties. When things got going at the Loft, the mass swaying in half darkness felt like a subway train when the lights go out. Sontag loved it, and I loved showing her a scene she'd never encountered. I suppose we were friends, but I was always aware of the gap between us, and so was she. The last time I saw her was in the early eighties, at a luncheon held by the humanities institute at New York University. It was in financial trouble, and I'd been asked by its founder, Richard Sennett, to publicize its plight. It wouldn't be easy to turn that situation into a story, but I was willing to try. At some point Sontag rose from the table. Staring at me, she said, "To think that we need Richard Goldstein in order to raise money!" It felt like a pie in the face—proof that I was nothing more than a necessity. She may have been a champion of humanism, but she was incapable of realizing how cruel her bons mots could be.

Still, Sontag was the finest cultural interpreter of her era, and I've always been a fan. I dip into her work the way I listen to certain albums over and over. She had the courage to revise her thinking, which is a more remarkable trait than it should be in a critic. They may be momentarily correct, but they are never permanently right, certainly not in a time of rapid change; yet they are rarely willing to reexamine their most closely held opinions. Sontag was one of the few critics who didn't rest in peace. She once called America "the cancer of Western civilization," but she went on to write a brilliant critique of metaphorical thinking about illness. She made her name by privileging sensuality over morality, but in her later work she wrestled with the impact of unmooring aesthetic experience from ethical thinking. "By getting us used to what, formerly, we could not bear to see or hear, art changes morals," she wrote in her best book, *On Photography*. "In the long run it works out not as a liberation but as a subtraction from the self; a pseudo-familiarity with the horrible reinforces alienation, making one less able to react in real life." As usual her radar was acute.

Ecstasy and violence converged in pop culture during the sixties, as they would in radical politics. Art's attack on bourgeois taboos had been the model for our rebellion, but it also laid the groundwork for the blind ferocity that undermined our vision. Sontag was right to warn about this, but she didn't see the connection between x-treme culture and the economic forces that were transforming those fantasies into profit centers. Her political comments were sometimes bold, but often naïve. She was largely ignorant of left-wing theory, partly because she felt constrained by it and partly because it was regarded by the cultural elite as something even worse than reductive—*déclassé*. And Sontag was dependent on that elite. Even as she courted subversion she also craved prestige. She could never entirely break with the values of her class, and to me that was her greatest weakness as a critic.

That said, her work has aged well, unlike most of the apologetics that passed for solidarity in the sixties. I watched uneasily as intellectuals descended on radical culture and politics like tourists from the developed world. They were enchanted by what should have made them skeptical, and since they generally lived safe lives they were quite susceptible to the thrill of chaos. How else to account for the decision by the *New York Review of Books* to print a diagram of a Molotov cocktail on its front page during a riot in the Newark ghetto. The shocking thing about that cover was not that it ran, but that it felt right. Everyone who was anyone in the hip milieu, it seemed, wanted in on the incendiary action. The result was a profound retreat from the liberal tradition, and not just in the streets. Freudians unmoored from Freud saw the oceanic future, and several of them promoted what Norman O. Brown called "holy madness" as an alternative to repression. I found such work ominous. It was part of a larger rebellion against systems and standards that had spread from the arts to the academy. Anything beyond the pale of Western rationalism was worth a hearing, if not a book. On the more benign end of this spectrum were celebrations, by dazzled professors, of all things young and shaggy. This embrace of the new was necessary, of course; it broke the back of the hierarchical thinking that underlay normalcy. But it lacked precisely what was needed most: a critique of our headlong plunge into ecstasy as liberation.

The best thing about the sixties was the willingness to try nearly anything that hadn't been tried before. It was a truly stimulating strategy, because it allowed young people to imagine the future in practically limitless terms. But it placed all our impulses on an equal footing, suppressing our ability to think and behave strategically. What Gertrude Stein said of Oakland was also true of the counterculture—there was no *there* there, no will to form institutions that could transmit values, only a feeling that everything worth learning could be known in an instant. What we needed more than anything was perspective, but we isolated ourselves from anyone who could provide it. Driven by polemics—and publicity—we were rudderless in the current of our convictions.

Perhaps this is always what it's like to live in revolutionary times, the sense that everything is coursing toward a destiny that seems irrational and immanent. And certainly the r-word was sounded more and more often, in antiwar rallies as well as in commercials for refrigerators. But in 1967 this uprising seemed more like a Jim Morrison meditation on killing your father and having at your mother. One thing about Oedipal fantasies, as opposed to genuinely revolutionary ones, is that you don't really want them to succeed. You count on your parents to resist your most destructive desires. This is what I felt about America. It never occurred to me that one center of authority after another would give way, and that the nation would entangle itself in a ravel of rage and fear.

The breakdown of civil society had many causes, some more justifiable than others, but more than anything I blamed intellectuals. They were the guardian angels of my childhood, the authors of books that shielded me from the brutishness of my neighborhood. I expected them to stand against the approaching chaos. I should have realized that they were as likely as any other group to fold under the pressure of conformity. And now there was the added inducement of fame, the great intoxicant, harder than even McCarthyism to resist. But it wasn't just that intellectuals refused to occupy the pedestal I had placed them on. The pedestal itself was gone. It had been smashed, along with other signifiers of the order, and what took its place was a slope on which many people scrambled to a top that didn't exist. I was one of those climbers, as deeply invested in the futile scrum as any Sisyphus. The uncertainty I saw in my heroes was a mirror of mine. Something was coming down the pike that none of us could stop, or even understand. It frightened me. But even as I recoiled from the approaching storm I was drawn to it. There would be many good stories to report.

The Unraveling

I remember the moment when I decided that rock as a revolutionary force was dead. It happened in the spring of 1968, when I heard a seven-minute opus called "MacArthur Park." I'll mention just one of its all too many verses, something about being pressed "in love's hot, fevered iron, like a striped pair of pants." Actually the word *striped* was sung in two syllables—as in *stri*-ped—because, you know, this song was art. It had deep meanings, hidden references, and a refrain that was its own parody. A cake left out in the rain ... the icing melting ... the recipe lost forever ... There was only one permissible response to imagery like that: a heartfelt "Heavy!"

Of course, icky words are not an impediment to a great pop composition. The lyrics of my youth were often insipid, but at least they were inspired by real emotions. What passed for rock poetry in 1968 lacked any relationship to recognizable experience. It was a set of floating metaphors for a culture that was growing detached from everything but its own tropes. Dylan had withdrawn from the scene, and when he returned he was writing more traditional, less flamboyant songs. A serious motorcycle crash was the ostensible reason for his retreat, but I suspected that he'd caught a terminal case of disgust at the fake pieties that flooded rock in his wake. The synthesis of musical modes pioneered by the Beatles had become a rote exoticism with vaguely Eastern vibes. Every musician in Topanga Canyon was strumming a sitar. Meanwhile the Fab Four were heading for a breakup, and I could see the signs in their latest compositions, which were far easier to attribute to either

Lennon or McCartney than their classics had been. There was a rumor that Paul had died in a car crash, a precursor of the famous "Paul is dead" canard of 1969, which no amount of official denial could dislodge, because the truth was not the point—it was all about the feeling of doom projected onto a beloved star. These were symptoms of a deeper disintegration. I observed them, horrified but fascinated. It was like coming across a really nasty porn film from which you can't avert your gaze. This was more than just the triumph of plastic—it was a symptom of exhaustion.

The decadence that overran the counterculture had happened so quickly. I scrambled to describe it, fighting off the fear that doing so would threaten not just my commitment but my career. I'd been called a fascist by Mark Rudd, a leader of the radical students at Columbia University, because of my dismissal of *Sgt. Pepper*. I was haunted by the thought of being booed off the stage, the way I'd seen students harangue the old socialist Irving Howe, who had warned them about the consequences of doing politics by passion alone. (The election of Richard Nixon in 1968 proved him right.) But I couldn't continue to celebrate something that no longer thrilled me. On the contrary, I felt a seething contempt for hip enlightenment. All sorts of vacant slogans were in the air. The peace sign was mandatory; any criticism brought the admonition "You're bringing me down." It reminded me of Communism, with its obligatory optimism, except that in the Eastern bloc countries I had visited, nearly everyone thought the professed morality was bullshit. Here, where freedom allegedly reigned, millions of kids spouted empty platitudes. This was worse than even hype, because it was self-created.

I suppose I should have focused on the fun of it—the gushy sentiments of flower power, the sheer joy of a song like "Yummy Yummy Yummy" ("I got love in my tummy"), the outsize theatricality of concerts. But I'd seen one too many L.A. bands with fire bursting from their headdresses as they rhapsodized about love. Psychedelic music was giving way to fake opulence, and a new genre called art rock appeared. These were lushly orchestrated ballads with fabulous stereo effects. They had their own delight as kitsch, I suppose, but by then I had lost my capacity for enjoying it. Too much was at stake, given the mission I'd assigned to rock. I could only rail against the simulacra of the music I adored. I knew it would earn me the ultimate accusation—*bummer!*—but it was as close as I dared come to issuing a warning. My column was rarely a pleasure to write, and it couldn't have been fun to read, because there's nothing felicitous about doubt.

I bonded best with other skeptics, and they weren't easy to find, since most of my peers were convinced that I needed to mellow out and trip more frequently. My favorite holdout against this kind of thinking was Bill Graham, the rock impresario who managed the Fillmore Ballroom, booking the great bands I'd seen in San Francisco. I met him in 1968 as he was about to open the Fillmore East in a former Yiddish theater on Second Avenue. Graham was not a child of security like most of his customers. Born in Berlin, he'd escaped from the Nazis in a children's refugee program and grown up in the Bronx with American foster parents. The intent expression on his face, the grimness around the eyes even when he was amused, was the only way in which his past life intruded. He was one of the few people I could trust with my apprehensions about the zaniness pretending to be a higher sanity, since he shared those qualms. Pondering the latest bizarro excess of the counterculture, we would shrug to each other like old Jews expressing fatalism toward the future. I could read the meaning of this gesture because at heart all Jews of my generation are survivors. My parents never mentioned the death camps, but I was aware of them as a boy in my nightmares. Graham had been shaped by the real thing. He didn't do drugs, as far as I knew. I figured that he didn't dare.

I spent many nights at the Fillmore East in the line of duty, sitting so close to the stage that my body vibrated from the sound and the fillings in my teeth hurt. After several hours of this barrage I would fall into a daze under the influence of blobby projections on the screen. I have trouble remembering the details of those shows, since I saw so many. But I do recall the night I noticed a musician in the B-band warming up the crowd. He was a Groovy look-alike, another long-haired, lanky kid with a sinus-driven thrum in his voice. I'd thought of Groovy often since our acid trip on Lake Tahoe, and I wondered whether he'd become a drug dealer, a patient in a psych ward, or a rocker. Any of those alternatives seemed possible. By then I associated him with an experience that was both outside my life and deep within it. On LSD I'd felt as if my defenses were a celluloid scrim. He could see through it to the murky core. I didn't trust anyone with the power to do that, not in the midst of a confusion that made me feel as fragile and hollow as the Japanese paper lamp shade in my living room. I was pretty good at hiding my anguish, even from those who knew me well. Only my mustache, uneven because of the hairs I bit out of it as a nervous tic, gave me away. But I couldn't hide myself on acid.

The Groovy look-alike stepped to the mike, his face pale in the blue lights. His band was pure California mellow. The soft thump of the bass and the low patter of drums matched his supple voice. The beat was barely there, and the melodies seemed as indefinite as a breeze. But most of all I remember his wispy tenor. It blurred the lines between guy and girly. I closed my notebook and let the music take me.

I wasn't sure whether it was the singer or the association with Groovy, but I felt a vibration in my pelvic region, as if fingers were running down my spine. It wasn't a unique experience—my body was often suffused with arousal when I listened to rock. But this was so much like an overtly sexual feeling that I clenched my legs together and touched my crotch to reassure myself that I wasn't getting hard. I looked around. Everyone was sitting alert with their eyes closed, transfixed.

The set went on for maybe twenty minutes. Then it ended abruptly. There was no applause, just a kind of sigh moving through the audience. The B-band left the stage, a new set of equipment appeared, and the clang of guitars in the semidarkness reminded me of the real reason I was here tonight. It wasn't the kid from California. I had come to see some hard-driving British group, the Moody Yardbirds or whatever. I figured that they had brought this laid-back kid along, plucking him from a honeysuckle bush in L.A. as a gentle prelude to the bum's rush of their act. I settled down for what I anticipated would be a very long set, but then I heard a commotion in the aisle. It was that kid, surrounded by a knot of fans. Now I *really* wasn't sure if he was Groovy; acid had created an indefinite image in my mind, and the kid almost fit it. He smiled at me—was that a sign of recognition or a California courtesy nod? I thought of approaching him, if only to find out whether he really was my old acid buddy. But what did it matter? Seeing him had brought me back to that afternoon at Tahoe, when Groovy's long face looked like a Disney doggy and his uncombed hair bristled like a mane.

The kid called the next day. He was following up on the eye contact we'd made, and he invited me to visit him at the Albert, the hip hotel for musicians in New York. This was proof that he was just another peace-signer with a hard-on for success. I was sure that his first words when I arrived would be a West Coast version of, *Rich, baby, for you there's some hash in the butterfly.*

I realized right away that he wasn't Groovy. The thrum in his singing, which had reminded me of my friend, was missing on the phone, and so was the laid-back attitude. This kid sounded as hungry as me. But he was definitely my type: string-bean body and an edge of delicacy that he couldn't quite suppress. "Let's do a doobie," he said in an L.A. accent that spoke of surf and serenity. As we chatted I pictured myself stoned on his grass, gazing at his superstar grin while he sprawled across the bed, leaning on a skinny elbow, his wares showing through his jeans.

I'll call the kid Denny. (It seems apt to name him after a fast-food chain that probably supplied a major part of his diet.) He'd grown up in a tract-house exurb of San Francisco, amusing himself with war games in the chaparral. Then came puberty, and he met its tests in the usual budding rocker way: he withdrew to his guitar. That was when he began to create his own songs—typical shit about flowers and gentle people. His mother listened like a fan, and she told him that he had an enchanting voice. His father said nothing. He'd hoped for a son more attuned to the manly arts of football and fishing, but Denny dreaded the sight of a salmon squirming on the hook, and as for sports, when he was remanded to a neighbor's care for lessons in the pigskin arts he stood dreamily with the ball at his side, immune to all coaxing. The neighbor gave up, and his father retreated, subtly but permanently.

This is the scenario that disposes a boy to become an artist, and, listening to Denny's bio, I decided that he had the makings of the real thing. Maybe it was just the genius that I ascribed to anyone who turned me on. There was nothing terribly original about his songs—they were Beatle-bangle *chazerei* to my jaded mind—and his professional life wasn't special: migration to L.A., small gigs in smaller clubs, a nibble from an independent label with ambitions to be gobbled up by the Warner combine. I asked if he had an album in the works. "Eventually," he sighed, which I took to mean, *I need your help.*

I was sure I could wring a story out of Denny—every child of the vast basin between the Pacific and the desert had a sensitive soul to me. More to the point, I got the gist of his message: I could have him if I was willing to write about him. I felt the indisputable evidence of a stiffie, but I was sure he couldn't possibly find me attractive. It never occurred to me that we might have enough in common to inspire a buzz between us. It could only be my power to promote his career. I had been in such situations before, and I saw the exchange of sex for publicity as a kind of payola, so I always backed away. I might have made an exception for Denny—he was such a classic of the nerdy/arty type. But I could tell from the way my fingers trembled as I gripped the phone that this wouldn't be the forgettable sex I was willing to have with guys. He would ride off into the neon sunset, while I would think of him forever, just as I still think of Groovy. I couldn't afford another phantom lover; so, no, I wouldn't have a "gay-off" with this dude.

I told him that I couldn't make time for him—too many deadlines to meet. I expected him to sound disappointed and maybe a little hurt. Instead, he said something that hit me like a bullet. He said I was afraid to let myself love.

I was used to people making inappropriate remarks. The sixties were an age of faux candor, nuggets of wisdom meant to be therapeutic but actually just manipulative. And here was this kid implying that I didn't want to write about him because I dreaded the way he made me feel. Troubadours from the land of eternal sunshine weren't supposed to be wise. It pissed me off, but I was stunned by his insight.

"That's why you're such a good critic," he said. "The music is an echo."

"Of what?" I asked, trying to sound casual.

"Of what you need."

I didn't have to respond. He seemed to sense my thoughts. "Stop worrying about getting laid," he said. "Start thinking about giving love."

That was pretty much where the conversation ended. I shook it off as hippie drivel—a more genital version of the injunction to "Be here now!"—and I never wrote about Denny or saw him again. But I've thought a lot about the spell he cast. Groovy had the same ability to propel me into a state of childlike wonder. I realize now that this allure was a quality my favorite rock stars also possessed. Something about their bodies bathed in light, slamming into their axes or wrapped around the mike, captivated me. It could happen in the clamor of a hard-edged blues or the ebb and flow of a ballad. When it came from a woman, I felt a deep identification, as if I were inhabiting her. With a man, it was a different sort of intimacy—I was jamming with him, locking guitars. I didn't think of these sensations as queer. All I knew was that they were thrilling.

So the kid was right about why I was an effective critic. It wasn't just my way with words. It was my passion about the music and what it meant to me. I might pretend that virtuosity was what counted in rock— that was the manly thing to admire—but actually it was about longing and craving, the need to possess and to adore; desire in all its permutations, unbounded and uncanny. I tried to evoke that mythic dimension in my pieces. I'd described Mick Jagger as a pop incarnation of Shango, the African thunder god, and Jim Morrison as the Lizard King. But I never really captured the emotions that rock conjured up in me. The terror of knowing myself stopped me from writing about, or even perceiving, what I really felt. It was accessible only with my eyes closed or in the darkness of an arena, when everything repugnant about me vanished in the sound, and I was lost in ecstasy. Music was the only way I could connect with my latent feelings, the only time I felt whole, and this had been true ever since I was a teenager, locked in loneliness. Like Jenny, the sad girl Lou Reed sings about, I was saved by rock 'n' roll.

> *Despite all the amputation*
> *You could dance to the rock 'n' roll station . . .*
> *Baby, baby, ooohhh.*

The encounter with Denny made sex with my wife even more intense. The feelings I had for her were genuine, but they also affirmed my membership in the holy order of heterosexuality. I still had doubts, and I eased them with the occasional chick. (I actually had a wrestling match with another rock critic over a woman—he got me in an illegal hold, and I was on crutches for several weeks.) But my greatest escape from myself was what it always had been: writing. Ironically, the best way to flee into reality was to cover the new unreality, and it wasn't hard to find. As the order lost credibility, so did its spiritual consistency. A Mexican peyote shaman seemed far wiser than the Cardinal blessing the troops in Vietnam. Krishna Consciousness was a lot more devout than a catered bar mitzvah. The problem was that anything could be a mantra, just as anything could be a jingle. How to tell the polyester from the polytheism?

I saw a role for the critic in me. But despite my best efforts, I couldn't dislodge the slogan of the moment: "Be here now!" Its inventor, Richard Alpert, had morphed psychedelically into Baba Ram Das. I couldn't resist referring to him as "baba au rhum." Still, I had my moments of weakness when it came to free-floating religiosity. I remember remarking to Judith, in an intoxicated state, that Jesus was in all of us. (She kicked me.) Before my military physical I consulted an ancient and very trendy Chinese work of prophecy called the *I-Ching*. There were hundreds of passages in the text, and throwing coins would lead to one of them. By pure chance, I got a passage called "The Army." It was a *Far-out!* moment, tantamount to realizing that, though I didn't believe in astrology, I was a classic Gemini. I never lost myself in the cosmic vibes, but I could understand why people with mystical leanings were drawn to Alpert's partner in revelation, Timothy Leary. In certain enlightened circles, he was referred to as an incarnation of the divine. To me, he was all too human—and that's the kindest thing I can say about him.

No one knows how many young people took LSD in the sixties. Several million is my best guess (and what's a memoir if not a guess?). I suspect that most of them look back on tripping as an adventure they don't regret, though they wouldn't recommend it to their grandkids. For some, it was a very important experience; I have a friend who was inspired to become an artist while tripping. The comix, the posters, the curvaceous mode of music and decor, all attest to the profound influence of acid on the counterculture. But the drug was a crapshoot. It could access parts of the brain where inspirations reside, or it could induce a harrowing panic attack—the infamous "bummer." You might be a very fucked-up person and have a wonderful time, or be very together and end up in a state of dread. Most people came to their senses after the drug wore off, give or take a few recurring "flashes," but some acid-heads never came down. Others believed they were endowed with the power to control others, and still others decided to follow them. Cults arose around this mutual illusion—can you say Manson? On LSD, it is easy to see God or be God.

The most dangerous trips involved a lasting confusion of fantasy and reality. I never had that problem, perhaps because my suspicions cut so deep that I always knew when I was having a hallucination. I wasn't tempted to leap from a ten-story building, convinced I could fly, and I never became psychotic, though I knew people who did. I had friends who struggled for years to climb out of the rabbit hole they'd fallen into. One of them joined a rehab program that required him to perform elaborate rituals of neatness. He had to iron his socks and hankies every day. To me, that was worse than ego death.

The casualties of acid were easy to spot. They had a floating look, and if you let them they would share all sorts of exotic beliefs. Pharaonic spirits were inhabiting the body of my buddy Joel, who, by 1968, had left his communal farm in the Catskills and renamed himself Mithra (though he preferred the more casual Ra). Planets were converging in apocalyptic signs for him, amid astrological calculations that went beyond any Zoroastrian scheme. And Joel was far from unique. Even freaks who functioned well might harbor ideas that failed the test of reason. The truth was in the vibe, the higher reality made sensate. LSD was an agent of this thinking, but not the cause. The psychic chaos that the drug sometimes produced was consistent with the climate of the time. Acid is a template on which many things can be inscribed. For all that it might put you in touch with your inner drives or enable you to access the oversoul, it could also inspire an undue confidence in your feelings. LSD rarely fostered doubt, but, then, very little in the sixties did. It's often said that the boomer generation was narcissistic, but the real problem was negligence—of one another and finally of reality. That was the decade's greatest contradiction: its capacity for radical change was also a tendency toward madness. Acid fostered both.

The original advocates of LSD understood its power, and they urged careful attention to what was called "set and setting." I heeded their advice to trip in parks or forests, and always with a "guide," a kind of designated driver who could talk me down from a panic attack or give me Valium if all else failed. I was much too self-conscious to drop acid at a concert or a tribal gathering; the prospect of blowing my mind among thousands of similarly disoriented kids didn't appeal to me. And as for psychedelic sex, I can only say that orgasm is not the point. I would get lost in the fleshiness and forget the need to come.

I was reckless about all sorts of things in the sixties, but not LSD. The same cannot be said for Leary. To him, acid was an elixir that should be widely and casually dispensed. Dosage was whatever it took; undesirable effects were the remnant of ego games that could best be dealt with by taking more acid. Working to better the here and now through politics was futile. It would merely lead to more of the same.

The only activism worth embracing was to change the world by altering consciousness. This was a just-add-water cake-mix vision of America, where the spirit would triumph over Moloch, courtesy of chemicals. The counterculture had its own version of the Rapture; John Lennon would call it "instant karma," a flash of revelation that could happen through either meditation or the shortcut of a drug. Though the mystique of acid has long since faded, something like that concept has survived, thanks to the rise of an industrialized pharma culture with labs churning out mood-altering meds for an ever more diagnosed nation. This is Leary's real legacy.

Class consciousness was not his strong suit. He was ignorant (willfully, I thought) of the impact that racism and poverty might have on someone's drug experience. The distance between Leary and Martin Luther King was unbridgeable, and since I was closer to the idea of passive *resistance* than I was to pacifism, I approached his psychedelic revolution with my antennae of doubt bristling. At least the Beats had embraced the idea of voluntary poverty; Leary preferred pleasure to self-denial. He was quite willing to hole up in an estate about an hour north of New York City, in a part of Dutchess County where the horses were better fed than the help. There, under the auspices of a nonprofit called the League for Spiritual Discovery—LSD, get it?—he hosted various illuminati (Allen Ginsberg hung out there) along with renegade academics and any guru who could shake his ashram. I didn't merit an invitation to Leary's lair, but I was useful enough for him to grant me an interview in town. Like many of my subjects, he couldn't resist publicity.

I met him in the East Village, outside the theater where he was holding forth weekly at a "psychedelic celebration" called *The Death of the Mind*. It had something to do with everyone's favorite incarnation of the Buddha, the young seeker Steppenwolf. It featured a light show by Leary's associates, the same pair who had advertised themselves in the *Voice* as being available for psychedelic fashion shows, industrial shows, and bar mitzvahs. Everything fit together: enlightenment, entertainment, subsidiary rights.

As we walked up the street Leary greeted admirers among the passersby, his hands folded together, guru style. We popped into the Second Avenue Deli. It struck me an odd haunt for a man whose followers would probably regard everything on the menu as the product of a savage slaughter. But I could tell from his expertise in ordering pastrami that he knew his way around a mile-high sandwich dripping grease. This was another earthly delight for a man of big appetites, as was sex. From the way he cased out the room, I had the feeling that he would just as soon fuck a woman with one of the pickles in the briny bowl on the table as eat it. Lust was an acceptable lifestyle in the sixties, but the idea was to be casual about it. Leary had the lubricious air of a man who had come only lately to the sexual feast. He'd arrived at every pop spiritualist's dream, a milieu where prophecy is a greater aphrodisiac than even power.

He had that floaty look. There was dried pigeon shit on his sweater. But he also radiated the sleek serenity of a yogi and the well-tanned face of a movie star. He'd come a long way since his days as a professor at Harvard, which had severed its connection with him, ostensibly because of his very public experiments with LSD. Listening to his rap, I concluded that the real reason was intellectual mediocrity. His spiel was a blend of ideas bobbing around in the cultural soup. I could hear chunks of Jim Morrison and Susan Sontag, along with New Age rhetoric via the New Left, in the quotable lines he flung at me. As in: "The police-state mentality always tries to repress sensual experience; it never works." Or: "The average man has got to come to his senses." There was no personal dimension to our conversation; he was as slick and mediagenic as any celebrity intellectual. Indeed, he was following the trail blazed by Marshall McLuhan, whom he admired, up to a point. "He knows about psychedelic art," Leary said, "but he's all external; he hasn't seen the inside yet. It'll be fascinating to see what happens when he finally takes LSD." This was the way he divided up the world. There were those who sensed the truth and those who truly grasped it on acid. He might as well have been a Christian missionary bringing the light to pagans.

As for the media's response to his preaching—the usual combo of fascination and feigned horror—he seemed to regard it as something of a miracle. "When you think of the history of new movements," he said, "no country has ever been as tolerant as America of a force that's going to wipe it out. In any other time or place we'd be in danger of our lives." He'd already done a stint in jail as a "narcotics offender," but prison was something many activists endured with far less attention than he got. He wasn't political—or black—enough to be in mortal danger. I wanted to hurl that accusation at him, but I saved my wrath for the article.

I think I reacted the way I did to Leary because his narcissism corresponded to a part of me that I despised. But unlike me, he had no capacity for self-doubt, and without that it's possible to believe in anything. There was a sweeping certitude to his ideas, and beneath it an even more offensive philistinism. He blithely explained that the theater had been taken over by careerist intellectuals. "Plays by Tennessee Williams, for instance, are the memoirs of a neurotic, not art. Art must involve the senses. All original drama is psychedelic. The theater, remember, was originally a religious experience. It all stems back to religious motives— someone with a vision turns other people on." This was the same old shaman routine, much less attractively packaged than Morrison's, but, then, Leary didn't have an original thought in his head. His ability to think systematically had been undermined, not by drugs (there were plenty of smart acid-heads), but by fame. He was caught up in the vortex of the time, the conviction that his own impulses were more important than reasoning. I was quite familiar with these illusions, but I was only an expert on pop culture. He was an expert on the death of the mind.

Freed from the standards of scholarship, he dispensed pronouncements with no attempt to prove them. For example, he proffered LSD as a cure for homosexuality. I tried to imagine Allen Ginsberg dosed straight, or Tennessee Williams newly enlightened and rewriting Stanley Kowalski as a rock star with fire spurting from his headdress. I'm going on about this because it was so emblematic of the unraveling, the dance of expectation and ecstasy, the indifference to the consequences of our schemes. And there were consequences, believe me.

On acid the magic of infancy returns in HD. Colors prismatize, sounds resonate with overtones, the shapes and patterns that allow us to function become suggestive. Something like driving is impossible, at least on planet Earth. (I understood that very well, having survived a road trip with Dennis Wilson tripping at the wheel.) Having children, however, is something LSD does not impede, and lots of stoners did. Childhood had a special status in hippie culture. It was the state of innocent wonder to which everyone longed to return. I never knew anyone who fed their babies LSD, despite many rumors to that effect. It was commonly believed that the benefits of the drug came naturally to kids. They were vectors of love, and a great deal of affection was showered on them. These were not the cleanest girls and boys, but they were less unruly than you might think, considering that they ran around freely and were clearly the center of attention. I know a number of people— some quite famous now—who grew up in such households. They've got their resentments (what kid doesn't), but they're very close to their parents.

However, raising children requires skills that tripping is likely to suspend, such as keeping an eye on the little ones. That was a lesson Leary and his largely childless cohort didn't think to teach, and this lapse led to some devastating incidents. One of them involved a three-year-old boy named Godo. He'd been described in *Life* magazine as "the most beautiful child in creation, with pure blond hair to his shoulders, pudgy little cheeks and blue eyes that are steady and make you want to weep." In the photo that ran with this piece, Godo is posing with his father, Vito, an artist and dancer who was a star of the L.A. freak scene. Bohemians there have always attracted the wrong kind of attention—think beatnik movies set in Venice—and in 1966, Vito was a regular on the kind of TV show where the host berates his dissident guests. He was also a darling of skin mags with pretensions to interests higher than flesh. "A name that represents nonconformity, artistic freedom, originality," one journal of ass and the arts gushed about him. "One of the most diversified sculptors the world has ever known." (I don't think any museum agreed.)

Godo was raised to expect the spotlight, and his exploits only added to his legend. It was said that if the police showed up at his parents' place, a bead-curtained loft that looked a lot like the set of a beatnik movie, this magic child would answer the door. "Fuck off, cop," he'd snarl, and the officers would leave. I believed those stories because I knew how indifferent most cops and city bureaucrats were to the lives of hippies. As a result, no one inspected Vito's loft for safety hazards. At some point a trap door on the roof gave way, and Godo fell through.

A few months afterward, I was in L.A. to cover a hippie riot, something I regarded as inevitable, though I didn't think it would happen on the Sunset Strip. I associated that boulevard with delta-wing diners and relentless glare. But its disposable identity made the Strip a perfect gathering place for kids—not the Laurel Canyon crowd, but flotsam from the endless suburbs, who looked like neon butterflies. They staked their claim to turf around a club called Pandora's Box. By the time the police moved in to clear them, there were maybe a thousand longhairs hanging out on the pavement. The confrontation that followed wasn't violent by the standards of, say, the Watts riot, but it was bloodier than anything these strays had seen. Night after night of protest followed. A song by Buffalo Springfield summed up the mood of darkening paranoia.

> *It starts when you're always afraid*
> *Step out of line, the man come and take you away.*

Suddenly, the hippies were being lumped together with rampaging blacks in a city gripped by anxiety. It wasn't just the fear that another race riot was imminent and that this time a dusky mob would surge out of the ghettos and torch West Hollywood. There were huge antiwar demos, one of which, along the Avenue of the Stars, had been broken up by club-swinging police, leaving hundreds injured. Maintaining order on the streets was an obsession. Long-haired loiterers were busted on a charge that had been used for vagrants strolling in pricey districts. It was called "suspicion." (The courts would later deem it unconstitutional.) L.A. cops, in those days, were the closest America got to the spirit of a Leni Riefenstahl movie: leather-clad storm troopers on motorcycles, impassive behind wraparound shades. "Whip-dick" was their favorite word for hippies, and bashing these kids was a sport for them. No one in charge intervened.

During a lull in the protests I contacted Vito. He was eager to be interviewed, which struck me as odd, since I thought he'd want to be left alone with his grief. I showed up at his loft feeling like an intruder, but he didn't look like he was in mourning. We Jews sit on crates for seven days after someone in the family dies, and we say the kaddish for eleven months. Vito was ebullient. He seemed more like a press agent than a bereaved parent, and he had a lot of Godo memorabilia to show me. Nothing was off-limits, not even his most painful recollection of the child. He told me about the last time he'd seen Godo, lying on a metal hospital table, strapped down and spread-eagled, a towel covering the hole in his head, his fists clenched. "Help me!" Godo cried. An hour later, he was dead.

Why was the child strapped down to a table; why wasn't a tracheotomy performed; why was the trap door on the roof left to rust? These were plausible questions, but they came with delusions of persecution, as if some diabolic force had failed to treat Godo or fix the door. Vito saw himself as the victim of a fascist conspiracy to demonize the freaks by framing him. This rap went beyond the anguish of a parent dealing with guilt. I decided that he was one of those people—I'd run into many—whose identity hinges on playing to the media. He was already producing the next sensation, another magic child. That's why he was so glad to see me; he wanted the world to know the auspicious news. His eyes shining, he pointed to his wife's belly. "My baby is already dancing in her stomach," he said with a delight that spoke of radical detachment from the tragedy in his midst. I was used to the rote optimism that passed for hippie style, but this went far beyond the usual buoyancy. It struck me as a perfect example of the attitude I saw all around me, a desperate clinging to joy in the face of looming chaos.

I worried about turning into Joan Didion, whose literary career consisted of compiling grotesque examples of the unraveling of reason, so that sensible readers could be horrified and amused by it all. I hated her perspective because it came from far above and outside the counterculture. She had the symptoms right, but not the causes. She saw the widening gyre, but not its axis. In order to understand why people behaved as they did you had to experience it on the ground, and that was where I drew my conclusions from.

Many kids around me thought we were entering a revolutionary situation. I agreed, up to a point. But it seemed to me that this was different from the insurrections of the past and the uprisings in what was then called the Third World. Our revolution was sparked by promo and hype as much as ideology. This combination had a huge influence on how people processed the circumstances around them. It heightened feelings of personal power and diminished the ability to make judgments that were urgent and necessary. It occurred to me that advertising had something in common with acid: they both distorted the relationship between impulse and reality, novelty and change. For hippies whose rebellion wasn't grounded in concrete politics, this confusion was profound. Moving among them felt like being in the middle of a commercial for a future that would never exist outside of merchandising. Everything is beautiful in its own way. Banal ballads are actually wise. Life is transient and transferable. Of all the gauzy rock songs that were called progressive, the one that best captured the tenor of the late sixties didn't appear until 1977. I can still recall its melancholy refrain: "All we are is dust in the wind."

I didn't believe that. We weren't dust in the wind; we only had dust in our eyes. And yet . . . and yet. I couldn't forget the kids I'd met in the Haight, the softness in their faces, unencumbered by the ambition that seethed within me; how deeply they moved me and how much I wanted to protect them. What would happen to these kids once the dust hit the fan?

Groucho Marxism

I'm not saying there was no great music after the Summer of Love. The encroaching sense of danger was a perfect setting for rock, and I found a lot to get excited about: John Lennon's wicked ruminations, the wry romanticism of Joni Mitchell (at her best when she wasn't trying to be anthemic), John Fogerty's neo-Americana. His song "Bad Moon Rising," with its nod to horror films, vividly depicts the ominous mood of 1968:

> *Don't go 'round tonight*
> *It's bound to take your life*

I still wrote about music, but now it was only part of my beat. The real action in youth culture was in the streets. The hippie riots on Sunset Strip were soon replicated in other cities as nomadic tribes of freaks met the forces of law, order, and real estate development. Even Toronto, that bastion of Canadian sanity, experienced a nasty crackdown. Only the quiet contempt that passes for tolerance in New York kept the local hippies from receiving the same treatment (for the moment). But the greatest threat to their safety came from civilians who were out for pussy or prey. Hippie chicks, as they were already called, became easy pickings, and rape was a major problem for kids living on the street. So were hard drugs like speed and heroin, as well as the sinister presence of the Hell's Angels. In those days, their lifestyle was less about freedom than authority. For me, biker brutality would be embodied by the infamous Altamont concert of 1969, when the Angels who had been hired to provide security stabbed an acid-addled fan to death. The incident occurred just below the stage as the Rolling Stones performed, and it was captured on film. You can see the look on Mick Jagger's face as he watches the murder after the fact, on an editing console. There's a shock of . . . is that recognition? For a moment he looks like he's pondering his role in the enveloping madness. Then he recovers his composure—ever the pro.

I wasn't surprised by this turn of events. The insulation of urban hippies prevented them from seeing their privileged position in neighborhoods where poverty was endemic. Spiritual or not, these kids were targets for the anger that welled up in residents who had no choice about where they lived. The police had a similar attitude, and all that was necessary for them to exercise it was tacit permission from their commanders. Soon everyone I knew had a friend who'd been roughed up by cops or ripped off by thugs. It was as if the blood of hippies was being offered to the entire society as an outlet for its anxieties. The hippies reacted to their new role by refusing to be sacrificed. Though passive resistance was the strategy of choice, it became hard to maintain once the brutality landed on them from all sides. Enlightenment was proving insufficient to resolve the conflict between the hip and straight worlds. Now it was time to put up a fight.

A similar shift went on in the black community, where the pacifist teachings of Martin Luther King had been supplanted by the bark of Black Power. The ideological rift between the old militance and the new was clear, but the difference in sensibility seemed just as interesting to me. This wasn't only a new attitude toward violence; it was a new style that owed as much to the counterculture as it did to Malcolm X. Afros and dashikis were a corollary to long hair and tie-dyes, with a different meaning, certainly, but serving the same purpose of creating a group identity. Meanwhile, the counterculture borrowed many of its slogans and much of its slang from blacks. These two groups moved in separate spaces, but their consciousness crossed over. As a result, the Aquarian Age, if it ever existed apart from the musical *Hair*, gave way to a white version of Black Power—the image of a hippie with a Molotov cocktail.

A year earlier, the kids I wrote about were "too busy grooving to put anybody down," as the Monkees warbled. Now they saw themselves as part of a global struggle. Someone borrowed a page from the Vietcong playbook and called 1968 "the year of the heroic guerrilla." The term applied not just to Third-World revolutionaries and insurrectionary blacks but also to students resisting the war, and even to hippies. It wasn't a vanity. People who are subject to the same treatment soon conceive of themselves as a class, and the perception widely held was that everyone who wasn't white and straight (i.e., normal) faced the same enemy, embodied in the cop with a club. The ability to identify one's oppression with a much larger situation was as pretentious as anything else in youth culture, but it was also a real expression of the empathy with the underdog that many young people felt. The result was a new political formation that went by an amorphous but inclusive name: the Movement. I was glad to see this fusion take shape, and I wondered what role rock would play in it. The answer was blowing in the tear gas.

I don't want to give the impression that no one believed in the pacifist hippie vision. One of them was Don McNeill, my best friend at the *Voice*. We were pretty much the same age, and we formed a kind of triumvirate with another young writer, a disillusioned West Point cadet named Lucian Truscott IV. He'd come to the *Voice* after writing a series of letters with a distinctly conservative slant. Naturally he was invited to the paper's Christmas party, and he showed up in a full-dress uniform and sandals. Lucian was the scion of an illustrious military family—the only person I'd ever met with a number in his name—but he soon broke with his legacy (you can find the details online; they're worth checking out), and he fit right in at the *Voice*. He was hard-drinking but deeply caring, the perfect foil for Don, with whom he immediately bonded. Both of us saw Don as a model of the alternative-press ideal: he lived what he wrote about.

The hustle didn't exist for Don, which made him an unlikely New Yorker. In fact, he'd been raised in Alaska, the son of a journalist, and he inherited the itch to report, along with a set of values that drew him to the counterculture. Why he came to the hardest place for such a project to succeed, instead of joining the trek to San Francisco, I'll never understand. But he was the *Voice*'s correspondent in the hippie trenches—literally, since he was homeless. Once in a while he took a room at a midtown hotel, but many nights he relied on a bed in an unused upper floor of the office, or he moved among the crash pads of the East Village. One of the most distinctive things about the *Voice* was its willingness to hire people who were partisans of the subjects they wrote about. I felt that way about rock, at least at the start, and Don was just as dedicated to the hippie scene. Nearly every week he filed a piece about something I hadn't noticed, radical experiments in communal living and the kind of activism that would never reach the desks of journalists busy covering the more colorful manifestations of the mess.

Don managed to be both accurate and sympathetic to the people he wrote about. His attitude was a striking contrast to my fretful ambivalence. It rekindled the sentiments I'd felt in the Haight and repressed on the pavement of Manhattan. I suppose he signified upward mobility to me—he was so securely middle-class that he could afford to be indigent. In any case, we saw the struggle very differently. He believed in consciousness; I believed in fighting back.

The detachment I was so proud of, the mark of my rationality in the face of mental goo, was beginning to seem like the greatest of all illusions. There was no way to justify remaining outside the battle. The draft was an omnipresent threat, the war a patent danger to everything I stood for. I hated the lies that rationalized it, and the pretense of reason that masked a blind madness. Like millions of people, I was appalled by the photos of naked children fleeing from a wall of burning napalm; the Zippo lighters setting fire to peasant huts; the bodies coming home, which the military hadn't yet learned to hide. It was enraging and frightening to behold. Worse still for someone with my politics, the war was being prosecuted by the most progressive president since FDR, the man who'd led the drive to pass the Civil Rights Act of 1964 despite his prediction that the Democrats would lose the South as a result. (They eventually did.) That contradiction stoked my fury. Liberalism, the religion of my youth, was now a nice word for hypocrisy. The president had a crack in his moral center, and we, the young, had a duty—to each other, if not history—to drive a sword through it.

My shift from observer to participant in the uprising that came to be called the Revolution was a long and perilous process. Don McNeill played an important part in it. He was the reporter I most wanted to be. Craft and empathy were conjoined in his work; he witnessed and he empathized. His politics were in his limpid eyes. Though he never sported bell-bottoms and beads, he had a certain style in the only clothing he wore, a leather jacket, dark pullover, and jeans. His long hair brushed against the press card dangling around his neck, and he was skinny the way people who don't think much about eating are. I didn't think of him as a sex object. Though he was certainly my type, he didn't project an erotic aura. But I often found myself offering him a sandwich or a donut. I think it was my way of hovering over him.

Nothing in my experience had dislodged the feeling that it was risky to cherish people. The only way I could handle it was to argue with those I cared for, as I did with Don, incessantly. We had running debates about the fate of hippie culture and the proper strategy of resistance to fascism—that word was on everyone's lips. He seemed so out of touch with what was really "going down," yet I longed to believe that he was right. After all, I'd come of age in the civil rights movement. I wanted us to overcome. But the unrest fostered rage where hope should have been— and I was bursting with it.

Some of the fury was righteous, some compensatory. I was pissed at the government for saddling my generation with a wicked war. But I was also angry about being forced to reveal my homosexual feelings in order to avoid the draft, thereby acknowledging, if only to the army doctors, something that still shamed me. One of my greatest satisfactions is that no young person today will experience the ordeal of "queering out" of the military. Though I didn't realize it at the time, this act of desperation seared itself into my personality. In the project where I grew up, the word *faggot* had a double meaning, as it does in many working-class communities; it was what you called a queer, but also a weakling—and that's what I was in the eyes of the army. I wasn't good enough to be a soldier. At first I felt immense relief. I came home after my draft-board physical and fell into an exhausted sleep. But I had the most unlikely dream. I was in Vietnam, fighting alongside the other guys, dodging bullets and scurrying under barbed wire, having a hell of a time. This was a dream of belonging, not combat, but I woke up horrified.

The dream revealed that I was psyched for warfare. The only problem was finding the right enemy. Like most of my friends I thought Ho Chi Minh was cool, a poet who had once lived in Harlem and worked in a Chinese restaurant. How could I hate someone who looked like my image of an Asian sage? Better to strike out against the system whose might was at the core of this unjust war, of poisonous coups by the CIA, of FBI provocateurs planted in groups that were dedicated to change. This was the nation we had come to call AmeriKKKa.

The same passions that once drew me to rock, the lust for ecstasy and the need to escape from myself, now fed a fascination with the Revolution. I was on my way to becoming what the Rolling Stones called, somewhat derisively, a "street fighting man." (I didn't appreciate Mick Jagger's irony—after all, *he* wasn't being drafted.) The new counter-culture of resistance was immensely attractive. It summoned me. And what it said was: Don't hustle, don't seethe, don't be-here-now. Act.

By the end of the decade I would be faced with situations that required me to make a choice between reporting what I knew and hiding salient facts. Sometimes I chose to do the latter because telling the truth would have blown the cover of activists accused of crimes, people whose safety I valued more than the rules I'd learned in j-school. It wasn't an easy decision—I took the ethics of reporting very seriously—but hope-fully this chapter will explain why I acted as I did. I witnessed the violent reaction of the authorities firsthand, and it destroyed my confidence in American justice. I saw black defendants mistreated in courtrooms, and it made racism feel concrete and systematic. I watched young people who were in every sense like me—my long-haired peers—clubbed before my eyes, and it made the police seem as irrational as the men conducting the war in Vietnam; in fact, their brutality felt like part of the war, and it unleashed the solider within me.

Still, I carried a press card, and that gave me immunity. All I had to do was show my credentials and the cops would let me pass or swing their clubs at someone else. This was a profoundly guilt-inducing priv-ilege, but it also allowed me to observe the mayhem without feeling personally at risk. I could vent my emotions safely, unlike the protesters, and I loved running alongside them as they went wild in the streets. My political commitment was real, but so was the rush I experienced, a surge of adrenaline and a sense of transcendence that I'd only felt from music. I began to transfer my awe from rock stars to radicals.

I admired their stringent thinking, especially after the mushy logic of the hippies. I saw their certainty as sexy in a completely different way. The Movement's leadership was pretty much a fellowship, and, whatever the limitations of such an arrangement, hanging out with these guys felt like I was finally part of the combat unit that the army had declared me unfit to join. Of course, we warriors were committed to nonviolence—at least at first—but our idea of passive resistance didn't involve joining hands and singing hymns. Peacefulness was a tactic, not an inviolate principle. We were prepared to be as violent as we had to be, no more, but no less. Our major inspiration was Malcolm X's admonition "By any means necessary." I never thought that, when he excoriated white people, he meant me. I saw him as a big brother, and I think that's how many white activists felt about the black militants who maintained a distant but potent alliance with the antiwar movement. They were a manly example to nerds like us. The counterculture had transformed dorkiness into freakiness, which was a good thing, but adapting the Black Power attitude meant we could also do battle, and that felt very good indeed.

I stopped thinking about hippies and their plan to save the world by expanding consciousness. Only action in the streets could accomplish that. I decided that pacifism was the essence of bourgeois spirituality in soft times. But the times weren't soft for millions of people in the Third World; nor for U.S. soldiers in peril and the people they killed by the thousands, the ten thousands, the hundred thousands. Not for the wretched of the earth, including Newark and Watts. Yet even as I felt drawn to the earthly delights of insurrection, one thing about the hippie spiel stuck with me. It had to do with giving myself in sex.

That was difficult for a twenty-four-year-old with a narcissistic personality. At first I had to force myself to concentrate on pleasuring women. The need to come pounded within me like Keith Moon's drums, and it was hard to hold back. But the real difficulty was focusing emotionally on the person beside me. It felt perilous in a way that the particulars of sex didn't. It wasn't just a matter of muff diving. I liked the smell and feeling of a clitoris on my tongue, but to really consider a woman's gratification meant daring to experience the undertones I wanted to deny. Was there a relationship between these feelings and the mild buzz I had when holding my mother's hand to help her across the street? (She was on the way to becoming lame and blind.) Had she experienced waves of ecstasy while holding me as a baby? I was only wading in the shallows of these emotions, but once I allowed them to register they flowed through me, heightening my pleasure. The bliss of connection rivaled the joy of rock. As a result I had a lot more sex, and not just with my wife. (What else can you do on a waterbed at midnight?). But with Judith it was special. When my delayed climax finally erupted, I would shake wildly in a head-to-toe spasm. I began to think of this as the mother load.

Then I would leap out of bed and race to the fridge, because suddenly I was hungry. I would sit at the table, spooning something sweet and creamy into my mouth, letting it lull me into forgetting the intensity. Something always stopped me from keeping that feeling in mind, which was probably why it was easy to transfer my sexual affections. There was a barrier to intimacy that I couldn't surmount or even detect. In other words, I had room in my life for the Revolution. And by now it merited a capital R.

Don McNeill was changing, at least in his affect. He often looked grim, and his responses to my arguments seemed less confident. He fretted over the people he wrote about, how easy it was for them to shift from pacifism to respect for righteous violence. His uneasiness deepened my melancholy. It was a poignant reminder of the unraveling I'd observed for the better part of a year, which had swept up even die-hard hippies. Every incident of police brutality, every kid in a tie-dye with a bloody head, was a shot to the heart of love. The communes were ripe for organizing, and a new group arose within the Movement to accommodate that possibility, a cadre of media-savvy freaks who called themselves the Youth International Party, aka the Yippies.

From the start, the New Left distinguished itself from the old one by incorporating rituals of theatrical disruption. We didn't just march with banners and raised fists; we wiggled and whooped, shouted nonsense slogans, and pulled pranks that revealed the contradictions of power. Play was the key—it was part of the ideology of childishness that had been so important to the hippies and still was to us. But it also reflected the surrealist tradition, which I was familiar with from my time in the cultural underground. I watched the Yippie leader Jerry Rubin create a Dada event by showing up at a congressional hearing in a Revolutionary War uniform. A prior generation of radicals had been hounded by this same committee, and many of them showed great dignity under immense pressure. But Rubin's antics—at the witness table, he blew bubbles with his gum—completely degraded the proceedings. I have a vivid memory of him running giddily through the corridors outside the hearing room as stunned office workers peered.

The media lapped up these antics, especially when other Yippie leaders wore shirts made from American flags. Today flag neckties are the height of patriotic fashion for right-wing pols, but in those days such displays were considered defacement, and they were a crime. This created a perfect opening for the most creative radical activist of the sixties. He often appeared in a flag shirt; in fact, he was arrested for wearing one.

"I only regret," he said after his trial, "that I have but one shirt to give to my country." His name was Abbie Hoffman.

With his mane of curly hair (sometimes called a Jewfro), his thick and crooked nose, which had been broken a number of times by the police, and his streetwise Boston accent, he was the face of revolutionary action for my kind. It was Abbie who thought of sneaking onto the balcony of the New York Stock Exchange and tossing a barrage of dollar bills onto the floor. He hadn't devised such strategies from the Dada playbook, but from a close reading of McLuhan—the old pundit was good for something after all. Abbie was blunt about his intention to use television as a tool of subversion. Though he lacked the cool demeanor that McLuhan regarded as optimal for the new medium, he had a quicksilver tongue and a folksy persona that played great on camera. Watching him on a chat show was like seeing a political version of that Jewish funny-man type known as the tummler. But Abbie had honed his skills as a civil rights activist in the South. He'd been arrested dozens of times and menaced by police dogs. There's a Richard Avedon photo of him that shows the full impact of these experiences on his face. He was wizened, intrepid, and feisty, even in his writing. Few characters in literature are as true to their author's lifestyle as the one he created in his memoir *Revolution For the Hell of It* and its brazenly titled sequel, *Steal This Book*. The other leaders of the youth movement were either serious militants or jesters like Rubin. Abbie was a guerrilla clown, and he presented a new model for the revolutionary.

I met him on Fire Island, my favorite retreat from the streets. There, I swam nude, ate fish fresh from the sea, and hung out with people who were mellow in a way they couldn't be in the city. Cars weren't allowed on Fire Island, so it was easy to forget the tumult. My adrenal glands were on holiday—until I met a firebrand black feminist named Flo Kennedy. I remember her best for introducing me to the phrase "lateral oppression," which described the practice of minorities attacking each other. She also introduced me to her weekend guest, whom I recognized from the pictures I'd seen of him in action. At the moment I badly needed Abbie's help.

I had left my dog in the small cabin where I was staying. The dog was large and easily agitated; I'd bought him from a prior owner who had abused him. The vet called him a "fear biter." (I would often apply this term to cops.) When I returned to the cabin after an afternoon at the beach I realized that I'd forgotten to take my keys. The dog was locked inside. Since I was afraid of heights—a lifelong phobia—I wasn't about to climb up to the window and lower myself inside. I mentioned this to Abbie, who agreed to do the job. I told him he was crazy, but the look on face said, *Don't tell me about vicious dogs; I've seen 'em, smelled 'em, wiped their drool off my pants.* He hoisted himself to the window and disappeared. I expected to hear screaming, but instead the door opened and he stood there, holding the docile doggie by the collar. It was a fear biter, but Abbie was unafraid.

The Yippies—not to be confused with yuppies or any cohort of new money that calls itself hip and vibrant—the Yippies were, well, I never really knew what they were, except that they smoked dope, watched a lot of TV, and plotted the overthrow of the government. Over the next year, I got to know Abbie and his wife, Anita, quite well. I would stop by their apartment on St. Mark's Place from time to time, and through them I got to meet other radical leaders including Jerry Rubin (who later became a stockbroker and marketeer) and Tom Hayden (sexy despite his terminal earnestness; I saw what Jane Fonda would see in him). These activists were among the defendants who came to be known as the Chicago Seven. They were tried on charges of conspiring to start the riot that sullied the Democratic Party convention in 1968. Because I had witnessed several meetings of these alleged plotters—I'd earned their trust as a journalist—I was summoned to testify at their trial. That subpoena is one of the few artifacts from my youth that I held on to, and I still regard it as a mark of pride. To my regret I never got called to the witness stand, but even without my help all the defendants were acquitted of the conspiracy charges. Only Abbie spent time in jail. He'd taunted the bemused judge, a hack named Julius Hoffman, even scolding him for having the same last name. (He called it a *shonder fur de goyim,* a shame in front of Gentiles.) Finally the judge had enough. As Abbie was carted off for contempt of court, I heard him shout to his wife, "Water the plants!"

One member of the Chicago Seven suffered a special fate. Bobby Seale, a founder of the Black Panthers, was part of the coalition that had led the protest at the convention. Like several of his white codefendants, Seale was verbally disruptive at the trial, but unlike them he was chained to a chair and finally gagged. I would see several black men receive this treatment in court—and worse. I was present at a hearing for George

Jackson, a felon who had written an eloquent memoir called *Soledad Brother*. I won't go into the contention of prison officials that Jackson was violent toward his guards; such things were often acts of self-defense. But at this hearing he was shackled to a chair. Suddenly the lights went out. Everyone hit the floor, and I heard the sounds of a scuffle. When the lights came on again, Jackson was bloody; he'd been beaten by guards. The official explanation was that he planned to escape, but it would have been impossible in the heavily secured courtroom. Still, there had been several attempts to spring him, including one by his younger brother that turned violent. In the ensuing shootout, a judge who had been taken hostage was killed, along with his abductors. It was very complicated, but not if you were sitting, as I was, near George Jackson's mother. I saw the look on her face as her son emerged from the darkness, helpless and bleeding.

Images like that were seared into my mind—black men muzzled and chained while a white judge, white guards, and nearly always a white jury proceeded blithely with the proceedings. Perhaps I should have considered whether it was necessary to restrain men who were, in some cases, capable of violence. But no one raised on news photos of lynchings could have assimilated these sights. They convinced me that I was living in a racist state where black men were the objects of fear and loathing. The evidence was manacled before me. And my own freedom to behave as badly as I pleased only added to my rage.

Meanwhile, back at the ranch of New Journalism, I was about to lose the last of my literary heroes. The celebratory tone of Tom Wolfe's work had turned acidic, and he no longer wrote about the zany individualists who created the style of the sixties. Now his dominant subject was the Manhattan cultural establishment, and he skewered its pretensions in gleeful detail. I relished his exposé of the *New Yorker*, in which he described the hothouse environment around its editor, William Shawn. My friend Ellen Willis, a pioneering feminist and the first significant woman rock critic, wrote for that magazine, and she had hilarious tales about what couldn't be said in its decorous pages. She wasn't allowed to use the word *wig* or refer to anyone as short. (Shawn was a diminutive man.) Another friend, the pop music critic Jon Pareles, had a similar ordeal at the *Times*, where the honorific *Mr.* had to be used before every male name. Pareles fumed about this rule well into the seventies. Would he have to call Iggy Pop of the Stooges "Mr. Pop"? Or Meat Loaf "Mr. Loaf"? No, he wouldn't, but the problem showed how far mainstream publications were from the spirit and letter of youth culture. Tom Wolfe had an unerring ear for that sort of contradiction, and he used it to devastating effect when he covered a fund-raiser for the Black Panther Party at the home of Leonard Bernstein. Wolfe captured the strange interplay between the militants and the culturati whose patronage they were soliciting. The result was one of his most famous pieces, "Radical Chic." It was a great read, but Lenny was an easy target, and Wolfe couldn't—or wouldn't—grasp the complexity of the situation. It didn't suit his purpose to imagine that someone like Bernstein might have real feelings of solidarity with the Panthers. I knew otherwise because I, too, admired them.

Today the Black Panthers are part of the retro universe available to anyone with a search engine. For many young people their image is mashed up with the caricatures of blaxploitation films from the seventies. But I got to see the real thing when the cameras weren't rolling. I often ran into Panthers at Movement meetings, where they were guests of honor. It was a mark of pride for a Panther to attend a demo-planning session. I once spent an afternoon at their office in the Fillmore district of San Francisco, where they ran community programs. There were no media stars in the house, none of their extremely photogenic leaders, just people dropping by to hang out and join the running debate, which was so recondite that I could barely follow it. This was lefty discourse with an internationalist gist. I'd hoped for something more quotably black-and-proud, but I realized that I wasn't at a James Brown concert. I was watching real-world Marxists discuss ideology, and of course it was boring.

The Commies of my youth—my friends' parents—would never have talked politics in front of me. It was too risky at the height of McCarthyism. In those days, people like them covered their faces when they were dragged before Congress. That changed in the sixties, when the New Left reinvigorated Marxism as a critical system, even as it turned against the Soviet Union. While covering teach-ins on occupied campuses, I saw undergrads fling dialectics around like fastballs at a game. I watched Spartacists and Trotskyists battle over tiny clods of turf, their numbers swelled by the government agents among them. But these were middle-class people, and I never felt comfortable with their jargon.

The Panthers didn't strike me as middle-class, and so I saw their formality as a marker of upward mobility. I wondered whether they'd trained themselves not to talk ghetto, the way I'd taught myself not to talk Bronx. That would have been a very sixties thing, all of us lifting ourselves through language and being reborn in the Revolution.

Many people reinvented themselves through radical politics in those days, so it didn't bother me that some of these militants were former criminals. It was what they became that mattered. Unlike black activists who took their cue from Malcolm X, the Panthers pursued alliances with whites, and they welcomed other minorities, including gay people. Though the conflict between blacks and Jews was simmering in the sixties, I never heard a Panther make an anti-Semitic remark. They rejected black nationalism as sectarian, and opposed the Nation of Islam. If I had to place them on the Marxist spectrum I'd call them Mao-oid. They swam in the sea of the people, as the Chairman instructed, but "the people" meant every group that was oppressed, not just a certain class or race. The Revolution would be made by a coalition of the stigmatized, and the Panthers were working to expand its ranks. Best of all, for my purposes, they had an unerring sense of style.

I lavished attention on their long leather coats, black berets, and perfectly coiffed Afros—all part of the Panther mystique, as were their graphics. They created the prime image of the resurgent left, a clenched black fist. It would appear, in many colors, on buttons for all the movements that surfaced in identity politics: fists for students, Chicano and Native American activists, militant feminists, and the Gay Liberation Front. Nearly every form of agitation in the sixties borrowed from the Panthers' iconography. Their emphasis on community self-defense inspired all sorts of groups, from the Gray Panthers, who advocated for the elderly, to the Pink Panthers, who responded to homophobic assaults. It's no accident that the Guardian Angels, hardly fans of Black Power, wore red berets. The extent of this influence reflects one of the most salient features of black insurrectionary thinking in the sixties—it motivated all sorts of people who never thought they could stand up for themselves. The Panthers were architects of the future. That was one reason why the government saw them as a threat.

On the fringes of the Movement, menacing rhetoric was an art form in 1968. An anarchist group called Up Against the Wall, Motherfuckers specialized in disrupting orderly demonstrations. Valerie Solanas had a cadre of one called SCUM (the Society for Cutting Up Men). It got more respect than it deserved, even after she shot Andy Warhol. Then there was the Weather Underground, named for a line in a Dylan song—"You don't need a weatherman to know which way the wind blows." Their signature was bombing federal buildings, and though they made an effort not to kill anyone, they didn't always succeed. Three people died when one of their devices accidentally exploded, demolishing a Greenwich Village brownstone. These were futile acts with fatal results.

Rational politics wasn't a strong suit with leftist fringe groups in the late sixties. Yet nearly all their members escaped the fate of the Panthers, whose leadership was hounded and sometimes ambushed by the authorities at all levels of government. Why did these black militants summon up the most primal emotions in their enemies? It wasn't just because they were armed (that was legal in California), or simply because they were effective (at its height they operated in twenty cities and their newspaper had some 250,000 readers), or merely because they were so good at spectacle. (You can check out the clips of them marching on the Oakland courthouse, chanting, "The Revolution has come! Time to get you a gun.") They inspired terror because of what they revealed about race—the nightmare and the reality. Race was a fantasy that shaped our identities. It had been central to my coming of age in the early sixties, and now it was at the core of the nation's destiny.

As a program, the Revolution was never very popular, but as a concept it pervaded the counterculture in 1968. Even the Beatles felt compelled to address it. The official lyric of their song "Revolution" reads, "When you talk about destruction . . . you can count me out," but in one recorded version John Lennon sings "count me in" as well. That was pretty much the way I felt. Though I was caught up in the mania, I had my doubts. An uprising of the oppressed was easy to imagine, but how could it possibly succeed? Who would provide the weapons to resist the heavily armed government? And what would happen after the inevitable bloodbath? I was certain that the end result would be a backlash of stunning proportions. There were some very dark forces in the military, and the prospect of a coup seemed credible to me. So I found myself torn between wanting the Revolution and dreading it. This wasn't just a political dilemma. It was a conflict between warring aspects of my personality, one part learning to love and the other eager for the rush of rioting. Many young people were faced with a similar dichotomy—we wanted to fight, but also to boogie. A quote from the anarchist icon Emma Goldman decorated a lot of dorm walls: "If I can't dance, it's not my revolution." And dance we did, all the way to the billy clubs.

As the unraveling accelerated, wild rumors spread, some of them deliberate hoaxes. One of the most notorious appeared in a hip satirical magazine called *The Realist*, which published "evidence" that Lyndon Johnson had fucked the corpse of JFK in the neck wound. Even a year after that story appeared, when the editor admitted that it had been fabricated, some of my friends believed it, and how could I convince them otherwise when so many unfathomable things were actually happening? Who could have imagined that the CIA would send a harmless gas through the New York subway system in order to experiment with aerosolized LSD as a weapon? It was inconceivable, but apparently true. Our most paranoid fantasies about the government were less extreme than the plans actually hatched. Please consider this when you wonder how people like me could have set out to destroy liberalism and its compromised emblem, Lyndon Johnson. I'm not sure that the foot soldiers of any revolution focus on the future they are ushering in. The urgency of the situation is the only thing that counts. For us, that meant ending the war, and the primary question was the one that inspired my favorite marching chant: "Hey, hey, LBJ, how many kids did you kill today?" The answer: more than we could bear.

I still wrote about rock occasionally, but it was much less central to my life than radical politics had become. My column mostly chronicled the adventures of the New Left. Songs without a political message were like a march without slogans to me, and I was big on slogans—my favorite one was "Don't trust anyone over thirty." I can only imagine how strange this concept of generational solidarity must seem to young people today, prompted to think that only cliques and networks matter, and bound together by the illusory intimacy of social media, what Susan Sontag, referring to snapshots, called "self-surveillance." But young people in the sixties were united much more broadly by a war we didn't believe in, and also by a set of great global expectations. From this perspective it seemed clear that America had to be rescued from its own forms of tyranny. I'm well aware that Tea Party partisans say the same thing, but the point of our movement wasn't to defend wealth and property. This is the difference between their radical sentiments and ours. They want to preserve their privilege; we wanted to overcome it. Our enemy was the government and the military-industrial complex. Their enemy is the government and . . . us.

I'd been following the Yippies since their first major demo, in 1967. This was the event that launched Norman Mailer's career as a New Journalist. The target was the Pentagon. Abbie Hoffman had calculated astutely that the sight of ten thousand kids (and several famous authors) chanting before the building, in an attempt to levitate it, would terrify the authorities. They could easily have coped with a purposeful march, but this was a signal of how cryptic our resistance had become. The open display of irrationality was intended to reveal the true nature of a "rational" war. But it was also an attack on the illusion of coherence. By violating the rules of plausibility, we embodied the disintegration of the order. Abbie called this strategy Groucho Marxism.

I could never decide whether he enjoyed the violence that his tactics unleashed, or whether he regarded it as a necessary evil. Perhaps he felt exhilarated by escaping into reality, as I did. I can't say, but I do understand the fire that was in his eyes. To commit violence for a just cause is a pleasure—you literally see red. But to present yourself for abuse, to let your head run bloody in the name of a belief, is an even more powerful experience. A violent act propels you to focus entirely on your feelings. You stop thinking. But receiving violence in a demo empties your feelings and replaces them with the purity of a principle. Your thoughts crystallize. This is why many protesters go limp when they are hit. It's a kind of consummation. I realize that this sounds like masochism, but such terms are useless when it comes to forcing change. Injustice doesn't relent of its own accord. It demands victims and the witness of the nation, and nothing plays better on TV than the blood of the beautiful being shed.

As our rebellion spread and we approached the brink of confrontation with the state, I could sense the shift on all sides, from protest to mayhem. An explosion seemed inevitable. I thought of America as a swollen boil. Over the fateful spring and summer of '68 it burst, and so did what little remained of my equilibrium. Jolt after jolt shattered my sense of order. Holding back became impossible.

In April, as the trees budded, I covered a bloody student uprising at Columbia University. It was sparked by newly discovered evidence that my alma mater had been doing research for the defense department, with a direct bearing on the war. Moral considerations aside, this meant that the university was supporting a military operation that could place its own students at risk once they graduated. But the protest also had a local agenda. One of the issues was Columbia's decision to build a gym in the park used by Harlem residents. The community would be granted limited access to the facility through a separate entrance. This was an outrage to an already seething neighborhood. Prominent militants joined black students in occupying a dorm, renaming it Malcolm X University. White students seized other buildings, with much of the faculty declaring its support. Soon the whole place was shut down.

When I arrived to cover the protest, it looked like a cross between a strike and a Living Theatre performance. I remember one student climbing a tree and shouting for all to hear, "This is a liberated tree, and I won't come down until my demands are met." Inside the dorms there was a festive air, with pizzas donated by sympathetic merchants, and guitars everywhere. I spent a fine afternoon flirting with students and shilling for quotes. This had the makings of yet another piece about the heroic struggle of the young. But then the administration made a deal with the black occupiers, who marched out of their occupied building with raised fists. That left an opening for the police to move in.

As they entered the campus, in the dead of night, all telephone connections were severed. Then the clubbing began. It had the look and feel of a baby seal hunt. Students were kicked, pummeled, and dragged by the hair down flights of stairs. Their screams echoed across the quad, along with the ululating rebel cry of Arab women that everyone knew from the revolutionary film *The Battle of Algiers*. It rang from every dorm. By the time the raid was over, seven hundred people had been arrested and a hundred fifty hospitalized. I toured the university chapel, now a makeshift infirmary where dozens of students lay bleeding. But the image that stays with me is the plaza before Columbia's library. It had been full of people when the raid began, and at some point the police charged the crowd. After the space was cleared I saw dozens of sandals littering the sidewalk. Students had jumped out of their shoes to get away.

How did I remain immune from the clubs, even though I looked just like the protesters? The answer lay in the magic credentials that dangled from my neck. As usual, I was protected by my press card, and it allowed me to witness the bloodletting up close and untouched. At some point that night I stumbled into the dorm next to the building where I'd once studied journalism. About a hundred students cowered in the lobby, and soon after I joined them they locked the doors. But the police used battering rams, and the doors came off the hinges and collapsed. As the cops barged in, I flashed on an old silent-movie cartoon with antique officers swinging their clubs in a cloud of smoke. I raced up the stairs to the mezzanine, and from there I saw the cops beating people in the lobby. The whole thing was in slo-mo—that's the kind of response adrenaline will produce. The shrieks of the students became a hissing in my ears. The police began climbing the stairs. I calmly opened a window and jumped, falling two stories and hitting the ground on my feet.

I picked myself up and walked to the subway, my mind a block of ice. I took a train to the *Voice* office and spent the next few hours writing my piece. Then I handed it in and headed home, still in an uncanny state of calm. When I closed the door behind me a cramp gripped my belly, and I dropped to the floor in a spasming ball. I had met my deadline; only then could I feel pain.

By that point I had come to regard political violence as part of my daily life. Only three weeks before the skull bashings at Columbia, Martin Luther King was assassinated. I was not so well insulated when I heard the news. I felt as if the top of my own head had exploded. As city after city erupted in flames, and Lyndon Johnson appeared on the White House lawn to plead for restraint—I remember him saying, "For God's sake, live within the law"—I noticed how shriveled he seemed. The president's impotence was nearly as devastating to me as the murder of King. I wandered through streets full of people in a daze, the traffic moving slowly, almost somberly. There are moments in the film *Taxi Driver* that remind me of the eerie ambience that night.

I saw a car parked, with its radio playing. A group of Black Muslims in suits and bow ties were sitting inside. One of them opened the door so I could hear more clearly. We listened together, not looking at each other but sharing wordless grief. It was a moment I will never forget, that recognition of what it means to lose an idea of what is possible. King's concept of America as the "beloved community" was powerful even to these separatists, despite their dogma. One of them reached across me to turn up the volume. I was prepared for the cold courtesy that Black Muslims typically extended to whites. One of them had rung my bell erroneously a few years earlier. "Pardon me, white devil," he'd said politely. This time there was no etiquette to express our feelings. I saw their silence as a vision of the future. But their willingness to share the radio with me was more mysterious. I think it showed a sense of how fragile we all are when a leader is killed. This is the purpose of assassinations, even when they are committed by a lone, crazed gunman. They produce a profound feeling of vulnerability.

Then, in June, Bobby Kennedy was murdered. Like some white lefties and quite a few black people, I'd regarded him as the great hope of electoral politics. Most of my friends preferred Eugene McCarthy, who was running a more cerebral antiwar campaign. He didn't appeal to me, for the same reason that the peace movement never seemed as urgent as the struggle for civil rights. I didn't believe in peace; I believed in justice, and that didn't seem like the same thing. I'm not saying I was right about Bobby, only young and subject to the charisma that he had in abundance. He was visceral in a way that invited not just optimism but ecstasy. Crowds surged to touch him, tearing at his clothes. Watching him campaign, as I did once, was an almost mystical experience. After Johnson declined to run for reelection it seemed likely that Kennedy would be the Democratic nominee. The announcement had just been made that he'd won the California primary. It was after midnight, and I turned off the TV. Then Robert Christgau called and told me to turn it back on. That's when I saw the ballroom erupt in screams.

I watched for several hours and finally fell asleep in front of the set. When I woke up they were announcing Bobby's death. The networks showed pictures of him lying on the floor of the kitchen where he'd been shot, his face pale and distant, the tie around his neck askew. His helplessness was terrifying to behold, and the feeling persisted long after that night. It was something I wouldn't experience again until I saw the column of black smoke rising over the Manhattan skyline on 9/11. But this was far more personal. The sense that all the heroes of my political life were being killed made me feel emasculated, literally. My balls shriveled up against my belly for protection, and for several weeks I was unable to get an erection, no matter how I enlisted my fantasies.

By July I was ready for a Mayan death star to strike the White House (as one of my friends predicted). Everyone around me seemed hooked on apocalyptic expectations. Hysteria had become a habit; I was living on what might be called, in today's elaborate diagnostic terms, adrenal bulimia. But I focused my feelings on Don McNeill. He represented every hopeful and delicate impulse that was being crushed. And now he slunk around the office, his shoulders sagging. I felt more protective toward him than ever, but I was too frantic to offer him the support he needed—also too overcome with guilt. A few months earlier I had pushed him to write about the Yippies. I argued that he couldn't understand how the hippies he reported on were evolving unless he hung out with Abbie Hoffman. I tried to convince him that antiwar demos were now part of his beat. I suppose he came to agree, because he decided to cover a Yippie protest at Grand Central Station. I offered to go with him, mainly because I didn't think he knew how to handle himself around flailing clubs. But there was only one press card. In those days the police thought they could decide what constituted the media, and we were issued just a few credentials, which meant that most of our reporters had to share them. Since Don would be writing the piece, he got the card.

What I didn't realize was the depths of resentment that the police felt toward reporters. Anyone wearing press credentials was a target for the guardians in blue. There are many pictures of journalists being beaten at demonstrations in 1968. (My favorite shows a *Times* photographer dragged down by cops who are choking him with his camera straps.) It had become apparent to me that I was safer without an identifier. I could easily pass as an ordinary protester, and when you're looking for someone to club, the taller target is the tempting one. I credit my survival to my shortness.

The demo that Don covered, billed as a Yip-In, had happened in March, just a month before King was killed. It was already clear that the police were ready to bust heads, especially when the protesters showed up in the main hall of Grand Central Station, with its celebrated vaulted ceiling featuring signs of the zodiac. The chaos must have been glorious to behold, chants ricocheting off the marble floor and walls. I wasn't there, so I wouldn't know, but I do remember what happened to Don. At some point, the police lifted him up and shoved him headfirst through a plate-glass window. His wound required stitches. Our staff photographer took a picture of him that ran, I believe, on the front page. Don is looking directly at the camera, blood dripping down his face and onto his press card.

After that incident we were told to buy helmets. (For years afterward I never went to a demo without one.) And Don became even more precious to me. I blamed myself for his baptism by billy club. Finally I forced myself to ask how he was coping with his injury. "Everything's cool," he replied. He was going to his place upstate to mellow out. I knew he needed a break. We'd already decided to cover the next big demo together, perhaps under a joint byline. This protest was being organized by antiwar groups determined to disrupt the Democratic convention in Chicago, where Johnson's vice president, Hubert Humphrey, would be anointed as the party's nominee. I would write about the chaos that ensued, but Don wasn't there with me. The conversation I've described was the last time I saw him alive.

Sometime during that time-out in the country he walked into a lake and drowned. He was twenty-three. The *Voice* obituary concluded that his death was accidental, but a guest at his house told me a more complicated version. According to him, they were tripping, and at some point he and Don had a sexual encounter. Apparently it was Don's first gay experience, and afterward he wandered off by himself—end of story. I know it's difficult to keep track of someone while you're in an altered state, but I was furious at this guy. Couldn't he tell how troubled Don was? Why hadn't he stayed with him? Unreasonable as my feelings may have been, this behavior struck me as the epitome of what lay beneath the mellow veneer many people cultivated in the late sixties. It wasn't indifference but something even worse: a casual faith in letting people in distress do their thing.

The trauma of Don's death remains so painful that my hands are trembling as I recall it. Everyone at the *Voice* was devastated. His memorial service was the only time I saw my colleagues cry. The editor seemed steeped in grief, and in the weeks that followed he withdrew into his office. A few years later the paper was sold to the first of many owners, each of them less connected to its original mission. But for a while I kept a picture of Don in my desk drawer. It was the one that had run after he was injured by the police. While pacing out a paragraph, I would stare at his face, blood dripping from his forehead and a look of stunned confusion in his eyes. Like so many images from my youth, that picture is now online. When I see it today the Neil Young song about childhood and memory fills my raw and raging mind: *I was helpless. Helpless. Helpless.*

The Whole World Is Watching

Youth fare was our best ally. If you were under twenty-five, you could fly anywhere in the country at half price. That made it easy to move thousands of demonstrators to Chicago in August of 1968—the cost from New York was only fifty dollars. The *Voice* sent several reporters to cover the Democratic convention and the protests in the streets. I had made a prior trip, tagging along with the radical leadership, a coalition of Panthers, Yippies, and the first major New Left organization, Students for a Democratic Society. They were scheduled to meet with the police department and the mayor's office. Only the activists knew that a journalist was present.

There, at opposite ends of a long wooden table polished to a sheen, sat Tom Hayden, Abbie Hoffman, and other members of the boisterous crew that would come to be known as the Chicago Seven. They were in no mood to be judicious. Permits or not, they were going to occupy the city's parks for the three days of the convention, and their agenda included a musical marathon called the Festival of Life. When asked how many people could be expected, they blithely estimated one hundred thousand. (The actual crowd was twenty-five thousand at most.) One of the leaders—I'm not sure who, but it was probably Abbie—told the officials that his followers were planning to drop LSD into the city's reservoirs. I remember questioning him about whether that was really possible. Of course not, he replied. Everyone knows you can't lace an entire water supply with acid, and besides, fluoride would neutralize the drug. But the bureaucrats at the meeting weren't aware of that. They looked pie-eyed.

Afterward they spread a rumor that the police were going to open unused sewer tunnels as mass jails. Hyperbole was the standard mode of address on both sides. It added to the sense of unreality.

I thought about sitting this demo out. I already knew what a police riot, as we called these encounters with the law, looked like. And I had vivid memories of the racial backlash, Chicago-style. In 1966 I'd covered a housing march led by Martin Luther King in a suburb called Gage Park. Five thousand white residents attacked us in a frenzy. I watched as King fell to the ground, hit on the head by a rock. He later told reporters he had never seen such violence. The march ended abruptly, and we were herded into buses under a hail of abuse. (I remember shouts of "Kill coon King!") The organizers told us to lie under the seats. As the bus careened through the streets, rocks crashed through the windows. I looked up long enough to see a nun throwing a stone. This left a vivid impression, and it recurred as I pondered returning to Chicago. But I decided to go. It was too good a story to miss, and by then I was hooked on the spectacle of violence, the greatest show on earth.

I also had a new role to play. I'd volunteered to help organize the free concert in one of the parks, and I started making calls. I had visions of rock stars casting an aura of significance over the event, as if to say, *We're all protesters now.* But this was no Monterey Pop. The hip elite weren't going to show up in their finery, and there wouldn't be any record executives to sign the best acts. Most of my connections were through press agents, and they were none too eager to see their clients associated with this protest. I contacted a few musicians whose numbers I kept in my Rolodex. They were all sympathetic, but no one was willing to commit. The basic response was: I'd love to overthrow the government, but I've got a gig that day. Some expressed concern for the safety of their equipment, which struck me as bogus in an era when guitars and amps were being smashed by performers like insects underfoot. A few said they were worried about getting arrested, though, of course, that was a time-honored tradition in pop. I suppose it was one thing for Jim Morrison to get busted after whipping out his dick onstage, quite another for him to be associated with political disorder (though, in fairness, my inquiry never got past his publicist). I suddenly became aware of how safe even the most radical rock experience was. You blew your mind and went home to groove another day. Pop stars were revolutionaries of representation, unwilling to put their bodies on the line for a Yippie riot.

Only the most political performers showed up in Chicago. One of them, Country Joe McDonald, would come to regret that gig. He got attacked in his hotel by men wearing armbands, probably security guards. I was glad that I'd decided not to reach out to Janis Joplin. I didn't want to get a regretful rejection from her. By then she had let her manager convince her to leave Big Brother and the Holding Company and take up with a band of seasoned studio musicians. I had a nagging suspicion that she'd become a true pro, and I was loath to be proven right.

I shouldn't be so hard on these musicians. They had every reason to fear what was about to take place in Chicago. Anyone with more sense than I would have picked up the signs. The whole country was inflamed, raw with anxiety and resentment, a land charred by fires of rage. One poster, devised by a British airline, caught the sense that everything was hanging by a thread. AMERICA, it read. SEE IT WHILE IT LASTS.

Nothing expressed this sense of chaotic dread like the scene on campus. Student strikes, following the example of Columbia, shut down hundreds of colleges and universities. To me, this revolt was tangible proof that generational solidarity had power, and, even more remarkably, it could cross borders. All over the West, even in the Soviet satellites, young people were in the streets. Mexico City erupted; Paris was in turmoil, along with London and Berlin. Back home, the expanded FM radio band had made room for new progressive-rock stations, featuring playlists that included a number of antiwar anthems. "Vietnam Rag," by Country Joe and the Fish, contained the scandalous couplet "Be the first one on your block/To see your boy come home in a box." Pete Seeger had a hit with his wry evocation of LBJ: "We're waist deep in the big muddy, and the big fool says to push on." These were auspicious signs, but by then I wasn't interested in pop and its artifacts. I rarely opened the records that arrived at their usual pace. I stopped spending long nights at the Fillmore East, and traded in my rock-critic drag for the worn T-shirt and jeans of a heroic guerrilla. On the few occasions when I interviewed musicians my questions were peppered with politics.

"What will you do when the Revolution comes?" I remember asking Neil Young as we sat on the patio of his home in L.A. He looked around him and replied, "I'll die defending my swimming pool." Even I got the irony in this zinger, and it almost made me face my rigidity. I greatly admired Young, though his politics were unpredictable. It seemed to me that he had the spirit of Dylan without the paranoia. His art was one of self-exploration, his tool the spare poetics of a Canadian prairie child. He was entitled to his interiority; I wouldn't have wanted him to face the guillotine for that. But I had seen too many bloody heads to indulge in self-reflection. Where had it ever gotten me, and what use could it be in the current situation? I wanted to put the anxieties of fame behind me and to use whatever suasion I had in the service of the future being born.

I traveled from campus to hippie enclave, covering the action. I learned to tie a wet rag around my face when there was tear gas in the air, and to smear Vaseline on myself to ward off Mace. It felt like I was applying warpaint, which, I suppose, I was. The writing that came out of these experiences was as exhilarating as my first pieces, when I focused on the fans and didn't have to deal with publicists. There was no need to fret about the compromises of my role. All anyone knew was that this cat was writing down everything they said, and it might end up in the paper. That was how I recaptured the sense of connection and tangibility that I'd lost. There were no celebrities in these uprisings; no dry ice behind the amps to give the illusion of an explosion. Everything happened spontaneously or by laborious consent, and the one thing that seemed inevitable was the deployment of police, whose version of a rave-up was cracking heads. The moment when they struck was primal for them and for us, a theater of cruelty that Antonin Artaud could only have dreamt of, where there was no real safety in the audience. Except, of course, for me. Assuming that I knew how to move fast, which I did, I could keep my skull intact. It was as close as I could get to being a war correspondent, which was the most heroic form of journalism to me.

And there were real martyrs—several hundred students killed in Mexico City when troops hidden on rooftops opened fire on demonstrators. A few years down the road, four students would be shot dead in Ohio by National Guardsmen who sent a fusillade into a rally. But in 1968 we were still regarded by the authorities as children of the white middle class, and that bought us a degree of mercy. This was not the case in France. There were news photos of Parisian cops swinging leaded capes at student protesters. I clipped these images hungrily. The city of Albert Camus and Jean-Paul Sartre, the birthplace of existentialism, was reenacting its history of rebellion. I yearned to cover it, in the tradition of Hemingway reporting on the Spanish Civil War. I imagined myself drinking hard (and eating well), sharing the barricades with students whose breath was as bad as their skin, and, as dawn broke over the smoky streets, fucking some shapely *enragée* in a room with a lingering scent of Gauloise. Nothing is hotter to me than a sexual fantasy combined with true belief. I seriously considered scrounging up the money to fly to Paris, but then I realized that I would have to report this story without credentials. There would be no time to explain to a cop in sporadic French that I was a member of the American press corps. I decided not to try it.

But a local underground paper ran a series of posters from the strike at the Sorbonne, and I put them up in my workroom for inspiration. They were more enigmatic than anything I'd seen here, featuring slogans over sketchy cartoons that perfectly expressed the anarchist roots of this student movement. As in: "All power to the imagination." "Demand the impossible." Or my personal favorite: "Under the pavement a beach." Googling those posters today makes me reach for my blood-pressure collar (LOL). They are the bridge between the anti-Nazi collages of John Heartfield and the street art of Banksy, as influential on the aesthetics of protest as Fillmore posters were on contemporary graffiti art. You can see the line leading from these bold *affiches* to ACT-UP and Occupy Wall Street.

I was struck by how similar the strategies of the French revolt were to Abbie Hoffman's sense of revolutionary theater. I mentioned this to him once, and I asked if he'd read anything by the Situationists, a French anarchist group of the time. "Only in the original Yiddish," he replied. Abbie was a very smart guy, but he didn't pay a lot of attention to the intellectual currents swirling around him, certainly not to philosophers with a European pedigree. A passing knowledge of McLuhan was as close as he came to theory. But ideas were absorbed by osmosis in those days; someone told someone, who told a friend, who wrote a song that Joan Baez sang at a rally, and soon it was common knowledge. Generational solidarity was a very effective communications tool, and rock was a tom-tom, its beat-borne messages cryptic to the straight world but quite clear to us. When you think about it, this is how Yiddish functioned for Jews, with an alphabet that couldn't be deciphered by those outside the tribe. Daniel Cohn-Bendit, a leader of the student strikes in Paris (back then he was known as Danny the Red; now he's a prominent Green), has recalled that he synchronized plans with radicals in other countries, without alerting the authorities, by using Yiddish.

What was the driving force behind our unity? The very situation we were born into, the combination of comfort and oppression. For us, I think, chaos and impulse were the alternative to the leaden regularity of an overly regimented system. We had never known an impediment to our desires; we'd come of age with a multi-billion-dollar economy dedicated to meeting our adolescent needs. We harbored a profound belief that change was waiting for the action that would realize it. These qualities—confidence and flight from stasis—are what's distinctive about anthems of youthful rebellion from the late sixties. A typical example is the repertoire of the MC5, a group of stoner revolutionaries who played during the protests at the Democratic convention (a hot dog vendor supplied the current for their amps). I saw them a year later in their hometown of Ann Arbor. They took to the stage in a clamor of clanging chords, screaming, KICK OUT THE JAMS!!!! I described their sound as "spasm rock." It was the classic message of rock 'n' roll but gone political, the adolescent's urge to resolve tension in an explosion of feeling amped by all the instability, the constant agitation, into a kind of hysteria. It was irresistible to me.

I'd seen the most incredible images on television: the heads of my political heroes blown apart, cities across the nation smoldering. Anything was possible—that was how it felt on a daily basis. I walked around in a state of disorientation, as if I were experiencing the aftershocks of an earthquake that hadn't happened yet. But the strangest thing about this sensation was that it drove me forward. The imminence demanded that I take action, and whatever I might do seemed very important, as if it could make a decisive difference. There's a joy in that conviction, a delight that overcomes the dread. This desire to know the brink, to leap over the edge and into the Niagara, is my most vivid memory of 1968.

The Democratic Party was about to nominate a man who, for all his progressive leanings, couldn't bring himself to oppose the war—another good liberal with a cowardly streak. In late August, Hubert Humphrey headed for Chicago to be consecrated, and we headed there too, thousands of us: radicalized hippies, hardcore lefties, adrenalized potheads, students who would soon be susceptible to the draft. Everything was converging. All signs pointed to a showdown. I had a feeling that we were about to kick out the jams, big time. What I didn't realize was that this moment of release would have enormous consequences. It would be the crucible event in a year when America experienced its gravest domestic unrest since the Civil War.

"You afraid?" I asked a kid from California. He filled his palm with a wad of Vaseline, then smeared it across his face to protect himself from Mace. "I dunno," he said. "My toes feel cold, but my ears are burning hot."

We were standing in Lincoln Park, not long after a curfew declared by the Chicago police. The cops had gathered on the rise above us, in formation. The festival I'd fussed and fretted over never took place, though there were a few impromptu concerts. The only event of note was a ceremony nominating the Yippie candidate for president, a hog named Pigasus. *Pig* was what we called the police. "Pigs eat shit!" had replaced "We shall overcome" as our chant of choice. As the police line tightened I saw kids holding Spalding balls studded with nails and tacks. My new friend from California pulled a canister from his pocket. It was pepper spray.

Following his lead, I wrapped a towel doused with water around my face. "Better take off those credentials," my comrade advised. "They're going after the press." And they were. Even Hugh Hefner had sustained a minor injury. But most journalists were safe inside the convention hall, which had been cordoned off from the demonstrations. I didn't see any other reporters in the crowd of kids, and I felt the tremble of elation that comes when you realize that you've got a scoop. But this wasn't just a professional high. The moment when I removed my press pass was also the instant when I crossed over from the regretful life of the insulated to the thrilling zone of risk. Everyone here had seen, if not shed, blood. They were the hardcore, and I was finally among them.

The police advanced a bit after midnight, behind two massive trucks. You could sense the fear in their bodies, the same foreboding that was gripping the whole nation. Though they were very well armed, with steel-tipped riot batons, shotguns, an assortment of pistols and ominous canisters in their belts, when you got close to them you could see terror in their tight lips, and you knew that nothing in their training had prepared them for this. They'd handled riots, but not with TV cameras following their every move; they'd shot at people in the ghettos, but not at the children of middle-class whites. These men were as alarmed and as pumped with adrenaline as we were. When you sense that in a cop, you know that what follows will be out of control.

It remained only for the signal to be given, and when it was, the police advanced down the slope. Floodlights mounted on their trucks shone bright orange. Then tear-gas canisters exploded—putt, putt, putt—and you could see that the police were wearing masks, which made their vision even more imprecise. Soon the kids were engulfed in an orange cloud, and we ran in every direction, looking for rocks to throw and windows to smash and something to feel besides fear. Because one thing about tear gas: if it doesn't knock you out, it makes you crazy.

That was the first night. The following day was the main event, which began with a demo in the park that bordered Michigan Avenue, just across from the Hilton, where many of the delegates and much of the press corps was staying. Tear gas was useless here, because the wind would send fumes into the hotel. Already reporters were throwing things out of the windows—rolls of toilet paper and even typewriters. Some demostrators threw balloons filled with cow blood from the stockyards. These missiles burst on the cops, along with bags of animal shit, smearing their uniforms like works of abstract art. That was when they really waded into the crowd. Cameras were snapping; TV trucks were gathering. And meanwhile, in the convention hall, Hubert Humphrey's name was placed in nomination. When one speaker excoriated the city for the violence in the streets, the mayor of Chicago, an old-school boss named Richard Daley, could be seen in TV close-up, shouting what seemed like "Fuck you, you Jew son of a bitch."

I don't remember when the National Guard arrived, but we knew that they'd be more disciplined than the police, and we cheered as they positioned themselves between us and the pigs. It was clear from their eyes where their sympathies lay. Kids started putting flowers in the barrels of their rifles. A few soldiers mustered peace signs. The folksinger Phil Ochs, who had been performing through it all, yelled into a mike, "If any of you are human beings, take off your clothes." To my astonishment, a number of soldiers removed their helmets. It was one of the most moving moments I experienced in the sixties, proof that my hunch had been right—they were young, and the young were one.

I stood in a knot of journalists, the few who dared to cover the demo from its midst. To my right was an editor from *Esquire* whose job was to protect the star writer from Paris whom the magazine had imported to cover this event. He was none other than Jean Genet, the sacred monster of modern French letters. Genet was transfixed by the beefy flab of the Chicago police. "Those bellies!" I heard him exclaim in French. The police were clubbing people within earshot of our group, and the editor from *Esquire* was worried that his charge might submit to a steel-tipped embrace. He ushered Genet along like a parent dragging an unwilling child across the street.

Suddenly I realized that someone had his arm over my shoulder. It was Ed Sanders, the poet I'd met in 1962, when he ran the Peace Eye Bookstore. By now his beatnik band, the Fugs, had had an unlikely hit and he was something of a celebrity. "Stay with me," he said. I still remember the protective look in his eye. It always came as a shock when someone who didn't want something from me showed concern for my body or my soul. But I didn't stay with Ed. I had my escape route mapped out in advance—I always did at demos—and I crossed a bridge a few blocks away. Whatever the danger, I had to witness the action.

I ambled onto Michigan Avenue, where the police were still deployed. By now night had fallen, and they were foraging for stray protesters. I needed the safety of a group, and I let myself get swept up in the crowd around the Hilton. A line of cops started pushing everyone back against the plate-glass windows that framed the lobby, flailing away at whomever they could reach. I heard glass break behind me. People were falling through the windows and into the hotel, shrieking with one breath and apologizing for stepping on toes with another. I saw clubs moving in slow motion—the same cartoony experience I'd had at Columbia. I stared at a kid whose arms had been twisted behind him in the crush. I felt the *Guernica* in his eyes; the same terrified expression that the big horse had in the painting was on his face.

All of a sudden floodlights on TV trucks broke the darkness. The street looked like a studio, and in the glare everyone started shouting, "The whole world is watching." It was a spontaneous chant, born of the knowledge that we were on the air, live, just as Hubert Humphrey was accepting his party's nomination—the networks showed a split screen. We had accomplished what we'd come for, spoiled the party for the party of war. Even better, we'd taken our hero Henry David Thoreau's advice: "You must live in the present, launch yourself on every wave, find your eternity in each moment." I found something else as well: the joy of knowing that I was risking it all for the Revolution.

Once again, my diminutive height came to my rescue. I managed to scurry under people's legs, and I slipped out of the crush at the Hilton. I scampered down the street, shaking badly. A few blocks from the hotel, I heard a police car screech to a stop. Three cops got out, ready to arrest me, or worse. I sprinted up the stairs of the Art Institute of Chicago and took refuge in its arched arcade. In the street below I saw people who weren't even in the demo carrying TV sets. (Black residents would call this "the white riot.") My eyes burned with gas. My hands shook with fury. "Pigs eat shit!" I screamed. Suddenly I heard a gun go off. For the second time in my life, I felt all the hairs on my body stiffen, as I had at the White Castle riot.

The cop standing behind me must have fired over my head, or maybe his gun had blanks. At any rate, I wasn't hit. Instead I had a kind of blackout, mentally disappearing from the spot. When I came to, I was three blocks away, with no memory of how I'd gotten there. A police car skidded along the street under a hail of rocks. A kid standing next to me was preparing to heave one. "The first time's hard," he said to me, "but after that it's easy."

I don't think I threw anything. I was too overcome by an immense feeling of fatigue, sudden and almost paralytic. I sat on the sidewalk to catch my breath, and slowly I made my way back to my motel. I plopped onto the bed and turned on the TV. Everything I'd been through was on the air—the clubbing, the turmoil, the hapless politicians in the convention hall, and that incredible chant: *The whole world is watching.* The blurry black-and-white images rendered all of it far more extreme and significant than it had seemed while I was actually going through it. I learned a lesson that made me rethink my dismissal of McLuhan. TV was not teaching us to think in depth or turning us into a tactile society, as he claimed. But it made strange things seem realer than real.

Something similar was happening in Czechoslovakia, where, a year earlier, I'd seen the glimmers of a liberal Communism that was fated to be repressed. Just a week before our marauding through Chicago, Soviet tanks had entered Prague. I'd seen footage of students pleading in vain with Russian troops. It added to my sense that we were fighting a global battle against a tyranny that was much bigger than the U.S. government or even capitalism. Years later I would understand that this was a battle between a patriarchal order and the forces of change, and the streets of Prague and Chicago were bloody with the effects of machismo run amok. But whatever drives people to risk their lives in the name of liberation, whatever the moment contains that makes revolutionary energy decisive—it was missing in Chicago. Something stopped us.

We had glimpsed the precipice, seen the potential for vast violence, felt the viciousness of a threatened state, and sensed the power of the backlash that would surely ensue from its collapse. Call it cowardice and you won't be entirely wrong. But it was also the product of an unexpected perception. The moment of our victory in the streets was also when we had to confront the consequences of our acts. Did we really want our country to fall apart? That was the question Chicago presented, and for most of us the answer was a definitive, if unarticulated, no. It was like the hatred you feel toward your parents when you're young. You may want to kill them, but you don't want them to die. This is the origin of the love that eventually replaces filial rage. It doesn't usually arrive until the parents are feeble, and that was how the government now seemed to me. Suddenly I felt bound to its fate. I'd left New York determined to smash the state, but I left Chicago an ambivalent patriot. It prevented me, or saved me, from the fate of a warrior. And this, I've come to think, is why our revolution fizzled.

To my mind, the same decision was made in the black community, where the ghetto riots never evolved into a true insurrection despite the efforts of a number of radicals to organize a fighting force. It wasn't just the fear of retaliation. Malcolm X's famous slogan "By any means necessary" poses an implicit question: What, exactly, is the reason for this necessity? For most black people, including the rioters (some of whom were middle-class), the answer was similar to ours. There was a widespread underlying faith in the possibility of change—even Abbie Hoffman had named his son America. This belief inspired rebellion, but also restraint. And change would come. Fitfully, and not entirely for the better, a new America would be born. From rage, renewal: that's the lesson of the sixties, dude. But at the time, the only thing that seemed to be approaching was . . . exhaustion.

I've already mentioned the Weather Underground and its futile attempt to end the war by setting off bombs. But they were rationalists compared with the Symbionese Liberation Army. In 1973, this cultish cadre would shoot a school superintendent with cyanide-laced bullets. Later they would achieve fame by kidnapping Patty Hearst. By then I didn't want to even hear the R-word. This violence was not only useless and immoral, but dour. The pleasure principle was missing. And the man who could have brought creativity to the remnant of the Movement was hors de combat. I would later learn that Abbie Hoffman had been struggling with severe depression. He would kill himself in 1989. The Revolution was a crucial distraction for him, even more than for me. When it was over, he lost his best defense. And so did I.

The Reckoning

I took the train from Chicago to New York, composing my piece while the heartland streaked by, rusting and resentful. I wrote about crossing the line from reporting to participating, but it took some time for the full feeling of what I'd been through to register. I'd never felt so exhilarated as when I watched kids being clubbed at the Hilton and escaped without a scratch. Now I knew what it was like to exist in a state of pure sensation, to lose myself in the ecstasy of a riot. But the aftermath of that high was sickening. What kind of person did it make me? What had become of the idea, so central to the civil rights movement, that violence was abhorrent because it reduced people to inhuman objects? And what, finally, did we accomplish? We'd destroyed the president who betrayed us, but we had no alternative to offer. And Richard Nixon was lapping up the blood in the streets.

Back in the city I noticed the used needles on the sidewalks, the blathering burnouts, the mood of grim forbearance. It seemed worse than the usual Manhattan response to a summer that lingered too long. There was a pall in the air, as if everyone were breathing the stench of having failed to do what seemed necessary but horrible to behold. We had a stake in the system, hate it as we might, and the prudence it dictated stopped us in our tracks. It felt suspiciously like maturity, and not many of us were ready to accept that gracefully. We had struggled against growing up, but in the crucible of history we did. I certainly did, and it left me feeling prematurely old.

Amid this dejection I interviewed Joe McDonald, of Country Joe and the Fish. They'd been brave and committed enough to play at the Chicago protests, and I wondered what Joe thought of the Revolution now. I wanted him to offer some alternative to my glumness, but instead he affirmed it. "There isn't going to be any revolution," he said tartly. "Let's be realistic."

Why not? I asked.

"Because you have to control things, and most people I know aren't ready for that. They want a leaderless society." Contempt flashed in his eyes. "Three years ago we were hobos singing our hearts out about the virtues of the open road. Last year, we were Indians. Now we're revolutionaries. Man, if the Revolution ever comes for real, they'll probably use Andy Warhol munitions. You throw it and this big sign comes on— Pow!"

We heard the sounds of a demo in the street below his hotel. We ran to the window. Kids were carrying Vietcong flags. Joe drew the blinds. "I'm not into that anymore," he sighed. What was he into? I asked. His wife and kid, he replied—the standard of the mature man, delivered with the venom of a defeated partisan. Like me, he had played a role that proved to be, for all its promise, a stylization, and now it was his life. "I've been a poet, a guru, a politico," he said. "I'll be anything you want. Tell me what you want me to be."

I had no answer.

"Well, I'm in the entertainment business. It just so happens that the people I entertain are freaky."

Joe paid a price for his realism, and it showed in his music, which became almost laconic. "Only the symptoms of energy remain," I wrote. I could have been talking about myself, but I was still invested in the belief that my mission was more than merely entertaining. I had to find a new subject, something that could inspire the prophetic rhetoric that my readers expected from me. For the better part of a year I thrashed around for a subject. Nothing made my blood beat. Then I heard about the planning for a rock festival on a farm in upstate New York. "Three days of peace, love, and music," the poster said. I needed that kind of inspiration. If anything could rekindle my ardor it was the lineup at Woodstock, even more definitive than the one I'd seen two years earlier at Monterey Pop. But I wasn't going to make the same mistake of mixing with the industry elite, so I declined an offer to travel to the festival in a

VIP helicopter. I wanted to experience the scene the way I once did—as a fan—and that included getting there. So I joined some friends and we drove up the New York State Thruway. But the road was so jammed that the police shut it down, and I never reached my destination. The news coverage was all of Woodstock that I got to see. I have to say, I was relieved. Now I wouldn't have to face the fact that I had no spunk left for this sort of thing. Epiphanies in the mud were no longer my idea of grooving.

Clearly it was time to leave the field of rock criticism to a not-yet-jaded generation, and already the *Voice* had taken steps in that direction with a new column rotating among a group of writers. It skewered the negativity of "professionals" like me, insisting that the music should be about pleasure, period. I watched from a distance, too melancholy to feel resentful. I understood the need to focus on joy rather than judgment, and I pondered what Joe McDonald had told me during our interview: "Two years ago we believed in music like a god. Well, it's nothing to believe in. The only emotion I associate with it is pleasure." The problem was, I couldn't make that link. My head was hurting, not from the crashing sound of guitars but from Joni Mitchell's homage to Woodstock, in which she channeled a magic world where bombers turned to butterflies. "We've got to get ourselves back to the garden," she warbled. What garden? The one where it was forbidden to eat the fruit of real-world knowledge? Better to be expelled—or perhaps to be the serpent. I fumbled for a way to articulate these feelings, but I couldn't summon up the language to describe what I felt. The only honest response would have been silence, but I wasn't ready for that. I am a writer. When all else fails, we write.

At this point I was so desperate for a theme that I reviewed the L.L. Bean catalog. I also covered a march against hunger held in an affluent community in the Connecticut woods, where well-fed people carried neat signs to the village green. This was a feel-good gesture with no impact, the perfect expression of an exhausted ideology. My piece was laced with irony, and far from newsworthy, but the *Voice* published it. (I don't think they ever turned down an article by one of their writers.) Then I went too far—I asked for health insurance. I'd seen my father-in-law die in a hospital that admitted him only on the last day of his life. He'd been a freelance writer. I wanted to protect my family against that fate.

As Robert Frost wrote, "Home is where, when you have to go there, they have to take you in." That was how I thought of the *Voice*, and the owners encouraged writers to regard the place as a family. But the look on the editor's face when I made my request shattered that illusion. Dan Wolfe told me something I should have known all along. "Richard," he said in a tone that took the full measure of my naïveté, "this is a business."

I guess it was a reasonable call. I had the look, and probably the stink, of a washed-up writer. But I reckoned that I had given the paper my best work without asking for much besides attention. All I needed now was some shelter from the storm. But I knew there would be none. That's when I left the *Village Voice*. I slouched uptown to see Clay Felker, and he made me an offer. I would become a contributing editor at *New York* magazine, with a modest salary—and health insurance. I stayed for about three years, until Felker and his backers bought the *Voice* in 1974. He asked me to be the arts editor, and I eagerly agreed. On my first day in that job I strode into Dan Wolf's office. It was vacant now. I walked up to his empty desk and sat in his chair.

I was sorry to leave *New York*. During my stint there, I wrote pieces and edited packages on pop culture, including a special issue about Latino life in the city. It earned the magazine a sit-in from activists, ostensibly because of the title I'd chosen, "The Big Mango." The invaders were from the Young Lords, a gang that had evolved into a Pantheresque political group. Its ranks included several Latino militants who would go on to illustrious media careers. I met with them, and I had the impression that they bore no animosity toward me or the publication. They simply wanted in, and they were using the most effective tactic of the time. I was relieved, because all I cared about was being reassured that I hadn't done anything racist. I liked the fact that they were ambitious. It was an antidote to the sense of futility that was endemic around me.

I often found myself thinking about how other radicals had coped with the failure of their revolutions. How did the young visionaries of 1848 deal with the suppression of their noble dreams? What did partisans in the Paris Commune think when their defeated comrades were executed by the thousands? How did Communists who deeply believed in the triumph of the proletariat live with the tyranny of Stalin? Some of them recanted in best-selling books, others clung to the long view of human history while settling down to raise ungrateful children. None of it consoled me, because our revolution hadn't even happened, and yet we had to suffer the feeling of impotence in its aftermath.

Most of us made an uneasy peace with our expectations, but nothing was settled. It felt as if we were lying in wait, with no leaders worth heeding or new strategies to reanimate us. Peace marches grew more virulent, but the war went on under the tarantula designs of Henry Kissinger. Universities reopened in a chastened mood, and student militants were largely isolated. Black radicals were fighting a futile battle against the culture's capacity to subsume their power in erotic fantasy— as in the vast success of superpimp films. Meanwhile, in the white mainstream, retro reared its fashion-savvy head, an invitation to consume the past even as we were consumed by the present. Those supreme rock rascals the Beatles released a song about getting "back to where you once belonged." I understood the feeling, and I shared the need, but I couldn't do that trick, because I'd never belonged anywhere.

Even if I'd wanted to turn to music for sustenance, there was little that seemed nourishing to me. The hits kept coming, but not the revelations. The pain of reckoning with the events of 1968 led to a retreat from incendiary rock, and the hottest new bands made music that sounded decorative rather than destructive. Jethro Tull, Led Zeppelin, and (God help me!) the Vanilla Fudge: they all signified a spirit of withdrawal from the edge. These groups inspired the lighting of matches but not the kicking out of jams. On the soft end of pop, there was a lot of mystical crap around. Tiny bells seemed to be ringing on every corner, while something called the Human Potential Movement was hot-tubbing toward Big Sur to be born. The peace sign cohabited with the smiley face, and the raised fist looked painfully passé. Meanwhile in Los Angeles, the Charles Manson "family" stuck their knives into Sharon Tate's pregnant belly, inspired by another prophetic Beatle song, "Helter Skelter." All of it, I thought, reflected a retreat from faith in radical democracy.

In the summer of '69, Life magazine ran a feature on hippie communes. But the real hippie life, at least in New York, had become a sitting target for the rage and violence of the slums. I'd seen the signs two years earlier, when a hippie chick from the suburbs and her less affluent boyfriend were murdered in the East Village by rapine thugs. That crime caught the media's eye because it epitomized the naïveté of the counterculture. The story gave every reporter an excuse to feel good about the compromises of the straight life. I was horrified to learn that the dead boyfriend had called himself Groovy. At first I thought he was my old friend, but as I've said, it was a common name. At the time I wrote that the outpouring of grief and gloating was the inevitable result of an alliance "between the fourth estate and the fifth dimension," the media and the kids who'd been inspired by all the coverage to attempt the impossible. Except it wasn't impossible. It was crushed—by commerce, chaos, and the anxieties of instability, which became unbearable.

The counterculture as I knew it was dead, yet its corpse remained, as lacquered and preserved as Lenin's body in Red Square. There was an enormous appetite for films, plays, books, and TV shows about the florid ways of hippies. I could have siphoned off my share of this market and found a niche as a syndicated columnist, but I imagined myself flogging that beat until middle age, fending off angina and struggling to describe a youth culture that I no longer understood. I'm not saying it's impossible for geezers to write about rock; there are several who do, quite well. I lacked their enthusiasm and their focus. My only recourse was to find a place where my peculiar blend of insight and vulgar energy would be welcome. But I wasn't what's happening, baby—not anymore.

The same forces that were pushing the country toward reactionary politics also stiffened the hierarchies of taste. The adventurous publication *Commentary,* which had once run essays by Susan Sontag, now veered toward neoconservatism, reflecting a trend among chastened intellectuals. "A conservative," said the pundit Irving Kristol, "is a liberal who's been mugged." But I *wasn't* a conservative, and I had been mugged. The perp apologized—he explained that he was a junkie. Judith, who was with me, insisted on confronting him. "How do you expect us to get home?" she fumed as he took our money. He gave us carfare.

To me, a neocon was a liberal who missed the pleasures of class privilege, who was sick of living communally and repressing sexual jealousy, who wanted to dress in something more status enhancing than a T-shirt and jeans, who yearned for assets and stability. This was the same prosperous crowd that had sponsored the radical hybrid culture of the mid-sixties; now it looked for safety. Every style that had once been transgressive was packaged attractively for this audience; museums and art spaces incorporated every radical gesture. Meanwhile on Broadway, Christian musicals with a hippie edge replaced the spirit of *Hair*. I could assess the state of pop culture in 1971 by contemplating *Godspell* and *Jesus Christ Superstar*. Better that, I told myself ruefully, than a musical called *I Protest*.

The mainstream press had embraced a tame version of the New Journalism, so the real thing had to move further out on the ledge. The result was a style called "gonzo," whose major practitioner, Hunter S. Thompson, had a rocker's sense of excess and a radical's insight into the grotesqueness of American politics. But his work didn't interest me—it read like a night in a bar with a maudlin drunk. Still, the magazine that published him, *Rolling Stone*, was one of the few bright spots in the media. It had emerged from the sixties scene to mingle literary reportage with rock criticism, the perfect combo for me. The editor offered me a dream assignment—an interview with William Burroughs. I was ready for my comeback.

Burroughs received me at his "bunker," a loft on the Bowery that came with a built-in orgone box. He had a practiced rap and he laid it on thickly, including the part about men and women being different species that weren't meant to mate with each other. He was as droll as his writing, and as deadpan in his delivery, but when I asked about the power of love he got serious, or so it seemed to me. Love was an invention of women, he said. It wasn't something men needed. I had struggled to believe that needing love didn't make me unmanly, and I tried not to look as appalled as I felt. Another great American writer had turned out to be a pig.

I was trapped between my revulsion toward Burroughs and what I thought a piece on him should be. He was surrounded by a hip honor guard that cherished his dystopian genius. Numerous bands took their names from references in his work—Steely Dan was a dildo in *Naked Lunch*. His dour face was the perfect icon for the sour mood that dominated vanguard culture, and he was well on his way to replacing Norman Mailer as a hipster literary superstar. But by then I was sick of celebrated writers who advocated terrible things. I'd lost my tolerance for black clothing and Downtown irony. To me, this was another retreat from idealism, a backlash for left-wingers.

I'm not saying there was no good music around in the early seventies. I admired David Bowie—I just didn't trust him, and he didn't want me to. His persona was slippery, which is not the same thing as transformational. It was about changing your presentation, not your consciousness. I tried my best with glam rock but it felt brittle, very different from the sixties idea of gender as a flowing, unfocused, playful thing. That concept didn't go with the new longing for roles and authority. It seemed inevitable that formerly androgynous hippies would develop an interest in S&M as the decade progressed. Leather was the new tie-dye.

If I'd been nineteen and trekking downtown from the Bronx I would probably have been impressed by the style that was coalescing into punk. But I was burned out before my time. I felt like a puritan defending a bankrupt utopian vision, and I didn't think it would be welcome at *Rolling Stone*, so I decided not to file anything about my afternoon with William Burroughs. I'd never blown an assignment, and this felt like a big deal. But it wasn't just a negative reaction to him that had stopped me; it was the way the scene had changed. The drug of choice was no longer acid but cocaine, the perfect agent of numbness—and expensive to boot. It was cool now to spend a lot of money on getting high, and you could find a nice return on your investment from MDA, a variant of speed that provided the buzz of LSD without the unpredictable hallucinations. My friends called it Miracle Drug of America. When you wanted to come down after a night of partying you could pop a quack (quaalude). That great leveler, booze, was back as well. The idea was to maintain; to keep yourself on an even keel. I went to dinner parties where rounds of aquavit were followed by lines of coke. Music was playing, and in that hyped-up state I felt the rhythm as an invitation to climb an even slope toward a joyously vacant summit.

I had one more junket left in me. *Vogue* dangled an offer from the Brazilian government to fly me to Rio for a pop festival. The editors didn't seem to mind that Brazil was a military dictatorship. I couldn't help thinking of old *National Geographic* pieces about life in Berlin just after the Nazis took power, which blithely featured photos of swastikas waving in the breeze. But I shouldn't knock *Vogue*—I was a columnist there during the late sixties, and they suffered my insouciance gracefully. One day I was introduced to the publication's guiding light, the doyenne of American fashion, Diana Vreeland. She was the most carefully put-together old lady I'd ever seen, but I had no idea who she was. I whispered to my editor, a lovely woman with horse-country manners, "Who is she?" My editor tried not to roll her eyes, just as later she would sit primly at a performance in the East Village I had dragged her to, a play called *Che*, in which the male and female leads had real intercourse onstage every night. What can I say? *Vogue* spent good money on me, and it paid for my drugs.

Rio was fascinating. I had never been in a place where race relations seemed so mellow, though they were actually quite rigid. In America, all the racial resentment was out in the open; here it was most evident in the segregation by altitude. The black slums climbed the steep hillsides around the city, and they were subject to collapse during frequent storms, with deadly results. But these precarious *favelas* were central to Rio's mystique. I remember standing on the balcony of a luxury apartment in Copacabana during a reception held by an executive at the biggest Brazilian TV network. Naturally this honcho was an American. His flaxen-haired son pointed eagerly to the favela that rose a few blocks from the building. He traveled there often, he explained, porting his guitar to jam with the locals. He had no fear of being robbed, not in a friendly land like this, and his father made it clear that the programming at the TV network reflected Brazilian culture, which was "simple and fun-loving." I knew how sophisticated the scene in Rio was. It was hard not to spit in the honcho's face.

Somehow I managed to elude the police escort that was assigned to transport reporters to the festival, and I hooked up with artists who were part of a sly cultural movement called Tropicalism. Painters, musicians, and filmmakers worked with one eye over their shoulders. Films by left-wing directors had to be smuggled out of the country so they could be screened in New York. (A friend of mine actually did this.) Every now and then, I saw the police enter a café and drag someone off. As for the event I had come to cover, it was about as daring as the soap operas that dominated TV. The audience was chaotic and irrepressible—this was a city where several layers of conversation could be heard in every phone call—but the real life of Rio was missing from the stage. Still, one vanguard band had made it through the cleansing process. They were called Os Mutantes, the Mutants, and they sounded a bit like the Mothers of Invention. There was no translator present, so I couldn't really do an interview, but I promised to write about them. How could I not? Their antic style was to the spirit of cultural resistance in Rio what a similar group, called the Plastic People of the Universe, would be to Soviet-era Prague. By then I understood the crucial role that pop music played in countries where there was no political outlet for freedom.

Though the best-known Brazilian composers were in exile, the songs on the radio could be subtly antigovernment, and I soon learned to read the codes. Subterfuge reigned, as it always does when anger is risky.

It was a revelation to visit a military dictatorship. There were bullet holes in the Congress building from the latest coup. Soldiers were everywhere, and their behavior was quite unpredictable. Not even the police in Chicago had frightened me as much as these badly trained thugs walking around with machine guns. I returned to the States with the uncanny feeling that I was glad to be home. I wrote about the sterile quality of the festival in Rio, and the vitality of the cultural dissidents I'd met. I called the piece "The Sound of Silence." My editor at *Vogue* regretfully said she couldn't publish it. Too political.

Swallowing my dismay, I retreated to my favorite recovery zone, Fire Island. Judith and I had rented a house that was more like a shack, which was perfect for me. I took refuge in the restorative effects of body surfing, ample drugs, and sex, marital and otherwise. I didn't visit the Sunken Forest, where gay men frolicked among ambling deer—I wasn't ready for that. But I did walk around the beach naked, reveling in the long hair brushing against my back. The media and its discontents seemed distant on this island, and as fall approached I decided to stay. The crowds were gone, the water was still warm, and the shrubbery took on an auburn hue. I started to write an essay, very different from my journalism, about what it was like to grow up as a descendant of slum dwellers. I was experimenting with repetition borrowed from Allen Ginsberg. I watched the ferries from the mainland come and go, freed from the tyranny of schedules and deadlines—and also the news. No one I knew on Fire Island had a TV. So I was stunned to see the front page of a local tabloid that someone had left in the sand. Janis Joplin was dead.

She'd overdosed, of course—the rock-star version of a poetic death. A roadie, concerned when she didn't appear for a recording session, went to her hotel and found her body. This was in L.A., a very hard city to be alone in if you're fucked up. Janis had friends there, as well as a girlfriend, but perhaps they were too busy to see her. Her only visitor, it seems, was her dealer. The fatal dose might have come from him, or it could have been someone in the music industry charged with keeping her well supplied. There were a number of people willing to provide rock stars with drugs if it assured their dependence and loyalty.

Back when I toured with Janis, she showed no signs of heroin use; she didn't nod or scratch or leave the room to shoot up. As far as I could tell, alcohol was her only excess, and it seemed understandable given her insecurity. Her original band, as I've mentioned, was a major source of support, but her new group, a put-together ensemble, couldn't possibly relate to her in the same way. She was every bit the superstar by then, driving a psychedelically painted Porsche. Rockers of her caliber are the ultimate transients, and they soon lose the attachment to a community that can create stability in a whirlwind existence. That was why Janis had come to San Francisco in the first place—she needed to find a hometown where she was normal. But stardom had made her a citizen of the system, a ward of the industry, and she lacked the self-possession to survive in a constantly shifting milieu. That was my take on her situation, though I could only grasp it from afar.

I raced home from Fire Island and called Janis's publicist, the only person I knew who stayed in close touch with her. The publicist was a voluble and caring woman. We'd both wanted to be the friend Janis could call when she felt desperate, the catcher in her bottle of rye. But there was no way for us to keep track of her. Pretty much everyone in her circle was in the music business, and, like so many others, they practiced the hip ethic of nonintervention. No one stopped her from skirting the edge of the cliff. Like Don McNeill on the day he drowned, she was simply doing her thing, and, like the guy who left Don alone after seducing him, no one would feel responsible for Janis's death.

I'd known many junkies. There was Tom, the woman who had introduced me to the East Village, and the first person in my life to OD. A close friend of mine was hooked on a sedative with the enticing name of Placidyl. He had so much of it in his body that his sweat bore a metallic odor. I enrolled him in a rehab program, to no avail—he eventually put a gun to his head. These addicts were very dear to me. In the days following Janis's death I thought of them all, along with every rocker whose path to destruction I had witnessed silently, every acid casualty I'd iced out of my life, everyone I'd seen fall by the wayside while I clung on. Why hadn't I intervened?

I locked myself in and let the answering machine overflow. Deadlines came and went, but I couldn't work. I would sit at the typewriter in a state of profound wooziness, so that I couldn't construct a sentence. The words didn't come together, and when I finally managed to string out a thought I couldn't figure out where to go with it, how it fit into a larger whole. I went through a ream of typing paper, five hundred sheets, without producing a coherent piece. I knew then that I would never again write about rock. Every album in my collection carried memories of disillusionment. I would hear a song and burst into tears.

Writing had been the companion to all my adventures, the thing that enabled me to cope with life since my childhood. Now I had to face the possibility that I might never be able to count on that outlet again. To this day, when I think about what dying would be like—what it *will* be like—I recall the baffling sense of everything vanishing from my grasp. This was the feeling of writer's block. It was the real sound of silence.

That's when I felt the full weight of my loneliness, the hard truth that emerges in the course of a depression, the sadness that all the obsessive activity had kept from me. I threw away my beads and took my revolutionary posters off the wall. And then I cut my hair.

Aftermath (or: There's a Bathroom on the Right)

I wish I could write a coming-of-age story like *Almost Famous*, Cameron Crowe's frisky tale of his time on the road in 1973 with a rowdy but caring rock band. I'd love to wring that kind of juice out of my life, to tap into the myth of music as a tool for self-discovery and sexual awakening. Well, the myth was true for me, but it was far from heartwarming. There are many reasons why. Crowe's movie is set in the years when the anguish of the sixties had more or less calmed down. My trajectory was much more traumatic; also more intense. It was all about love and disappointment, yearning and satisfaction that led to yearning again. I learned to take risks and make real connections, but the death and destruction that I witnessed left me with a rueful self-assessment. I would have to learn to live within my means and without my dreams.

Eventually I found a new subject in the thorny issue of gender, and a new persona through the sex wars of the seventies. It seemed to me that the things I'd always hated—racism, warmongering, police brutality—were all aspects of patriarchal culture, and that the things I loved—such as androgyny in rock—were vectors of rebellion against those structures. I spent a good part of the next twenty years attacking machismo and its symbols, which were easy to parody, as are all forms of arbitrary power. Like any hegemonic class, the whiteboys, as my feminist friends called them, had no critique of their dominance. I was there to provide it.

I waged this combat on the page rather than in the street, but it was no less aggressive. I wrote with a shiv in my prose, although I had to fight the inner suspicion that I was carrying out a revenge mission on behalf of my own feelings of failed masculinity. Would I have become the sexist enemy I was fighting against if I could have carried off the macho thing? In the corners of my fantasies the question nagged at me. But if we have to wait for activists who aren't motivated by personal problems, nothing will ever change. Feminism gave me a potent analysis of power, and its love child, gay liberation, allowed me to resolve (at least provisionally) the question of my identity. Am I gay? More or less. Homosexual? Not only. My sexuality has always been a congeries, but I'm satisfied with the shake, full of stems and seeds as it may be. Identity politics supplied two things I badly needed: a struggle that inspired me and a place on the sexual map. It also allowed me to leave behind the feelings of pain and failure that had haunted me at the end of the sixties, culminating in my massive writing block. Janis Joplin's death was the trigger, but it persisted long after my grief settled into melancholy.

Years would pass before I crawled out of that hole. I had to invent a new style that didn't seem stylized, and a voice that wasn't artificial, as my previous persona of the hip arbiter had been. It was a slow and uncertain process. I learned to tolerate days, sometimes weeks, when nothing I wrote held together. But I pounded away at the typewriter, sitting there all night, crafting a paragraph that felt genuine, and then another. By 1971 I was finally able to complete an essay that had nothing to do with rock or youth culture. The theme was my deep attraction, sexual and otherwise, to WASPs. The piece was bought by *Harper's*, whose editor, Lewis Lapham, confessed that he had the same obsession with Jews. I credit him with giving me my profession back, but I still couldn't turn out copy on a regular basis. And I couldn't bear to live in New York—there were too many absent faces and aching memories.

So I retreated to a small town on the Connecticut coast, not far from the Rhode Island border. Judith and I lived in a commune until it broke apart, along with our marriage. I won't go into the details, except to say that our experiment in free love disintegrated in the usual explosion. At some point I was left alone in the house. That's when I had my last encounter with someone who reminded me of Groovy. By then he'd become a spirit that popped up in my memory. At odd moments I would think of the stud I met at Tom's house, who seduced me with the sound of his guitar; or the dude who introduced me to acid in San Francisco; or the kid from California who told me that I was afraid to love. I have no idea what became of any of them, and I suppose it doesn't matter—Groovy the man wasn't all that attracted me. It was also the type, maybe even the idea. He was the hippie I yearned to be.

After the sixties ended I didn't think I would ever meet such a person again, but I did. He was hardly a classic of the Groovy breed: too down-and-out, but by then I was full of self-doubt too. I bonded with him at an event that reminded me of how quickly the recent past becomes the stuff of nostalgia. I'd been sitting around the house in Connecticut, brooding; a college radio station was playing in the background, and the DJ said something about "a blast from the past." He was plugging an event called Sixties Night. Only two years after the decade ended, it was easy to imagine that it had all happened in a dream, but the need to revisit the era persisted, especially for those too young to have participated in the Summer of Love. They were snacking on milk and Oreos while I was chewing 'shrooms. Now they could experience a simulacrum of, at least, the vibe.

The venue for this sixties spectacle was a bar in Westerly, a Rhode Island border town so strapped for cash from its only industry, which was fishing, that it called itself the Cat Food Capital of America. But Westerly was only a short drive away from my house, so I decided to check out the gig. In those days, bars in smallish cities might have gay nights or polka nights, whatever brought out a special clientele. The performers often weren't billed; all that mattered was the theme, and in this case the era was the point. The owner had hung a frayed mandala in the window, and I could smell marijuana rising from the small knot of kids in the doorway. In their processed tie-dyes, they looked like mannequins in a retro-clothing shop. A car cruised by; empty beer cans were tossed at the crowd. I screwed up what was left of my courage and walked inside. Except for the bartender, I was the oldest cat in the joint.

Long hair was no mark of pacifism by then; it had become the signature of young working-class guys, and you never knew, when they raised a fist, whether they were greeting you or getting ready to beat you up. So I wasn't sure whether the dudes standing around were there to hit on hippie chicks. It would be quite a task for any musician to reach this audience. The amps buzzed loudly. The room was bathed in ultraviolet light to mask the corroded walls. This was the kind of place that paid off fire inspectors. I decided to stay close to the flickering exit sign.

Then I noticed the high-schoolers gathered around the cramped stage. These were the kids who wished they had been there when it was cool to be a freak. I could tell that they spent a lot of time in their rooms, letting the sound of a reedy voice suffuse their suffering spirits and awaken their deepest recesses of love. It wasn't all that easy in 1972 to find songs that inspired those associations. Regularity reigned, rhythm passed for blues, and there was no real place for the meanderings of acid rock. This was pure nostalgia for a world that never was but really could have been, and the music was the only part of it that remained.

Off to the side, I saw the performer tuning his guitar. His glum expression put me in mind of that Creedence Clearwater song about a touring band stuck in Lodi again. This was a guy who didn't rate a roadie; he had to carry his own equipment. He looked more haggard than hip, with his stringy hair and the makings of creases in his cheeks. Hard living isn't pretty after the age of, say, thirty-five, and he'd already crossed that threshold. At a signal from the bartender, he slunk to the mike and launched his act. A prerecorded track provided the beat, and he wasn't even singing a song from the sixties—not technically. This tune had come out in 1970, and it always made me want to shoot up a post office.

> *Everybody's beautiful in their own way*
> *Under God's heaven, the world's gonna find a way*

The set went on for maybe twenty minutes. When it ended, there was wan applause. I didn't think he deserved a warmer response, but I was well aware of what a poor reception feels like, and it brought out my sympathy. So I dragged myself over to the nook that passed for a dressing room, and introduced myself. I told him that I used to be a rock critic. He summoned a weary smile, as if he didn't care about my former profession. (That was a good sign.) Then he offered me a deal—if I put him up for the night, he'd take me to Woodstock. I didn't know what the fuck he meant. I thought it might have something to do with sex. He had the hustler look, though it may have been the desperation of a traveling musician who has to pay for his own room. I suppose that was part of his appeal.

"Very good stuff," he said, pointing to his pants pocket. I must have let my emotions show, because he explained that he was talking about

LSD. I tried my best to hide my disappointment. Not that I was looking to hook up with a guy, but I was hungry for company. He made me feel the loss of my wife and of the commune we'd joined with so much hope. I wasn't used to being on my own in a coastal town. I'd never heard anything as isolating as the sound of gulls on a narrow, empty street. I'm sure that's why I saw an erotic spark in his tired eyes.

I remember thinking, I'll take him home, he'll drop acid, and I'll watch him trip out. That was all I felt up for. I hadn't had sex with a man in several years, other than the intoxicated rubbing that took place in the commune as part of our group-love experiments. I tried to control my nervousness as we drove to my place. He gazed out the car window; I fiddled with the radio dial. It was cold for October. There was a coating of frost on the front porch. I grabbed an armful of logs from the wood-pile and threw a few into the pot-bellied stove that heated the living room. He plopped down on the couch, stretched his legs, and asked if I lived here alone.

"Now I do."

"Ah," he sighed, "the changes."

He leaned back on the sofa, so that his hair fell against the cushion behind him. "The whole thing sort of slides by," he said. "I mean, it's hard. So phony. But . . . so what. Right?"

He'd had a promising start, a nibble from a label, but he could never, "you know, grab it." I told him he was lucky. Everyone I knew who *did* grab it is gone. Not everyone, of course—not physically. But one way or another.

It didn't matter to me whether he'd fallen from the grace of a one-shot song that made the bottom of the Hot 100 charts, or whether he'd even gotten that far. Some people possess the mystery of music, its uncanny ability to put fans in touch with yearnings that have no object except for wholeness. That was what it meant for me to be in the presence of a rocker, even one who reminded me of a dog in a rainstorm, soaked and puny. I had to stop myself from trying to fluff him up.

He reached into his pocket and pulled out a wad of foil. Inside were two small tabs. I decided to go for it, and we sat before the fire, sipping tea, waiting. An hour later we were lying on the rug. He slipped out of his shoes and put his feet on mine, hesitantly. He slid them gently up and down my legs. I wriggled toward him until our bodies touched. We lay like that for quite a while, communing with the fire log sparking. I heard him breathe deeply, felt the brush of his aspiration against my cheek, caught its odor in my nostrils. He took off his shirt and put my hand on his chest. The hairs were downy against my fingertips. He put my hand on his cock. "Ta-da!" he said.

And then he kissed me. Lightly, with the tip of his tongue parting my lips and flicking my teeth. I felt a wave of nausea. I was no stranger to blow jobs, but I'd never been kissed by a man. Disgusting, I thought. But a line from a girl-group song reverberated in my mind. "It's in his kiss, that's where it is."

Somehow we got out of our clothes, and he wound himself around me, grinding slowly against my belly. Soon we were balls to balls. Every now and then I would open my eyes to see the embers in the stove glowing like tiny eyes. A dry radiant heat rose from our bodies and enclosed us. Rabbis in heaven were frowning down on me. I gazed at his black hair, the strands swirling around his eyes. In my altered state, he had Don McNeill's face, the friend lost to me. I realized that I'd wanted all along to hold Don, to nestle him and shelter him, but I never did, because guys don't do that—and we were guys.

I'm not sure how we untangled ourselves. It was daylight when I woke up, and my pal was gone, leaving only the foil wrapping from the acid behind. I raced from room to room, thinking he might be in the attic or even under my bed. Maybe he'd crawled off to sleep in the bath. But he was nowhere to be found. An awful scenario presented itself to me. He'd had a homosexual panic, walked to the end of the spit of land near our house, and plunged into the Long Island Sound, disappearing in the black brine. I flashed on him washing up among the beer cans. I would be responsible for that, forever.

Then I calmed myself down. There was no evidence that he'd panicked. I didn't even know if we'd had sex. The whole thing could have been an LSD hallucination, a wish come to life, not just for him, but for contact with what I adored in rock. I couldn't say that I'd finally fucked a rocker, since I wasn't sure I actually had. I couldn't even think of his name. The odor of his body, which lingered in my nostrils, was all I could remember. Hidden desire, repressed queerness, grace—whatever he meant to me, it was fleeting, evanescent, like the music and the emotions it produced. I thought of that Neil Young song about being helpless. Yes, I was helpless before the feeling of love and loss, always would be. Helpless.

In the Facebookable universe, I imagine, everyone has a page. But you won't find my Groovy there. I don't think anybody goes by that name anymore; it's part of the faded enigma of the sixties. And yet, there are times when I think I see him. Usually it's just some stringy kid with an advanced degree in tweeting. I have to remind myself that I'm living in a present that sees the past through a glass wryly.

The sixties are a blur that comes into focus only in the froggy faces of the rockers who've survived, in a retro style more lurid than it should be, in movies awash in historical details but stripped of their true complexity. Also in books that offer rueful retrospectives on the counter-culture by those who have nothing but tenure to show for their dreams. In these artifacts, the sixties are seen as either a puff of Acadian smoke or a dangerous diversion. The best defense against such distortions is to insist on radical subjectivity when describing that time, so there's no pretense of authority. That's the strategy I've followed here, though with some misgivings. I hate memoirs. They mainly exist to cast their authors in an unduly flattering light. I don't think I've avoided that entirely, but I've tried to present my motives as they were—ambivalent most of the time.

Still, few reporters deserve to be the center of the story; that's why I resisted writing this book for many years. I didn't want to end up with a spin on Nabokov called *Kvetch, Memory*. But not long ago something changed my mind. I read *Just Kids*, Patti Smith's account of her long rela-tionship with the photographer Robert Mapplethorpe. I was enchanted by her portrayal of their youth in the sixties, set in the bohemian milieu I inhabited at roughly the same time. Her writing manages to convey a sense of tragedy without losing generosity of spirit, a combination I find hard to achieve, partly because I'm not as great an artist as she is, and also because it wouldn't be true to my own experiences. I look back on my trove of recol-lections with a mixture of anger and regret, but if I delve beneath the pain I can locate memories of immense pleasure as well as more love than I deserved (though I didn't think I got nearly enough sex at the time). The transferential power of that love shaped me the way wind and water carve a rock. My inner life is an amalgam of my affairs, including those that ended badly. I needn't say more, because the pattern of my sexuality that these feelings formed fell into place after the scope of this book.

As did my second career at the *Village Voice*. I returned there in 1974, when Clay Felker bought the paper and hired me to be its arts editor. That position allowed me to bring in writers who fit the strategy I'd learned from the original owners, which was that reporters should work the beat they live. If you need someone to cover midnight movies, find an underground filmmaker to do it. If you want someone to write about the punk-rock milieu, get a kid who hangs out at CBGB. If you're looking for a performance-art critic, hire someone who empathizes with people rolling around in broken glass. Eventually I became the executive editor, with a specialty in turning young writers into, well, writers. And once my own block receded I filed a piece nearly every week. I wrote about artists, sexual politics, the media, and the incessant advance of hype. It was a concordance with my life that could only have happened at the *Voice*. My time there ended in 2004; I won't elaborate on my departure, except to say that nearly everyone I worked with is gone now, and the paper is not what it was. But the most remarkable thing you can say about a person or a publication that's been through many triumphs and traumas over nearly sixty years is that it's still around.

So is the profession that I helped to found. Rock criticism has changed a great deal—there are many more women, for one thing—but it's gratifying to know, or at least to believe, that during my tenure in the sixties I set a precedent that makes this form what it is. Other types of criticism put less emphasis on the personal, but a rock writer has to come across as an individual, not just an arbiter. The best of them have strong voices, different from mine yet not unrelated. This is a real distinction in an age when the author is supposed to have disappeared.

As for my own writing, it changed after my mother died in 2003. I lost the driving ambition that made me grasp for the spotlight, along with the energy to engage the latest outrage or sensation. It's not easy for me to be silent; I have a tendency to rant at anyone who will listen. But I know that wielding the sword takes time away from other possibilities. I still write, on an almost daily basis—I feel bereft when I don't—but rarely on deadline. By now I've learned to handle the horror of words that won't come and the flop sweat of literary failure. You have to persist, and it helps to have a day job. So I teach, at the public university where, half a century ago, I wrote my first article on rock for the school paper. I'm blessed to have avoided the kind of academic politics that makes journalism look like a Quaker meeting. I haven't ended up in a Rock Studies program where tenure hinges on one's opinion of the third farewell album of a band that's sold its catalog to Apple.

One of the courses in my repertoire is a seminar on the sixties. My students are fascinated by the era, but they don't know much about what made it work. It's up to me to take them beyond the tropes of "classic rock," to describe the logic of the decade and explain how its madness forged their reality. Multiculturalism, feminism, gender theory, even veggie burgers; all are products of a time when foolishness created a space for many wise ideas. When they ask, as they always do, what happened to the hippies, I tell them there's no easy answer. Some made a killing in real estate, some still live the communal life, some keep their commitments alive in social activism, and some are burned out. But most former hippies honor their past in a small corner of their existence, such as the record collection that they share with their grandchildren, as I do with my students. Every so often they make me realize that the meaning of a good song is constantly changing.

I once played John Fogerty's "Bad Moon Rising" for my class. A student mentioned that he'd heard it as a child. At the time he thought the refrain went, "There's a bathroom on the right." I corrected him— it's "There's a bad moon on the rise." But I realized that he'd given a perfect description of the difference between my youth and his: *Don't go 'round tonight, it's bound to take your life* . . . but, fear not, the nightmare will soon be over . . . *there's a bathroom on the right*.

At my ballsiest, I argue that the sixties can happen again. Not in their original form—we don't have the economy to sustain that kind of extravagance—and not with the same reckless naïveté. But the vision of that decade is imbedded in American history. Its roots lie in the periodic Great Awakenings of spiritual and political fervor; in the Transcendentalist ethos of Emerson, Whitman, and Thoreau; in the shake-ups of the Jazz Age and the ecstatic politics of the Beats. These eruptions of idealism, which nearly always involve new modes of life, are a major way we change. We are a nation of unreal possibilities made manifest, also a land where new ideas of liberty unleash new mechanisms of repression. This is the American dialectic. Leonard Cohen says the U.S. is "the cradle of the best and the worst." I believe that; I've lived it.

I was teaching my sixties course when Occupy Wall Street happened. Most of my students were disappointed that the protest fizzled, but I told them to be patient (something I wish I'd told myself when our revolution fell apart). This new movement is a harbinger of a generational politics still in formation. Its most important achievement, aside from crystallizing the perception of growing inequality, was to get kids off their butts, to let them experience what had been repressed: the politics of making noise. And it happened at a time when protest was supposed to be passé among the young. It's hard to imagine those joys when power is hidden and action is simulated in a video game; when the entertainment-industrial complex is so effective at delivering the libidinal goods. But an Instagram is not a life. There's nothing more energizing than feeling your power in a physical mass of your peers. That, I believe, is why thousands of young people poured into the streets in 2011 to proclaim not a program but a statement—we are being screwed.

I had my reasons to be wary of the Occupy movement. Disillusionment is painful, and I didn't want to join anything that might revive that feeling. Nor did I want to be reminded of my age by standing on my feet for hours. But one day, on an afternoon stroll, I ran into a demonstration blocking traffic. My blood pressure rose, along with the familiar feeling of regret that I'm no longer part of such things. I started to turn away, but a squirt of pepper spray hit the crowd and changed my mind. As usual, a cop had ignited a spark with his gratuitous brutality. I was gripped by a strange stirring, something like a man in a coma having an erection.

Over the next week I spent quite a bit of time at the Occupy encampment near the New York Stock Exchange. Tour buses took a detour to swing by, and I was surprised to see the passengers cheering. I also saw grizzled union members forming a protective circle. More than once they appeared when the city was about to move on the camp, sometimes very late at night, and in a labor town like New York they were intimidating to the political class. Between them and the tourists I realized that many people, across lines of age and class, felt held in check. They were sick of it, as was I—tired of walking around muttering to myself about the tyranny of a triumphant capitalism, the closed structure of wealth and influence, the recklessness and contempt of the financial class, the predation of wildcat development that homogenizes neighborhoods.

But pessimism had deadened my capacity to resist. I could no longer imagine a practical alternative to the present. Yet the urge to kick out the jams was still within me. I longed for the thrill of possibility, and above all I wanted to move.

Well, I did move, with some difficulty. After a few hours of marching I was exhausted. It was all I could do to raise an arthritic fist. And the police used every tactic in their arsenal to make the experience uncomfortable. They penned us up in areas much too small, so that we were crammed together like fish in a net. They declared a no-fly zone to keep news helicopters from overhead. They conducted mass arrests designed not just to clear the streets but to enter the protesters in a vast surveillance database. It was a nonviolent operation by the standards of my youth, though a number of heads were cracked—no amount of training can stop a cop from being sadistic in a panic. Still, despite the overwhelming show of force, the protest spoke truth to power. And I got to parade behind a kid with long hair flying, one arm around his girl and the other porting a didgeridoo. He wasn't Groovy, but he *was* the type. So it still existed after all. Doddering behind him, I realized that my adrenal glands were still capable of pumping, and that I still had the lung power to bellow. It didn't make me feel young again—nothing can do that. But it did make me feel alive. And that, finally, is worth a lot.

Alive I am. And kicking. Not ready for a nursing home. I can only hope that, by the time I've fallen and I can't get up, they'll have special places for sixties types, people who can't tell the difference between a contact high and dementia. Places with drugs so good you won't miss drugs, and an ambience that encourages you to lose your dread by living in the remnants of your youth. You'll have Be-In breaks, classes in art as self-realization, psychedelic music in the evening, and lava lights on all night. Kids will visit to hear your stories about the magic days as a nurse wipes up the drool. Munchies will always be available, Sara Lee cheesecake and other staples of the stoned. And there won't be any locks on the doors to prevent you from breaking on through to the other side, not until the wandering begins and you're tempted to walk to the water and sink under the waves, spreading your arms over the ripples the way I imagine Don McNeill did when he drowned.

One thing I know. After my senses have been stripped and the tambourine man has left for a more lucrative gig, after the Revolution is televised and banksters inherit the earth, when everything I value has been shorn of its original meaning, when my feet can't feel the beat and nothing but self-delusion remains, I will still have the need that drove me to devour as much as I could. I was born famished—for food, for sex, for fame, and finally for love. And I will die hungry.

Visit richardgoldsteinonline.com to read selections from the author's journalism in the sixties and to see pictures of his evolution as a rock critic.

A Note on Sources

This is not a history of the sixties. It is a collection of recollections. Fortunately, there's a published record of my encounters with rock stars and other celebrities during those years. The quotes from these people, and the descriptions of events I witnessed, are taken from those articles. But I didn't report everything I saw or knew—no journalist does—so I've pieced together conversations that were off the record or edited out of my pieces. I'm confident in the truthfulness of these passages because I remember nearly everything that famous people said to me. I can't make the same claim about people who weren't famous. I didn't take notes on our personal encounters, and it's impossible to recall precisely what occurred between us fifty years ago. I've done my best to reconstruct incidents involving those people in a way that feels authentic to me.

I've also taken steps to protect the privacy of those who had no idea that they would ever be written about, and in some cases I've altered their names or appearances so they aren't identifiable. I don't believe in ambush journalism, or in reporting that violates privacy, and the details of my intimate relationships are not for publication. So you won't find nearly as much here about the woman I was married to in the sixties as she deserves. Far too many characters in this book are dead, but some of them have children who may not know everything I do about their, parents' lives, and in those cases I've omitted information that might hurt the survivors. In addition I've compressed or combined some scenes and sequences for dramatic effect and I've corrected a number of small errors that appeared in the first edition.

I don't intend this memoir to be a definitive account. Nearly everything of importance that happened in the sixties is heavily contested, so I'm sure that much of what I saw and believed can be disputed. I've related my perceptions as they were, and owned up when they changed. As for my opinions of rock, they are what they are. There's no such thing as the truth about a piece of music; only a consensus. Sometimes I shared it, and sometimes not. So sue me!

Acknowledgments

First and foremost I'm grateful to my spouse, Tony Ward, whose name for this book—"That bitch!"—was aptly chosen, since the project intruded extensively on our life together. Not only did he put up with my need for solitude and assuage my many bouts of panic, but he offered superb advice, without which this memoir would have been an unbalanced mess. I'm grateful as well to my former spouse, Judith Hibbard, a gifted professional editor, who read the manuscript, offered her own version of experiences we shared, and helped me through the thorny task of writing about people without invading their privacy.

My agent, Sarah Lazin, provided the professional acumen I lack, patiently walked me through the many shoals of a project like this, used her extensive knowledge of rock music and journalism to advise me with great skill, and—something I will never be able to repay sufficiently—has been a caring presence in my literary life. In addition, I am fortunate to have an editor, Anton Mueller, who affirmed my standard for what a skillful editor does: He spotted the problems and left the solutions to me. All his colleagues at Bloomsbury who worked on this book deserve my deepest thanks, as do the many friends who encouraged me.

Music Credits

Lyrics to "Bad Moon Rising" written by John C. Fogerty, © 1969 Jondora Music (BMI).

Lyrics to "Everything Is Beautiful" written by Ray Stevens, Copyright © 1970; renewed 1998. Ahab Music Company, Inc. (BMI).

Lyrics to "The Shoop Shoop Song (It's In His Kiss)" written by Rudy Clark © Trio Music Co., Inc. (BMI).

Lyrics to "Dust in the Wind" written by Kerry Livgren, © Kirshner CBS Music Publishing (BMI).

Lyrics to "For What It's Worth" written by Stephen Stills. © Ten East Music, Springalo-Cotillion (BMI).

Lyrics to "Rock 'N' Roll" written by Lou Reed, © Oakfield Avenue Music Ltd. (BMI).

Lyrics to "MacArthur Park" written by Jimmy Webb, © Universal Polygram International Publishing, Inc.

Lyrics to "All You Need Is Love" written by John Lennon and Paul McCartney, © 1967 Northern Songs Ltd.

Lyrics to "Ball and Chain" written by Willie Mae Thornton, © Bro N Sis Music Inc. (BMI).

Lyrics to "See Me, Feel Me" written by Peter Townshend, © 1969 Fabulous Music Ltd.

Lyrics to "Blowin' in the Wind" written by Bob Dylan, © 1962 by Warner Bros. Inc.; renewed 1990 by Special Rider Music.

Lyrics to "Norwegian Wood" written by John Lennon and Paul McCartney, © 1965 Northern Songs Ltd.

Lyrics to "Give Him a Great Big Kiss" written by George Morton, © 1964 Screen Gems-EMI/Tender Tunes Inc./Trio Music Co. (BMI).

Lyrics to "Not Fade Away" written by Charles Hardin (Buddy Holly) and Norman Petty, © 1958 Wren Music Co. (BMI).

Lyrics to "Ballad of a Crystal Man" written by Donovan Leitch (Donovan), © 1965 by Donovan Leitch.

Lyrics to "Heroin" written by Lou Reed, © Oakfield Avenue Music Ltd. (BMI).

Lyrics to "Substitute" written by Pete Townshend, © Devon Music Inc. (BMI).

Lyrics to "Ballad of a Thin Man" written by Bob Dylan, © 1965 Warner Bros. Inc.; renewed 1993 by Special Rider Music.

Lyrics to "All Along the Watchtower" written by Bob Dylan, © 1968 by Dwarf Music; renewed 1996 by Dwarf Music.

Lyrics to "Working Class Hero" written by John Lennon, © 1970 by Yoko Ono, Sean Ono & Julian Lennon.

Lyrics to "Give Peace a Chance" written by John Lennon, © Yoko Ono, Sean Ono & Julian Lennon.

Lyrics to "San Francisco (Be Sure to Wear Flowers in Your Hair)" written by John Philips, © Trousdale Music Publishers Inc.

Lyrics to "Fun Fun Fun" written by Brian Wilson and Mike Love, © 1964 Irving Music.

Lyrics to "Vega-Tables" written by Van Dyke Parks and Brian Wilson. © 1967 Irving Music

Lyrics to "Take It Easy" written by Jackson Browne and Glenn Frey, © 1972 Swallow Turn Music.

Lyrics to "Surf City" written by Brian Wilson and Jan Berry, © Screen Gems-EMI Music, Inc. (BMI).

Lyrics to "Go Go Round" written by Gordon Lightfoot, © Witmark (ASCAP).

Lyrics to "The End" written by Jim Morrison, © by Admiral Morrison, Mrs. George Morrison, Columbus B. Courson & Mrs. Columbus B. Courson.

Lyrics from "Break on Through (to the Other Side)" by Jim Morrison, © 1966 Admiral Morrison, Mrs. George Morrison, Columbus B. Courson & Mrs. Columbus B. Courson.

Lyrics to "Light My Fire" written by the Doors (James Morrison, Robert Krieger, John Densmore & Ray Manzarek), © 1967 Nipper Music Co. (ASCAP).

Lyrics from "Let's Spend the Night Together" by Mick Jagger and Keith Richards, © ABKCO Music Inc. (BMI).

Lyrics from "The Under-Assistant West Coast Promotion Man" by Nanker Phelge (The Rolling Stones), © 1965 ABKCO Music Inc. (BMI); renewed 1993.

Index